MERIDIAN

Crossing Aesthetics

Werner Hamacher

& David E. Wellbery

Editors

Translated by
Bridget McDonald
With a Foreword by
Peter Fenves

Stanford
University
Press

Stanford
California

THE EXPERIENCE
OF FREEDOM

Jean-Luc Nancy

Assistance for this translation
was provided by the French Ministry
of Culture

The *Experience of Freedom*
was originally published in French in 1988
under the title *L'Experience de la liberté*,
© 1988 Editions Galilée.
The Translator's Note and endnotes
and the Foreword were prepared
especially for this edition.

Stanford University Press
Stanford, California

© 1993 by the Board of Trustees of the
Leland Stanford Junior University
Printed and bound in Great Britain by
Marston Book Services Ltd, Oxfordshire
CIP data are at the end of the book

"For the issue depends on freedom; and it is in the power of freedom to pass beyond any and every specified limit."

— *Critique of Pure Reason,*
Transcendental Dialectic,
book I, section 1

Translator's Note

For this translation of *L'Expérience de la liberté*, the order of the first three chapters has been rearranged. In the opinion of the series editors, Chapter 2 of the French edition raises issues that resonate with current Anglo-American philosophical debates on freedom. Chapter 2 has therefore been placed at the beginning of this volume.

Nancy's many allusions and references to French and German philosophical texts pose some challenges to systematic translation. Wherever appropriate, I have kept his terminology consistent with existing translations of these texts. In other cases, where Nancy attempts to free certain words from their given contexts, it seemed best to render these terms in a more literal manner.

I wish to thank Mr. Albert Liu for his generous advice and help in preparing this translation.

Bridget McDonald

Contents

Foreword: From Empiricism to the Experience of Freedom

Peter Fenves

"these mad abandon'd times"
—David Hume

Experience, freedom—these two words are perhaps the most potent slogans in the English language. Anglo-American thought has never ceased to draw on them in order to define its grounds, methods, and goals. Empiricism, as a doctrine of experience, and civil liberties, as the political content of freedom, are united in their effort to remove unjustified authorities. The championing of empiricism and the defense of civil liberties against a vast array of theological and political opponents are the chief occupations of much Anglo-American thought. Theological and political authorities are not, however, the only ones against which the words "experience" and "freedom" have been marshaled; as long as philosophy is held to be dogmatic and seen to insinuate certain obscure articles of faith, it too has been countered with appeals to experience and freedom. The Occidental other of Anglo-American thought, which is often called "the continent" and is not infrequently presented as philosophically incontinent—"seduced by language"—not only renounces empiricism but is also seen to remove the foundations on which a stalwart defense of civil liberties can be based. The remoteness of "continental" thought from the philosophy most often practiced in English-speaking countries lies as much in this renunciation as in the perception of this removal.

The championing of empiricism and the defense of civil liberties do not simply give a certain consistency to Anglo-American thought, nor do they merely give directions for its various theoretical and practical pursuits; these two endeavors are linked in a liberating imperative: accept no authority other than that of experience. Since experience alone is said to give words their meaning, this imperative also implies: free yourself from nonsense, from bunk and humbug. The appeal to experience is at bottom a call for liberation, so much so that empiricism can claim to clear away long-held opinions, dogma, doctrines, and, at its inception, the very idea of *a priori* justifications. In place of innate ideas and pure concepts there are works of experience—essays, inquiries, experiments, and laboratories, each of which constitute a labor of liberation wherein the given is made to release itself. If the five centuries of Anglo-American thought are successive elaborations on experience as liberation, the counterpart to these labors would be *liberation as experience*—liberation without labor or elaboration, liberation without empirical support, liberation that does not respect the boundaries of civility established by the protocols for civil liberties, liberation of experience from its service to the work of liberation.

Such liberation does not easily harmonize with Anglo-American thought, and yet it is no more in harmony with the motifs of labor and the thematics of the Will that have dominated much of its Occidental, "continental" other. It is possible that the thought of liberation Jean-Luc Nancy pursues in *The Experience of Freedom* has as great a potential to break open and expose Anglo-American traditions as the ones explicitly addressed in the text. The distinctive trait of Nancy's thought, like that of certain versions of empiricism, is the relentless questioning of necessity. From the outset Nancy removes freedom from its subjection to necessity, determinacy, and inevitability—a removal that does not, however, make freedom into mere indeterminacy, indifference, or arbitrariness, each of which is merely a negative mode of determinacy or necessity. The analysis of "existence" Heidegger first undertook in *Being and Time* leaves room for such freedom, and Nancy makes the dimensions of this room more precise, on the one hand by turning his attention to the legacy of freedom in Heidegger's subsequent writings, and on the other by returning to the phrase with which

Sartre launched "existentialism": "We are condemned to be free."[1]
Our condemnation to freedom expresses one more subjugation of
freedom to necessity, and so this slogan, far from recognizing
Heidegger's break with his philosophical tradition, repeats the formula common to classical metaphysics, Hegelianism, and
Marxism: freedom is the recognition of necessity. Against the still
sharply drawn background of these formulas—along with the
many associations and repercussions they set off, particularly for a
French readership—Nancy writes *The Experience of Freedom*. To
the degree that Nancy's text undoes the hold that the ideas of necessity and thoroughgoing determinacy exercise over thinking, it
resonates more readily with certain strains of Anglo-American
thought than with the versions of essentialism and existentialism
that want nothing more than to secure grounds, goals, and ver-
dicts.

If the championing of empiricism and the defense of civil liberties lay out the points of reference for Anglo-American thought,
then the direction this thought takes cannot escape certain moments of disorientation and errancy. These two points of reference
are not easily reconciled with one another. The locus of their conflict—a conflict with which more than one English-speaking
philosopher has tried to come to terms—is the philosophical concept of freedom, a concept to which the call for civil liberties ultimately refers and yet a concept that resists integration into the program of empiricism, for the experience of freedom, as the sole experience that would give significance to the word "freedom," is
unrecognizable, or at the very least under constant dispute. At the
outset of his famous treatise *On Liberty*, John Stuart Mill makes
clear that he will have nothing to say of the philosophical concept
of freedom: "The subject of this essay is not the so-called 'liberty
of the will,' so unfortunately opposed to the misnamed doctrine of
philosophical necessity; but civil, or social liberty."[2] Although
Locke tried to show that the phrase "liberty of the will" is meaningless—only a person is free, never a will[3]—the phrase nonetheless has a very determinate meaning; it designates the concept of
freedom with which philosophy has again and again struggled:

freedom as exemption from thoroughgoing determinacy. And this concept remains problematic as long as thinking—the occupation of the philosopher—means making indissoluble distinctions and seeking solid grounds. Although the precise experience of freedom is in dispute, there is still agreement about the nature of philosophical thought: it is at bottom the search for grounds. To think freedom in this context is to undermine it; to think freedom means, if one is permitted to draw on Hobbes's specious etymology, to suspend liberty in "deliberation."[4] Thinking is "de-liberation" as long as thinking means above all seeking grounds. From the perspective of this search, the thought of freedom is self-defeating.

Coming to grips with the self-defeating thought of philosophical freedom, distinguishing modes of determinacy and necessitation, showing the compatibility of thoroughgoing determinacy with spontaneous self-determination, seeking shelter for civil liberties in the defeat of systematic philosophy, even making ignorance of specific causes into the very guarantor of freedom—each of these strategies characterizes a particular way of handling the problematic concept of freedom, and each one tries to prevent freedom, which cannot be unambiguously experienced, from disappearing without a trace. Perhaps the most famous attempt to handle the problematic concept of freedom under the supposition that thinking means positing grounds—and one of the touchstones for Nancy's exposition—is the Third Antinomy of Kant's *Critique of Pure Reason*. An antinomy is generated when reason, seeking to complete the series of conditioning causes and reach an unconditioned one, demands an absolutely free beginning and is at once confronted with the counterclaim that any absolutely free beginning abrogates the rules of succession through which the unity of experience is established in the first place.[5] The doctrine of transcendental idealism, which presents space and time as forms of specifically human sensibility, has the virtue of rescuing reason from this conflict, and for Kant it is finite reason's only salvation. Having discovered the saving power of transcendental idealism and its idea of world-constitution, continental philosophy sets itself apart from its British precursors. But—and here is the point at which Nancy broaches the experience of freedom—Kant's "solution" depends on a self-subsistent subject who, having secured its own unity, constitutes a unified world, which can then assure it of its identity and location in space. But the very unity, identity, and location of this subject deny its uniqueness, its singularity, its being-in-the-world; freedom, as a result, cannot but appear as extramundane, "noumenal" causality. That empiricist challenges to the unity, identity, and efficacy of the subject—most notably, the challenge Hume proposes—avoid the Kantian "solution" of an *a priori* world-constitution makes their efforts into an invaluable palimpsest against which Nancy's endeavor can be read, and upon which the outlines of its thought of freedom come to light.

When Aristotle speaks of the modes of "responsibility" (*aitia*), this word cannot mean "cause" as long as causation is understood as necessitation. The analysis of causation as necessitation, by contrast, dominates modern philosophical systems and is perhaps as decisive a criterion of the modernity of a philosophical discourse as reference to the Cartesian statement "*cogito, sum,*" which is supposed to be "necessarily true" every time it is spoken.[6] Since the founding gesture of empiricism is the rejection of innate ideas, it could hardly accept causation as an *a priori* concept applicable to experience. In order to retain the analysis of causation as necessitation, it is therefore necessary to point out an experience of necessitation. But, as Hume insisted again and again,[7] there is no such experience; necessitation itself is never experienced, as long as experience means having an "impression in the soul." Talk of causality is from this perspective sheer nonsense, for the attribution of a necessary connection among impressions always falls short of—or oversteps—experience. Transcendental philosophy makes the justification of this overstep into one of its principal tasks, and it does so in order to secure the unity of experience. Without this overstep, necessity can have no home in experience, and causality would have to be understood as something other than necessary connection. Since necessity can never be experienced, all experience is a matter of "probability," which means, *a limine*, it becomes a matter of sheer possibility. Experience at the limit—which designates *finite* experience—would then be the experience of freedom.

But possibility is as impossible to experience as necessity. Such is the doctrine of the modalities of being to which empiricism is bound. Experience means having an "impression" in the soul, and each "impression" is actual; indeed, each one defines actuality.[8] And for Hume, the impossibility of experiencing necessity not only does *not* entail a new defense of the philosophical concept of freedom against the idea of thoroughgoing determinacy; it also gives him the chance to represent freedom as an inexplicable and thoroughly useless theological doctrine: "Liberty, when opposed to necessity, not constraint, is the same thing with chance; which is universally allowed to have no existence."[9] Once freed from theological dogmas—this plays no small part in every appeal to experience, including the appeal to "religious experience"—the concepts of freedom that philosophy has hitherto developed become moribund; to speak of freedom as opposition to necessity is to talk nonsense, since no experience, and certainly no "vivid" one, can be had of something that does not exist. As long as philosophical thought means making indissoluble distinctions and seeking solid grounds, it can make nothing of this concept and can therefore count it among the discarded items of theology. The defense of civil liberties, if they deserve to be defended,[10] will come from other quarters.

Freedom is therefore not a property of human subjectivity; it certainly does not, for Hume, distinguish human beings from other things. But it does not disappear without a trace. As freedom withdraws from the discourse of philosophy, the discourse of indissoluble distinctions and solid grounds, it leaves a trace of its retreat. The word "freedom" remains meaningful as long as it is opposed to "constraint," and so the retreat of philosophical freedom leaves its trace in a certain unconstrainedness, a certain *liberality*, the principal characteristic of which is an ability to make everything possible. Liberality cannot then be found in the mere givenness of impressions, since the givenness of these "experiences" is not free but, as Hume makes clear from the beginning, "arises in

the soul originally, from unknown causes."[11] Liberality expends itself, rather, in the "gentle force" called "the imagination," and the
imagination, true to its word, makes it possible for the soul to perceive anything. It is a name for making-possible, being-able: "The
uniting principle among ideas is not to be consider'd as an insepa-
rable connexion; for that has been already excluded from the imagination: nor yet are we to conclude, that without it the mind cannot join two ideas; for nothing is more free than that faculty."[12]
Freedom accrues to the imagination: a force whose very "gentleness," if not its gentility and urbanity, excuses it from forcing anything to occur; it is thus a force without enforcement, a force without necessitation, a *free* force, "for nothing is more free than that
faculty."

Imagination is as important for Hume's exposition of "human
nature" as gravitation is for Newton's elucidation of nature in general; but gravitation, which is perhaps gentle at times, could hardly be called "free." The word is therefore surprising, and the surprise is that we can speak of the normal, the everyday, and the natural; the surprise is that we can speak of something, some *one*
thing, at all. The imagination even lets us speak beyond the con-
fines of our nativity: "We are only to regard it [the imagination] as
a gentle force, which commonly prevails, and is the cause why,
among other things, languages so nearly correspond to each other."[13] Imagination "gently," generously, *freely* lets a world come into
being: it gives us—but we "are" nothing outside our imagination—the constancy of objects and it gives us the idea of causal
connections, two ideas that Hume shows to be mutually incom-
patible. Only a free force can let incompatibilities persist, and their
persistence constitutes our existence.[14] An independent and inter-
connected world resides in a gentility, a generosity, a liberality, a
freedom-ness that is itself emancipated from the traditional philosophical concept of freedom as mere indeterminacy, indifference,
or arbitrariness. Just as the liberality of the imagination is more
than mere exemption from determination or constraint ("negative
freedom"), so too is it less than self-determination or the overcoming of inner compulsions ("positive freedom").[15] Liberality, which

always escapes these alternatives, takes up residence in the imagination as long as the imagination names a space of sheer possibility, a space from which nothing, including the nonexistence of chance, can be excluded.

The gentleness of the imagination does not even exclude a certain violence, for the thought of the imagination wrenches Hume from the human. After lamenting the "despair" and "melancholia" into which his researches have thrown him, he seeks the reason why, at the very moment he wishes to conclude his inquiry into human understanding, he has found no mutual understanding at all and has indeed begun to "fancy [himself] some strange uncouth monster, who not being able to mingle and unite in society, has been expell'd all human commerce, and left utterly abandon'd and disconsolate."[16] Hume "fancies" himself an inhuman entity—and therefore exempt from a treatise of human nature—because of the fundamental character of his own "fancy," that is, because the imagination gives and takes away the specificity of the human in the same gesture: "The memory, senses, and understanding are, therefore, all of them founded on the imagination, or the vivacity of our ideas."[17] The thought of this abyssal foundation leaves one "abandon'd," without commerce, without relation, monstrous: in short, free. In the thought of the imagination as abyssal "ground" there is freedom. But this thought cannot be distinguished from imagination, for as long as it involves memory, senses, and understanding—and how could it not?—it, too, is "founded" on the imagination and can, without further violence, be called "experience."

The thought of the imagination is the experience of freedom. The word "experience," as Nancy reminds us, once had the sense of a perilous traversing (*peirō*) of the limit (*peras*): "An experience is an attempt executed without reserve, given over to the *peril* of its own lack of foundation and security in the 'object' of which it is not the subject but instead the passion, exposed like the pirate (*peirātēs*) who freely tries his luck on the high seas."[18] Such is the case with Hume, or at least so he thinks: "Methinks I am like a man, who having struck on many shoals, and having narrowly escap'd ship-wreck in passing a small frith, has yet the temerity to put out to sea in the same leacky weather-beaten vessel, and even carries his ambition so far as to think of compassing the globe under these disadvantageous circumstances."[19] The experience of thought—or, more precisely, of "methinks," which is not the same as the inquiry into the nature of personal identity—does not consist in "impressions" or in their "reflections" but, rather, in a perilous traversing of the limit to thought. Traversing in this way is doubtless "imaginary" but it is, for that reason, all the more fundamental. In the experience of this peril, thinking can no longer be understood as the making of indissoluble distinctions and the finding of solid grounds. At the limit of thought—or, in this case, at the conclusion to the inquiry into the nature of human understanding—"uncouth," *singular* monsters are born, and each of these singularities denaturalizes nature, as it finds itself so thoroughly "abandon'd," so absolved of relations that it cannot even find a self-determining "me" that thinks.

~

When Hume thinks himself an "uncouth monster," he can conceive of no community to which this uncanny entity could henceforth belong. Every section of *The Experience of Freedom*—to say nothing of Nancy's other writings[20]—sets out to expose the community of the uncouth and to show this uniquely complex community to be community *simpliciter*. Unlike Hume, he does not rely on nature and its unswerving passions to return the uncouth to the couth and the uncanny to the comfortable. Nor does he, as one awakened by Hume's devastating skepticism, try to discover a way back to the familiar.[21] Nor, finally, does Nancy, like Hegel and his successors, attempt to show why the familiar world is upside-down and how it, having become known, could be set aright. The uncouth never returns to couth; the unfamiliar never gives way to the familiar; the uncanny always haunts the known. And yet—or for precisely this reason—there is community. Such is the strangeness and the difficulty of the thought of freedom Nancy pursues: the abyssal character of freedom, its withdrawal from all grounds, implies the dissolution of every relation; but this dissolution—

which takes place without the labor of experience, without experiments and laboratories—constitutes community in the first and the last place. It is the free space of "fraternity," the immense site at which "equality" finds its incommensurable measure. Hume, who is not alone in this, conceives of his uncouthness as an expulsion from community for one simple reason: he, like the metaphysical tradition he inherits, has determined beforehand that community means partaking of a common substance, taking part in "common life" or, at the very least, sharing in "human nature."[22] If, by contrast, the experience of community were not of a common substance but of the very dissolution of substantiality as well as subjectivity—and what else does radical empiricism teach?—then the "abandonment" of which Hume writes would not mark the endpoint of inquiry into the nature of human understanding but a free beginning of thought. "Thinking" would no longer mean making indissoluble distinctions and seeking solid grounds; thinking would be the exposure to dissolution and groundlessness.

Attacks on the foundations upon which philosophers have purported to build systems are hardly new. Ancient and modern versions of skepticism as well as contemporary "antifoundationalisms" have thrived on such polemical strategies, and the point of these attacks, when they do not aim as in the case of Descartes to discover firmer foundations, is almost invariably the same: to give back the given, the natural, or the everyday. One outcome of Nietzsche's relentless critique of philosophical foundations—a critique that barred the way back to the everyday, if not always to the natural—was a certain irrationalism in which the appeal to and glorification of "lived experience" (*Erlebnis, le vécu*) contributed to its widespread reception. Nothing could be more alien to *The Experience of Freedom* than this appeal and glorification. Nancy does not conclude on the basis of subjectivity's inability to ground itself that it must seek a ground "beyond" reason and language in some ineffable "lived experience." Such experience, as Nietzsche taught better than anyone else, is just another, even more insidious ground. The experience of which Nancy writes is not "lived," nor is it, as all experiences of existence are for Hume, "vivid." It is as little an impression as it is a reflection; it is, on the contrary, the experience of exposure to groundlessness, the "experience of experience."[23] And *no* conclusion is drawn from the inability of subjectivity to give itself a ground and secure its own presence; rather, this inability, or destitution, is the unique fact to which *The Experience of Freedom* is dedicated. The immense dimension of this fact gives this text its broad scope, its uneven rhythms, and its constant alteration of tones and textures.

The unique fact is this: subjectivity—which names the substantial self that is supposed to have the power to support itself and to secure its identity—cannot keep itself afloat. The foundering of subjectivity does not mean that human beings, as weak and poorly equipped vessels, are not strong enough to actualize what they desire. With such a conception of human fragility Sartre arrived at the formula, "We are condemned to be free." For Nancy, by contrast, subjectivity is not simply impotent; if power implies causality, which it surely does, then the shipwreck of subjectivity means it has *none*, and this marks the end of subjectivity altogether. But in this end there is *finite* freedom, a freedom that does not amount to a limited space of action but is, rather, the opening—in thought, in experience—onto the limit, onto groundlessness, onto "existence" without essence. As the unique fact to which *The Experience of Freedom* is dedicated, the destitution of self-supporting subjectivity constitutes, according to the terms Heidegger deploys, the "facticity of existence." When Nancy compares Sartre's famous dictum "existence precedes essence" with the statement of Heidegger to which it refers—"the 'essence' of *Dasein* lies in its existence"[24]—he does not wish to castigate Sartre for misunderstanding or distorting the original formulation; the point of this comparison is to make the Heideggerian exposition of "existence" as sharp as possible. "Existence" here means being unable to give oneself a ground and thereupon to secure the unity, identity, and constancy that every question of essence—"What is that?"—presupposes. Existence does not then "precede" essence; essence recedes from existence as long as it is explicated as nature, idea, form, *to ti ēn einai* ("that which was to be"), *potentia* ("power"),[25] or even, according to the phenomenological tradition, as *Sinn* ("meaning").[26] Heidegger's replacement of the question of what something, including a human being, may ultimately be with the question after the "who" of the questioner is the starting point for more than one of Nancy's writings, because this replacement carries out the recession of essence from existence. No common name, no general title, and thus no concept of any sort can reply to the question "who?" And this failure of common names spells the end of any inquiry into essence; it marks the very destitution of essence, a destitution that Heidegger at times wished to restitute with appeals to "research" and to "work." The inability of the subject to procure a ground on which it can support itself does not require further work or deeper labor; it demands the abandonment of the idea of subjectivity in favor of the thought of abandonment, of existence, of freedom.

Of far greater significance to Nancy's endeavor than the confrontation between Heidegger and Sartre then is the altercation between Kant and Heidegger over the fundamental character of the transcendental imagination. The transcendental synthesis of the imagination names, according to Heidegger's well-known "destructive" reading of *The Critique of Pure Reason*, the abyssal foundation of subjectivity; it designates, although it does not fully acknowledge, the abandonment of the idea of self-supporting entities and the concomitant retrieval of *Dasein* "in" the human being. By opening a free space in which it first becomes possible to encounter things—a space called "time"—the transcendental imagination shows itself to be not precisely the origin of freedom but, rather, original freedom.[27] This freedom is as impossible to form into an image, and thus to "imagine," as it is to demonstrate on the basis of an impression or sensation. The unimaginability of original freedom does not, however, derive from its pure intelligibility or its noumenal character; it arises from the complexity or, better, the *heterogeneity* of the transcendental synthesis of the imagination. Far from settling the troubles Hume experienced when he discovered to his dismay that human understanding rested on the imagination, the uncovering of the fundamental character of the transcendental imagination in Heidegger's reading of Kant exasperates these troubles and makes them unavoidable; they become the ineluctable matter of thought. The discovery of the transcendental imagination as the abyssal foundation of self-subsistent subjectivity—as the destitution of essence and the destruction of all traditional bases on which answers to the question "What is man?" have rested—frees *being itself* from its determination and comprehension in terms of substantiality, subjectivity, nature, or lawfulness, and this freedom of being communicates itself, each time uniquely, to existence. The community of existence takes place in this communication, in this "sharing of voices,"[28] nowhere else.

The discovery of the transcendental imagination as the abyssal foundation of subjectivity not only undoes the idea of subjectivity as a self-supporting unity, but it also collapses the distinction between transcendental condition and empirical evidence. One mark of this collapse—and the one to which Nancy pays the closest attention—is Kant's disclosure of a unique "fact of reason." As a fact, it belongs to the domain of empirical evidence; as a fact of reason and a fact for reason, its exposition can only be carried out in nonempirical terms.[29] With the discovery of this fact Kant breaks through the impasse of the Third Antinomy and rebuilds traditional metaphysics on the basis of certain "postulates." But he also opens philosophical thought to *another* empiricism. No longer does the solution to the Third Antinomy *simply* lie in the idea of world-constitution; the resolution of this antinomy in favor of freedom shows, rather, the very limits of the world constituted in subjectivity and, for this reason, sets up an empiricism not of impressions or sensations but of (for want of a better word) liberality. The gift of this unique "fact" has no ascertainable origin; it always remains uncertain whether its "manufacture" is even a specifically *human* matter.[30] "The fact of reason" is as incapable of demonstrative support as philosophical thought, which, according to Kant, can neither base itself on anything earthly nor suspend itself from a heavenly peg.[31] By resolving the Third Antinomy in favor of freedom, this fact not only directs philosophy toward a rehabilitation of metaphysics but also, pointing in entirely different directions, abandons its erstwhile foundations and opens a space for the thought of "existence." The exposition of the "existence" opened in the space of a *factum rationis* demands that this fact be brought to its limit.

The "fact of reason" consists, for Kant, in moral consciousness: in an exposure, more precisely, to altogether necessary, unconditioned, "categorical" imperatives. Since the necessity of these imperatives does not lie in a "necessary connexion" among objects, their *mere possibility*—the sheer possibility that one can act on their basis alone, the possibility that pure reason can be practical—activates them and thus makes them actual: attention, respect, must be paid to them. The necessity of these imperatives lies in their possibility: this is not simply the rehabilitation of the ontological proof of God's existence but the formula for "existence" without ground and without rational demonstration, a formula for the deformation of the distinction between transcendental and empirical that is already under way in the phrase *factum rationis*. The empiricity of this fact cannot be gainsaid; or rather, to do so—and there is, according to Kant, an inclination in this direction—amounts to excusing oneself from the claims of morality and therefore from "the humanity in one's person."[32] To ground morality on empirical claims is, however, to undermine the unconditional character of its imperatives. So the "fact of reason" marks the point where the separation of transcendental conditions from empirical evidence no longer suffices. Nancy does not replace these terms with other ones, but takes the facticity of this fact to consist in a certain consciousness and pursues this consciousness—this familiarity with the demand to dissociate oneself from everything familiar—to its limit. Such a consciousness is, according to a word Nancy employs in *The Categorical Imperative*, a "haunted" one,[33] a consciousness or conscience that denies its familiarity with the "fact" of which it is conscious; it is a consciousness so driven to drive out the "fact" of which it is conscious, so ready to gainsay the experience of being implored to act unconditionally that it makes freedom into a mere matter of consciousness, something subjective, fleeting, epiphenomenal, delusive, a necessary deception.

Taken to its limit, moral consciousness denies itself and realizes this denial in acting for no other reason than to deny the unconditionedness and uncanniness of its imperatives.

To deny the unconditionedness and uncanniness of imperatives is, at bottom, to disregard the moral law not for the sake of pleasure or happiness but out of a profound contempt for the condition of insecurity and groundlessness it announces. Insecurity and groundlessness manifest themselves in the unascertainability of the "voice" that implores unconditional action as well as in the very condition of being unconditioned that this voice, each time uniquely, inaugurates. To act in order to spite—not in spite of—the condition of being unconditioned reaches deeper than the "radical evil" of which Kant wrote and in which he could see the roots of a purely ethical religion. Acting out of profound contempt for the unique "fact of reason," acting in order to wipe away the condition of being unconditioned, acting on the basis of groundlessness—this is not irrationality, especially if "reason" means rendering the grounds and causes of things; it is not irrationality but *wickedness*, and it can assert itself in appeals to empirical knowledge as readily as in calls to transcendence. "Uncouthness" would perhaps be another name for this action, if it were no longer conceived as isolation from everything human nature compels us to do but were, instead, seen as the furious denial of the uncouthness, uncanniness, and uncertainty of freedom; for wickedness wants nothing more than for freedom to disappear into stern necessity, and for commonality to mean nothing but partaking of a common substance, a specific nature, one place of nativity, one nation, a particular race. The experience of freedom cannot be dissociated from an exposure to wickedness, to a non-Humean—if nevertheless all-too-human—"uncouthness," which is not just the transformation of freedom into something subjective but, above all, the erection of "fraternities" on the ever firmer foundations that this transformation, this descent into evil, promises.

The experience of freedom cannot therefore be dissociated from an exposure to what Kant had called—although he denied it could ever take place and, as a result, made it into the limit of ethical

philosophy—"absolute evil."[34] Wickedness, which is not simply
moral depravity, defies the distinction between the transcendental
condition and empirical evidence even more forcefully than does
the "fact of reason." The *positivity* of wickedness drives the thought
of freedom Nancy pursues; it is its singular necessity, its unique urgency. So little does *The Experience of Freedom* rest content with
the free play of a harmless freedom that the very opposite of this
assertion—that it feverishly tracks down the harm freedom does to
itself—hits closer to the mark. With the acknowledgment of the
positivity of wickedness not only is every possible theodicy condemned to failure but so, too, is every other mode of giving
grounds for and thereby "justifying" the world. Friedrich Schelling,
taking his lead from Kant's last writings, made the positivity of evil
into the very starting point of thought, and the strangeness of this
thought—which excites ever more insistent appeals to homes and
homelands—plays no small part in setting continental philosophy
adrift from its Anglo-American counterpart. Of even greater significance to Nancy's endeavor than Heidegger's altercation with
Kant over the character of the transcendental imagination is therefore Heidegger's reading of Schelling's still too often neglected
Philosophical Investigations into the Essence of Human Freedom. In
his reading of Schelling Heidegger confronts a "positivism" of freedom developed from the distinction between "existence" and
"ground." In the groundlessness of existence evil posits itself as its
own ground. Such is, for Schelling, the positivity of evil. Since
Heidegger, by contrast, never fully acknowledged this positivity, he
can never arrive at the abyssal foundation of Schelling's treatise,
and this failure, which finds its echo in Heidegger's assertion that
Schelling's idealism prevented him from coming up with the idea
of *Dasein,* cannot but appear as the rumblings of a justification, the
implicit expounding, to use Nancy's words, of a "secret, imperceptible ontodicy."[35]

~

The positivity of wickedness—nothing has exercised so much
fascination in the last two centuries than this, "the flowers of evil."
And nothing has elicited more strenuous attempts to reconstruct

the liberties and communities torn apart in wickedness. German Idealism could see in evil the very labor of spirit; its insight into the negativity of evil and of death expressed itself in the affirmation that infinite spirit had to dwell in its own negation in order for it to recognize its freedom, to posit itself in destruction and to secure its self-presence in recollection. So persistent is this schema of recognition, reconstruction, and recollection that it dominates projects and discourses that have never heard of dialectics and want to know nothing of its operations; but every project and every discourse of reconstruction gives new life to theodicy, even those that set out to defend liberties and show how the defense of liberties accords with the plan of God, of nature, or even of human freedom itself.

When Nancy writes that the experience of freedom is not the experience of "classical empiricism, nor even that of an 'empiricism without positivity,' "[36] it is because (although this "because" anticipates Nancy's own discussion) the experience of freedom finds its urgency in the positivity of wickedness, a positivity that classical versions of empiricism are unable to handle. In Nancy's hands empiricism does not shirk positivity, but the positivity it touches no longer consists of impressions, sensations, or "brute facts." It consists of another species of brutality altogether: the insistence on a foundation at all costs, a furious insistence on a ground in the face of groundlessness, an insistence that expresses itself in acting so as to spite the condition of groundlessness, an insistence that, to put it bluntly, cannot stand ex-istence. And this positivity so alters empiricism that it could never again revert to its classical versions, nor to a new, romantic revision.[37] Nancy may at times call this alteration of empiricism "materialism," but the materialism he pursues does not propose to reduce psychic phenomena to their physiological bases; the very schema of phenomenon-foundation that materialism has traditionally shared with idealism has no place in his presentations of irreducibility, passivity, simplicity, elementariness, hardness.

No longer a doctrine of how words secure their meaning, no longer sure even of its own semantics,[38] empiricism in Nancy's hands becomes an exposition of groundlessness: an exposition of freedom, which removes every ground from existence, and an exposition of wickedness, which insists on a ground for—and therefore wipes away—existence. Nancy's empiricism does not set out to build a world out of fragmented and disconcerting experiences. It is the positivity of wickedness, not the givenness of sensations or impressions, that has torn the world apart, and every effort at rebuilding converts wickedness into a mode of a negativity that further work, especially the labor of recognition and recollection, promises to overcome. Nancy's empiricism exposes the event that takes place in the space of existence, groundlessness, liberality, generosity: it is the coming up, without ground, and the taking over, without possession, which is named in the word *sur-prise*. And this empiricism can only show the experience of "surprise" that every insistence on grounds, every demand for "necessary connexions," every application of the category ground-consequence, every claim to necessity and to be necessitated, misses. Surprise, however, *is* experience, and any empiricism without surprise, any empiricism devoted entirely to the customary and the everyday, fails to do justice to empiricity.

That something—it has been called "the positivity of wickedness"—drives Nancy's empiricism shows how little it, in a vain attempt to maintain its innocence, can excuse itself from an insistence on necessity. This insistence expresses itself with ever greater urgency in the final sections of this great book: decision, Nancy makes clear, cannot be avoided. The unavoidability of decision does not, however, amount to a "condemnation" to freedom; on the contrary, it is the *condition* of freedom, the condition that is mistaken for a ground whenever one wants to secure freedom—or even when one wants merely to defend civil liberties. For *freedom cannot be secured*, and this "cannot" expresses the unavoidability of decision. Freedom cannot be safeguarded, and so a decision for or against freedom—for or against existence without essence, for or against community without common substance—is always necessary and is always already taken. Freedom cannot be secured, and so every *labor* of liberation implies that this labor must at every moment be willing to abandon itself in favor of liberality, generosity, and abandonment—to give up its sacrificial designs and destinies. Mistaking the condition of freedom for its ground may have its roots in a desire to guard freedom against its enemies, *but it cannot do so.* Even under the guise of defending civil liberties, this mistake takes away the "surprise" of freedom—its overtaking, without possession, and its coming up, without ground. And it is precisely this mistake that Nancy, like every good empiricist, relentlessly tracks down.

For Nancy is precisely that: a good empiricist, so good in fact that he knows how thoroughly the "brute facts"—or the fact of brutality—undermine the exercise in semantic control that first gave rise to the doctrine of empiricism and that finds expression in its liberating imperative: trust no doctrinal words, give credence to experience alone. But the relinquishing of semantic control does not mean that words somehow lose their meaning in Nancy's writing, nor do they somehow regain their meaning in the "vivid" presence of the things themselves. On the contrary, language withdraws into precisely the same position as freedom itself: it cannot be secured, least of all by impressions, sensations, or "lived" experience. The insecurity of language makes *its* experience—not that of impressions or sensations—into the "experience of experience": into the experience of thought, when thought no longer means at bottom seeking grounds, and into freedom, when freedom no longer names a species of causality. Nancy has a name for the experience of language: he calls it "communication." Nothing is communicated in this communication but the very ability to communicate, and this ability, which has nothing on which to operate and does not therefore name a specific power, is, once again, freedom, and it freely gives, yet again, community.

THE EXPERIENCE
OF FREEDOM

§1 Are We Free to Speak of Freedom?

If nothing is more common today than demanding or defending freedom in the spheres of morality, law, or politics—to such an extent that "equality," "fraternity," and "community" have demonstrably and firmly been pushed, if at times regrettably, into the background of preoccupations and imperatives, or have finally even been considered as antonyms of freedom—then nothing is less articulated or problematized, in turn, than the nature and stakes of what we call "freedom." What has in fact occurred is a divorce between the ethico-juridico-political and the philosophical. Such a separation is nothing new in history, where it is for the most part constant, but in the modern world this separation has reached the point of rupture between what is in principle universally recognized under the name of "freedom," and what elsewhere remains questioned, under this same name, by a thinking still committed in a thousand ways to reinitiating its entire tradition.

We can repeat after Hegel, as a banal evidence of our world:

> No idea is so generally recognized as indefinite, ambiguous, and open to the greatest misconceptions (to which therefore it actually falls a victim) as the idea of Freedom: none in common currency with so little appreciation of its meaning.[1]

This is why a divorce has taken place between, on the one hand, a set of determinations that are relatively precise in their pragmat-

ic definitions and that are *freedoms*—a collection of rights and ex-
emptions—the suppression or even suspension of which we know
opens directly onto the intolerable itself, which is not intolerable solely from the point of view of moral values, but which is the intolerable, down to the very flesh and course of existences; and on the other hand, an "Idea" of freedom, called for or promised by freedoms—
yet we hardly know what this idea represents or presents of the
"essence" of "human beings," and we request that it not be examined,
specified, questioned, or above all implemented, so certain are we
that this would result in Chaos or Terror. In this way, *evil*—to the
point of *wickedness*, which we shall have to speak of further—has for
us come to be incarnated in all that threatens or destroys the freedoms most frequently described by the epithet "democratic."
Meanwhile, the essential "good" of a freedom in which the human
existence of human beings would be affirmed, that is, exposed and
transcended, has become totally indeterminate, stripped of all divine,
heroic, Promethean, or communitarian splendor, and is now barely defined, except negatively, and in relation to evil.

Nevertheless we know—by means of another knowledge no less
incontestable but kept in some way discreet, if not ashamed—that
"freedoms" do not grasp the stakes of "freedom." They delimit necessary conditions of contemporary human life without considering existence as such. They sketch the contours of their common
concept—"freedom"—as if these were the borders of an empty, va-
cant space whose vacancy could definitively be taken to be its only
pertinent trait. But if freedom is to be verified as the essential fact of
existence, and consequently as the fact of the very meaning of existence, then this vacancy would be nothing other than the vacancy of meaning: not only the vacancy of the meanings of existence,
whose entire metaphysical program our history has exhausted, but
the vacancy of this *freedom of meaning* in whose absence existence is
only survival, history is only the course of things, and thinking, if
there is still room to pronounce this word, remains only intellectual
agitation.

Under these conditions, the philosopher wonders if he can do anything other than "speak of freedom," in all the ambiguity of this expression: in one sense, he cannot but demand of thinking a think-

ing (and therefore a discourse) of freedom, for reasons essential to philosophy's constitution and destination (as we have already evoked in the preceding pages, and as we will specify later); but in another sense, he can only "speak about freedom," that is, *not* speak of *freedom* as such—he can associate a motif, but not assemble a concept or an Idea (or he can renounce freedom by taking refuge in the ineffable . . .).

"To speak of freedom" is accordingly to suspend philosophy's work. And this is in fact the very possibility of a "philosophizing" on freedom that finds itself, today, subjected to two kinds of obstacles.

The first kind of obstacle consists in the self-evidence of the common notion of freedom—which is always more or less that of a free will—coupled with the moral self-evidence of the necessity of preserving the rights of this freedom. Because self-evidence is involved, it is not necessary to question foundations; undertaking this type of questioning, however, risks weakening the self-evidence. Still, with some difficulty it is possible to avoid doing this, once certain rights are no longer simply defined as the free disposal of something (which presupposes its ownership, or its acquired use), but when they imply instead that the thing be placed at the disposal of the freedom to use it (for example, the work for a free right to work) and that it necessarily be placed at this disposal by an apparatus, usually that of the State, whose logic cannot be libertarian. In other words, once the right of all to the use of common goods—air, for example—requires regulation to enable this use (i.e., in the case of pollution), it is no longer merely a question of positing freedoms. It has to become possible to think the freedom that can posit and define these freedoms, regulating the conditions of their actual deployment. In all the ways that we orient ourselves toward the exploitation of the resources of the "Third World" or toward the management of automatic files and information banks, the rights of freedom today do not cease to complicate indefinitely their relations with the duties of the same freedom. In many respects, nothing has been displaced of what authorized and demanded the Marxian critique of the formal freedoms attributed to human beings who were "imaginary members of an imaginary sovereignty."[2] Still, the "self-evidence" remains, stubborn and inert, though what remains with this "self-evidence" is often, beyond the supposedly transparent imperative of a strict independence of individuals (but what is self-evident about the very concept of "individual"?), only a feeble and pale idea, obscured partly by its own realization. How could we not identify with these lines of Adorno:

> Ever since the seventeenth century, freedom had been defined as all great philosophy's most private concern. Philosophy had an unexpressed mandate from the bourgeoisie to find transparent grounds for freedom. But that concern is antagonistic in itself. It goes against the old oppression and promotes the new one, the one that hides in the principle of rationality itself. One seeks a common formula for freedom and oppression, ceding freedom to the rationality that restricts it, and removing it from empiricism in which one does not even want to see it realized. . . . The alliance of libertarian doctrine and repressive practice removes philosophy farther and farther from genuine insight into the freedom and unfreedom of the living. . . . But that freedom grows obsolete without having been realized—this is not a fatality to be accepted; it is a fatality which resistance must clarify.[3]

The second kind of obstacle is found in philosophy itself and in fact (as Adorno's text makes clear) constitutes the theoretical subsumption of the first obstacle. But what appeared there as self-evidence appears here as aporia. The philosophical thought of freedom has been thoroughly subordinated to the determination of an ontology of subjectivity. In the ontology of subjectivity, being is posited as the *subjectum* of representation, in which, by this fact, the appearing of all things is converted. The essence of being is to "appear to itself" [*s'apparaître*] in such a way that nothing is, unless supported in its phenomenality by the subject, and in such a way that the subject itself successfully passes the trial of phenomenality: "phenomenology of spirit." Freedom has not been considered as anything other than the fundamental modality of the act of appearing to oneself—this act in which the subject is always simultaneously *in actu* and *in potentia*, its act the potential for representation, its potential the act of phenomenality. This *actualization of potential*—which is fundamentally the instaurational gesture of subjectivity—thinks itself as freedom, which means as the power of appearing to oneself, or as the power of determining oneself according to representation and as (the subject of) representation. The corollary of this is a *potentialization of the act*—which is nothing other than freedom determining itself as free *will*, if will is defined according to Kant (and not as we tried to understand it above) as "the power to be by means of one's representations the cause of the reality of these same representations." For the ontology of subjectivity, freedom is the act (which also means the being) of (re)presenting oneself as the potential for (re)presentation (of oneself and *therefore* of the world). It is free representation (where I accede sovereignly to myself) of free representation (which depends only on my will).

From this point of view, the great classical philosophical notions of freedom all turn out to be, at a certain level of analysis, in profound solidarity. Although Descartes distinguishes between the freedom of indifference and the perfection of a free will instructed in the good or assisted by grace, and although Hegel steers between the bad infinity of the free will given over to its contingent satisfactions and the "actual and free will" that has "universal determination" for its object,[4] the essence of subjectivity is at work in each case. It is the self-determination of the will that is dialectically superseded in the grasp of necessity—or else it is the representation of the necessity that wills itself. In one case it is a question of releasing, for itself and in its punctuality, the "self" of "appearing to *oneself*," and this is what comprises the singular blend of contingency and necessity in the Cartesian decision to doubt. In the other case, it is a question of showing that this "self" appears to itself as Being, with its predicates of universality, necessity, truth, and so on.

When a contradiction is presented between the infiniteness and absoluteness given in the act of being, and the fact that the act of its freedom consigns it to a history that must not already be given, Hegelian History supersedes the contradiction, insofar as becoming is there the subjectivity of self-appearing being: but nothing appears to itself except this subjectivity preordained to itself, in which historicity as such is annulled. Ultimately, the completely developed (and not refuted, as German Idealism wished) metaphysical free will will have been the free will of indifferent being, which decides itself in dividing itself, and which in dividing itself appears to itself in the freedom of its necessity. The so-called Buridan's ass will have existed as the animal-subject that resolves its problem by cutting *itself* in two ("I = I") and by reconstituting itself, in the same instant and without history, in the representation of itself eating *and* drinking . . . [5]

Kantian freedom, to the extent that it is a "keystone," likewise is nothing other than that in which reason can and must appear to itself, confirming the delimitation of theoretical phenomenality, and opening—as the lineaments of a history, or at any rate of a destination—the having-to-be of a moral "second nature" that would be the *practical* phenomenalization of reason: its natured essence, its (re)presented subjectivity. The "keystone" is the point of equilibrium on which the forces of a construction founded in reason's (critical) self-(re)presentation are buttressed and secured.

The ontology of subjectivity is also the ontology in which being—as subject—is foundation. At the limit of the thoughts of foundation, where existence must be thought of as its own essence, which means as in-essential and un-founded, *freedom* as conceived by the philosophy of subjectivity is no longer *practicable* (but was there ever a different thought of freedom?). This is why the philosopher finds himself, dare we say, caught between the principial self-evidence of a "freedom" and the final aporia of this same freedom as foundation.

~ ·

Accordingly, it could be that we no longer have the task of thinking what was presented or transmitted to us under the name of *freedom*. Perhaps we must free ourselves from this freedom and consequently draw freedom back to itself, or withdraw it from itself, or even withdraw it in itself—not in order to recommit ourselves through a desperate about-face to the invention of some new discretionary authority (we would not be changing terrain, for despotism and freedom form a couple: the former figures, in a particular subjectivity, the ontology of the latter, whose benefits it simultaneously withdraws from other particular subjectivities), but in order to relate both the necessary thought of existence as such *and* an ethic of freedoms that would no longer be merely negative or defensive, to another concept or another motif whose name or idea we do not yet have. This should at least mean that we would have the task of delivering ourselves from the thought of "freedom" as a property of the subjective constitution of being, and as the property of an individual "subject."

But in fact it is not we who decide whether this will be the task of philosophy, even if it is necessary for us to make a decision. It is not an option offered to our free will any more than philosophizing freedom as such or any of its "orientations" was ever a matter of freely choosing a "freedom of thought."

If philosophy has reached the limit of the ontology of subjectivity, this is because it has been led to this limit. It was led to that point by the initial decision of philosophy itself. This decision was the decision of freedom—perhaps of the freedom preceding every concept of freedom (if it is possible to speak thus . . .) which belonged, for Plato, to the "philosophical natural": the generous availability and freedom of demeanor rather than self-representation—and it was in any case, and is still, the decision of a freedom necessarily prior to every philosophy of freedom. This was not and is not—in the history in which it never ceases to precede and surprise us—the decision *of* philosophy, but rather the decision *for* philosophy, the decision that delivers and will deliver philosophy to its destiny (and we will have to speak further of "destiny"). Philosophy too, as soon as it touches within itself the limit of the thought of foundation, or as soon as it is carried by way of itself to the unfoundable border of this thought, can no longer represent its own beginning as the originary unity of a Subject-of-philosophy appearing to itself in its freedom, or of a Subject-of-freedom appearing to itself as philosophy. (As Hegel represented it: "A higher and freer science [philosophical science], like our art in its free beauty, like our taste and love of these, has, we know, its roots in the Greek life from which it drew spirit.")[6]

On the contrary, the *difference* in the origin and the difference of the origin (as Derrida brings to light in his examination of the philosophical concept of origin and simultaneously of the philosophical thinking of the origin of philosophy)[7] requires us to think that *philosophy and its freedom do not coincide in a subjective presence,* and that every philosophical *decision* (and consequently the originary decision of philosophy and the origin of this decision)—every time that a "subject . . . takes the decision to philosophize," as Hegel claims,[8] or every time that philosophy "tries to change the procedure followed until now in metaphysics and to effect a revolution in it," as Kant claims—is delivered to itself by something that, unknown to it, has already been raised into thinking (and that might well be nothing other than *thinking* itself). At the same time, it must also be thought that this decision renders beyond itself something that arises, each time, from a freedom still to come from thinking (here again, perhaps: thinking itself). In other words, there is decision for philosophy and philosophical decision to the extent that thinking does not appear to itself in a subject, but receives (itself) from a freedom that is not present to it. Thus one could say that "freedom," in philosophy, was brought to us at the heart of an aporia that overcame itself as soon as it was formed (in Kant, Schelling, or Hegel), but that the theme of freedom brings us to a liberation with regard to its (re)presentation, in such a way that the resources of this liberation are not yet available to us. The thinking of freedom can only be seized, surprised, and taken from elsewhere by the very thing it thinks.

If there were not something like "freedom," we would not speak of it. For even when it is deprived of a referent or empty of all assignable signification, this word still carries, even to the point of indecision, or rather in the impasse of its meanings, the very *meaning* of *logos* in which philosophy recognizes itself: the opening of a free space of meaning. Thus philosophy has always already given itself over to the thinking of what it can neither master nor examine: and this is also what we understand, simply, by "being-free." We are therefore not free to think freedom or not to think it, but thinking (that is, the human being) is free *for* freedom: it is given over to and delivered for what from the beginning exceeded it, outran it, and overflowed it. But it is in this way that thinking definitively keeps its place in the world of our most concrete and living relations, of our most urgent and serious decisions.

§2 Necessity of the Theme of Freedom: Mixed Premises and Conclusions

Once existence is no longer produced or deduced, but simply posited (this simplicity arrests all our thought), and once existence is abandoned to this positing at the same time that it is abandoned by it, we must think the freedom of this abandonment. In other words, once existence, instead of "preceding," "following," or even "following from" essence (symmetrical formulas of existentialisms and essentialisms, captives—the one as much as the other—of a difference of essence between essence and existence), once existence itself constitutes essence ("*Das 'Wesen' des Daseins liegt in seiner Existenz*," "The 'essence' of Dasein lies in its existence," *Being and Time*, §9), and consequently once these two concepts and their opposition are no longer relevant to anything but the history of metaphysics, then we must think, at the limit of this history, the stakes of this other concept: "freedom." Freedom can no longer be either "essential" or "existential," but is implicated in the chiasmus of these concepts: we have to consider what makes existence, which is in its essence abandoned to a freedom, free for this abandonment, offered to it and available in it. Perhaps it will not be possible to preserve the very name and concept of freedom. We will return to this. But if the essence that is offered to existence does not in some way "free" existence in its most proper essence, then thought has nothing left to "think" and existence has nothing left to "live": the one and the other are stripped of all experience.

In still other words: once existence clearly offers itself (this clarity dazzles us) no longer as an empiricity that would need to be related to its conditions of possibility, or sublated [*relever*] in a transcendence beyond itself, but instead offers itself as a factuality that contains in itself and as such, *hic et nunc*, the reason for its presence and the presence of its reason, we must—whatever the modes of this "presence" and of this "reason"—think its "fact" as a "freedom." This means that we must think what gives existence back to itself and only to itself, or what makes it available as an *existence* that is neither an essence nor a sheer given. (The question is no longer exactly "Why is there something?," nor is it any more exactly this other question to which freedom seems to be linked in a more visible manner, namely, "Why is there evil?," but it becomes "Why these very questions by which existence affirms itself and abandons itself in a single gesture?")

Indeed, if the factuality of being—existence as such—or even if its haeccity, the being-the-there, the being-that-is-this-there, the *da-sein* in the local intensity and temporal extension of its singularity, cannot in itself and as such be freed from (or be the freeing of) the steady, ahistorical, unlocalizable, self-positioning immobility of Being signified as principle, substance, and subject of what is (in short: if in fact being, or if the fact of being, cannot be the freeing of being itself, in all of the senses of this genitive), then thought is condemned (*we* are condemned) to the pressing thickness of the night in which not only are all cows black, but their very rumination, down to their death, vanishes—and we with them—into a foldless immanence, which is not even unthinkable, since it is *a priori* out of reach of all thought, even a thought of the unthinkable.

If we do not think being itself, the being of abandoned existence, or even the being of being-in-the-world, as a "freedom" (or perhaps as a liberality or generosity more original than any freedom), we are condemned to think of freedom as a pure "Idea" or "right," and being-in-the-world, in return, as a forever blind and obtuse necessity. Since Kant, philosophy and our world have been relentlessly placed before this tear. This is why ideology today demands freedom, but does not think it.

Freedom is everything except an "Idea" (in a sense, Kant himself knew this). Freedom is a fact: in this essay, we will not cease discussing this fact. But it is the fact of existence as the essence of itself. The factuality of this fact does not belong to a transhistorically perceptive self-evidence: it makes itself, and makes itself known to experience, through a history. Not through the History of Freedom, the teleological and eschatological age of the revelation and realization of an Idea (by which a Freedom assured of its self-representation can necessarily only aim at being reabsorbed into Necessity), but by the freedom of history, which means by the effectivity of a becoming in which something happens, where "time is out of joint," as Hamlet says, and by the generativity or generosity of the new, which gives and gives itself to thinking: for all existence is new, in its birth and in its death to the world.

~

Existence as its own essence—the singularity of being—presented itself when history set a limit to thoughts concerning being as foundation. In such thoughts, freedom could not be given unless founded; yet as freedom, it had to be founded in freedom itself; this exigency determined the incarnation, or at least the figuration, of freedom in a supreme being, a *causa sui* whose existence and freedom were meanwhile, in the name of being in general, to be founded in necessity. . . . Once God is no longer the gratuitousness of his own existence and the love of his creation (to which a faith, not a thought, could respond), and once he becomes accountable to all existences for their foundation, "God" becomes the name of a necessary freedom whose self-necessitation actually determines the metaphysical concept of freedom (as the freedom of necessity, no less). In this way, being's free necessity appears to itself as the supreme being [*étant*], the Idea of which performs what we could call being's metaphysical turning away: broken off from its own fact, from its *da-sein*, it nevertheless *establishes* this fact, but it establishes it on a foundation and as its own foundation-*being*. Freedom of necessity is the dialectical predicate of being's subject-being. Along with all existences, being therefore finds itself subjected.

But freedom, if it is something, is the very thing that prevents itself from being founded. The existence of God was to be free in the sense that the freedom that sustained his existence could not become one of its predicates or properties. Theology and philosophy had certainly recognized this limit, or this dilemma. Conceived of as freedom's necessary being, God risked (if one did not elaborate subtle *ad hoc* arguments) ruining both himself and freedom. ("Is not freedom the power God lacks, or which he only has verbally, since he cannot disobey the command that *he is*, the command of which he is the guarantor?" Georges Bataille, *Literature and Evil.*) The freedom of the gods (if one must speak of gods . . .), like every freedom, makes them susceptible to existence or nonexistence (they can die): it is not their attribute, but their destiny. In return, a being taken for *being* as such, founding the freedom on which it is itself founded, designates the internal border of the limit of onto-theology: absolute subjectivity as the essence of essence, and of existence.

This limit is reached as soon as the logic and signification of *foundation* in general, that is to say, philosophy, is achieved. The end of philosophy deprives us of a foundation of freedom as much as it deprives us of freedom as foundation; but this "deprivation" was already inscribed in the philosophical aporia consubstantial with the thought of a foundation of freedom and/or with the thought of freedom as foundation. In philosophy itself, this aporia was perhaps already announced and denounced at the same time that Spinoza attributed freedom exclusively to a God who was not a foundation, but pure existence, and of whom Hegelian Spirit and then Marxian Man were perhaps also the inheritors, raising the question—still unperceived as such—of an existing and unfounded freedom, or of a freeing of existence down *to* its foundation (or down to its essence). Thus, the end of philosophy would be *deliverance from foundation* in that it would withdraw existence from the necessity of foundation, but also in that it would be set free from foundation, and given over to unfounded "freedom."

At the limit of philosophy, there where we are, not having made our way, but having happened and still happening, there is only—

yet *there is* (which is no longer an affidavit, but a seizure)—the free dissemination of existence. This free dissemination (whose formula might well be only a tautology) is not the diffraction of a principle, nor the multiple effect of a cause, but is the an-archy—the origin removed from every logic of origin, from every archaeology—of a singular and thus in essence plural arising whose being *as being* is neither ground, nor element, nor reason, but truth, which would amount to saying, under the circumstances, freedom. The question of being, the question of the meaning of being—as a question concerning the meaning of what arises into existence when no entity can found that existence—perhaps has no other definitive meaning than the following, which, properly speaking, is no longer the meaning of a "question": the recognition of the freedom of being in its singularity.

Thus it is no longer a question of winning or defending the freedom of man, or human freedoms, as if these were goods that one could secure as possession or property, and whose essential virtue would be to allow human beings to be what they are (as if human beings and freedom circularly returned to each other in the heart of a simple immanence). Instead, it is a question of offering human beings to a freedom of being, it is a question of presenting the humanity of the human being (his "essence") to a freedom *as being* by which existence absolutely and resolutely *transcends*, that is, *ex-ists*. In all movements of liberation, as in all vested institutions of freedom, it is precisely this transcendence which still has to be freed. In and through ethical, juridical, material, and civil liberties,[1] one must free that through which alone these liberties are, on the one hand, ultimately possible and thinkable, and on the other, capable of receiving a destination other than that of their immanent self-consumption: a transcendence of existence such that existence, as existence-in-the-world, which has nothing to do with any other world, transcends (i.e., continues to accomplish) the "essence" that it is in the finitude in which it in-sists. Only a finite being can be free (and a finite being is an existent), for the infinite being encloses the necessity of its freedom, which it seals to its being. It is therefore a question of nothing other than liberating human freedom from the immanence of an infinite foundation or finality, and liberating it therefore from its own infinite projection to infinity, where transcendence (existence) itself is transcended and thereby annulled. It is a question of letting freedom exist for itself. Freedom perhaps designates nothing more and nothing less than existence itself. And *ex-istence* does not so much signify what can at least be connoted by a vocabulary of the "ecstasy" of being, torn from itself: it signifies simply the freedom of being, that is, *the infinite inessentiality of its being-finite, which delivers it to the singularity wherein it is "itself."*

That existence presents itself in this way, and that it offers itself for this type of thought and task, is attested by the event and experience of our time: the closure of the order of significations, the closure of the very regime of signification as the assignation of meaning into the beyond (translinguistic or metalinguistic, trans- or meta-worldly, trans- or meta-existential) of a presence that consequently would be devoted to its own representation. According to this regime, freedom ends—or begins—by being understood as the unrepresentable (invisible) "in view" of which one would have to arrange representation, whether political (delegation of freedom . . .) or aesthetic (free giving of form). This presence-beyond, or this essential presence beyond all (re)presentable presence—with regard to which it is important that Freedom should have furnished its supreme Idea, or rather the Idea of the Idea itself (isn't the intelligible form of every Idea in the freedom with which it forms and presents itself?)[2]—is henceforth, undoubtedly since Hegel but with an exemplary insistence since Heidegger, confronted with the exigency of what could be called, for symmetry's sake, the hither-side [*l'en deçà*] of a difference: a difference of being *in itself,* which would not simply convert being into difference and difference into being (since precisely this type of conversion between pure substances would become impossible), but which would be the difference of its *existence,* and in this existence, inasmuch as it is its own essence, the difference and the division of its singularity. With the existence of the singular being, an entirely other possibility of "meaning" would be offered—freed—before us, on the edges of an epoch which has barely begun to hatch.

There is in fact a hatching [*éclosion*] correlative to closure, even though we perceive nothing of it and find ourselves delivered to dereliction, and even though we lack the words and thought for hatching (an image too organic and "natural" for what is also an irruption): there is a hatching because the event of closure itself makes history, and because what it brings to an end on the internal border of the limit it touches corresponds equally on its external border to an inauguration. "To inscribe the epoch in its essential outline," Granel writes of Derrida, and of Heidegger behind him, is to inscribe it "such that it is visible from the monster of the future, which gathers itself in that epoch and which no one can see."[3] This retro-spection anticipated without fore-sight is not a divinatory magic: it has its possibility insofar as history precedes itself as much as it succeeds itself in the present time, which thought experiences and in which thought inscribes an outline. If something like a "present" or an "epoch" can be presented, this is because it is not simply, immediately present (neither to us nor to itself: on the contrary, it has always, always already, drawn at one and the same time the two sides of its limit, and thus allowed itself invisibly to profile the contour without figure of that to which the present itself happens (and from which, at the same time, it withdraws).

History in its effectivity is certainly always that which advances without seeing ahead and without seeing itself, without even seeing itself advancing. This does not mean that it would be the inverse of a history conscious of itself, a blind and obscure force: for it is this very opposition that must be completely suspended here, in order to think a different historicity of history. And this task itself doubtless depends on a different thought of freedom. History is perhaps not so much that which unwinds and links itself, like the time of a causality, as that which *surprises itself.* "Surprising itself," we will see, is a mark proper to freedom. History in this sense is the freedom of being—or being in its freedom. Thought is placed today—by history and by its own history—before the necessity of thinking this unforeseeability, this im-providence and surprise that give rise to freedom. We have to think freedom and think in freedom (it is definitively *also* our most ancient and profound tradition), simply because there is nothing else to think (to preserve, not foresee; to test, not guide) besides the fact that being has a history or that being is history (or histories in the plural), which means at least the coming and the surprise of a renewed hatching of existence. This is the point we have reached: being, in its history, has delivered the historicity or the historiality of being. This means the end of a relation of foundation—whichever one—between being and history, and the opening of existence to its own essentiality as well as to this scansion, or singular rhythm, according to which the existent precedes and succeeds itself in a time to which it is not "present," but in which its freedom surprises it—like the spacing (which is also a rhythm, perhaps at the heart of the former rhythm) in which the existent is singularized, that is to say, exists, according to the free and common space of its inessentiality.

～

What one could call, in some sense, the axiomatic of the spatiotemporal effectivity of existence—that which requires existence to exist *hic et nunc* and at every moment to put at stake its very possibility of existing, at every moment delivering itself as its own essence (which is by this very fact "in-"essential)—does not signify the axiological equivalence of what is produced according to the places and moments of history. Evil and good are correlative possibilities here, not in the sense that one or the other would first be offered to the choice of freedom—there is not *first* evil and good, and *then* freedom with its choice—but in the sense that the possibility of evil (which proves to be, in the last instance, the devastation of freedom) is correlative to the introduction of freedom. This means that freedom cannot present itself without presenting the possibility, inscribed in its essence, of a *free renunciation of freedom*. This very renunciation directly makes itself known as *wickedness*, in a moment in some way preethical in which ethics itself would nevertheless already surprise itself. Inscribing freedom in being does not amount to conferring on being, as a singular existent, an indifference of will (resurrected from classical thought) whose ontological tenor would strike indifferently the moral tenor of decisions (as some have occasionally gratified themselves to think, in a posterity

skeptical of Nietzsche). On the contrary, inscribing freedom in being amounts to raising to the level of ontology the positive possibility—and not through deficiency—of evil as much as of good, *not
as indifferent, but insofar as evil there makes itself known as such.*

Before being able to establish what is anticipated here, it is important to posit the following: in a certain way, nothing is more constantly attested by the history of the modern world, and as one of its
most properly historical marks, than the free and resolute renunciation of freedom. We know that this can go as far as the absolute
horror of a "humanity" (willing itself "superhuman") exemplarily ex-
ecuting a whole other part of humanity (declared to be "subhu-
man") in order to define itself as the *exemplum* of humanity.[4] This
is Auschwitz. But freedom is also renounced everywhere that existence, as existence (which does not always mean *life*, pure and simple, but which implies it), is subjected and ruined by a form of
essence, an Idea, a structure, the erection of an (ir)rationality: in
Marx's Manchester, in our "Third" and "Fourth" worlds, in all the
camps, all the apartheids, and all the fanaticisms. But also and very
simply, if we dare say it, it is renounced where the essence, concentrated in itself, of a process, of an institution (technical, social, cultural, political) prevents existence from existing, that is to say from
acceding to its proper essence. Freedom is renounced in the exchange of this essence for the identification with the other (with the
Idea), and renounced freedom combats the freedom of the same and
the freedom of the other. (Which does not mean that existing
would take place without identification, but that identification is
something other than a substitution of essence.)

That this happens, and even that this seems to outline itself in a
manner indicted more and more often as evidencing the general
barrenness of today's world, is what demands of thinking the greatest circumspection and an extreme vigilance, especially if it tries
to make freedom its theme. But that this, instead of forbidding us
to think, demands precisely to be thought, which is to say finally to
be related to and measured against the unapproachable freedom
from which thought itself proceeds, also reminds us that with the en-
durance of thinking (if we must also understand by this the strength

to hold its ground, in the face of the evil that defies thought, from the deepest point of its freedom), there must also be its hope: this is not the hope that things "finally turn out well," and even less that they "turn into good," but it is that which, in thinking and of thinking, must, *simply in order to think*, tend in spite of everything toward a liberation as well as toward the very reality of the existence that is to be thought of. Without this, thinking would have no meaning. All thought, even when skeptical, negative, dark, and disabused, if it is *thought*, frees the existing of existence—because in fact thought proceeds from it. But hope, as the *virtus* of thought, absolutely does not deny that today more than ever, at the heart of a world overwhelmed by harshness and violence, thought is confronted with its own powerlessness. Thought cannot think of itself as an "acting" (as Heidegger asks it to be and as we cannot not require it to be, unless we give up thinking) unless it understands this "acting" as at the same time a "suffering." Free thought thinking freedom must know itself to be astray, lost, and, from the point of view of "action," undone by the obstinacy of intolerable evil. It must know itself to be pushed in this way onto its limit, which is that of the unsparing material powerlessness of all discourse, but which is also the limit at which *thinking*, in order to be itself, divorces itself from all *discourse* and exposes itself as *passion*. In this passion and through it, already before all "action"—but also ready for any engagement—freedom acts.

~

It is always too soon to say *what* hatches, but it is always time to say *that* it hatches. Being's difference-in-itself, or existence's (at least as soon as we give back to this word a weight that no foundation could support), does not make meaning available as *signification*, but is the opening of a new space for meaning, of a spacing, or, we could say, of a "spaciosity": of the spacious element that alone can receive meaning. This means the spacing of a time, the time that opens at this moment, in the passage from one epoch to another or from one instant to the next, that is, in the passage or transfer [*passation*] of existence, which succeeds itself and differs in its essence, opening and reopening the spacious temporality in accordance with which it exists: the opening of time, *the first schema*, the first draw-ing without figure of the very rhythm of existing,[5] *the transcenden-tal schematism itself* no longer as a "surprise attack" ["*coup-de-main*"] on the secret dissimulated in a "nature," *but as the freedom* with which the existent surprises the world and itself prior to every de-termination of existence. And this means that time in turn is opened onto a new spatiality, onto a *free space* at the heart of which freedom can exist, at the heart of which freedom can be freed or renounced, the free space of the clearing of meaning in general (but there is no "meaning in general," its generality is its singularity), as well as the free space of communication, or that of the public place, or that in which embracing bodies play, or that of war and peace.

That which exists, insofar as it exists, in itself, cannot be except for this space-time of freedom, and the freedom of its space-time. This is why the question of freedom (the question we ask in regard to freedom—What is it?—and the question that freedom asks—What is to be done?) henceforth begins neither with man, nor with God, at the heart of a totality of which Being would be the substantive pre-supposition, and as such foreign to the freedom of existing. It begins with the being of a world whose existence is itself the *thing-in-itself*. We must therefore think freedom, because it can no longer be a quality or property that one would attribute, promise, or refuse to the existent, as a result of some consideration of essence or reason. But it must be the element in which and according to which only ex-istence *takes place* (and time), that is, exists and "accounts" ["*rend rai-son*"] for itself.

Freedom must be the element or fundamental modality of being, as soon as being does not precede existence, or succeed it, but is at stake in it. "*The essence of freedom is not properly viewed until we in-vestigate freedom as the ground of the possibility of being-there*, as what *is even before being and time*."[6]

That there is no existence, that nothing exists, or at least that no one exists, except in freedom, is the very simple proposition that philosophy not only will always have indicated or foretold, but will always have more or less clearly recognized as its ownmost motif and motivation, the *primum movens* of its enterprise. That ontology must become an "eleutherology" does not constitute, in this sense, a discovery. But what reveals itself—what hatches for us in the history of thought—is that the eleutherology always presupposed by philosophy, both as the theme of its logic and as *ethos* or *hexis* of its practice, must itself be elaborated, less as a theme than as the "thing itself" of thinking. In this sense, the "treatise on freedom" that philosophy has not ceased to articulate will perhaps have to be abandoned, since it has never really elevated its object to the status of the "thing itself" of thought. Finally, the theme, the concept or concepts, and the name of freedom will perhaps have to give way—let us say, for the moment and provisionally—to another ontological "generosity."

Regardless of what happens in this regard, it will be a question of bringing an *experience* of "freedom" to light as a theme *and* putting it at stake as a *praxis* of thought. An experience is first of all the encounter with an actual given, or rather, in a less simply positive vocabulary, it is the testing of something real (in any case, it is the act of a thought which does not conceive, or interrogate, or construct what it thinks except by being already taken up and cast as thought, by its thought). Also, according to the origin of the word "experience" in *peirā* and in *ex-periri,* an experience is an attempt executed without reserve, given over to the *peril* of its own lack of foundation and security in this "object" of which it is not the subject but instead the passion, exposed like the pirate (*peirātēs*) who freely tries his luck on the high seas. In a sense, which here might be the first and last sense, freedom, to the extent that it is the thing itself of thinking, cannot be appropriated, but only "pirated": its "seizure" will always be illegitimate.

§3 Impossibility of the Question of Freedom: Fact and Right Indistinguishable

When freedom was presented in philosophy as the "keystone of the whole architecture of the system of pure reason" (thereby leading to a completion—a procedure undoubtedly engaged in all of philosophy), despite the *theoretical* determination of this presentation, which set aside a positive exhibition of freedom, or rather, in other terms, which set aside the possibility of *establishing* freedom as a *principle*, what was in question was in fact, and at first, an ostension of the existence of freedom, or more exactly an ostension of its presence at the heart of existence (and thus maybe the first definitive ostension of existence as such, *avant la lettre* we might say—unless Spinoza is to be counted here). For Kant, freedom does not arise as a *question* but instead as a *reality* or as a *fact*.

Freedom is not a property of which we must demonstrate our possession, nor is it a faculty whose legitimacy we must, in the Kantian sense, deduce.[1] It is a *fact* of reason, truly the only one of its kind, which also amounts to saying that it is reason's own factuality, or reason as factual reason. The "keystone" is reason in its fact, reason factually principial and principially factual. The factuality of phenomenal experience needed to be justified, since the authorization of knowledge was at stake (we will not ask up to what point this knowledge, as the knowledge of pure reason, plants in turn the root of its legitimacy into the fact of freedom . . .). But here what is involved is the experience that reason *produces* [*fait*] (another valence of fact: not only its positivity, but its active and/or passive effectivity) from itself, and which consists in the experience of the obligation of free will or free action (which, under the circumstances, and as I will show, amount to the same thing), or even in the obligation of will or action *to* be free. It is the rational experience of reason *as* "practical reason."

Commentators have often been surprised by the text of §91 of the Third *Critique*, which posits the Idea of freedom as "presentable in experience." This surprise has been underlined and problematized by Heidegger, whose analysis we will recall later. It would have been less accentuated if Kant's permanent insistence on this motif had been remembered. "The Canon of Pure Reason" already states: "Practical freedom can be demonstrated by experience," which also has as a correlate that "pure reason, then, contains . . . in that practical employment which is also moral, principles of the *possibility of experience*, namely, of such actions as . . . *might* be met with in the *history* of mankind."[2] In fact, the Second *Critique* opens onto this alone: it is indeed, writes Kant, a critique "of practical reason" and not "of pure practical reason" because it is concerned solely with establishing "*that there is a pure practical reason*," and that, once established, pure practical reason has no need of any critique that would come to limit its contingent/eventual presumption: practical reason would not be able to "surpass itself," as theoretical reason can and irresistibly tends to do. If *there is* a practical reason, "its reality" is proven "by the fact itself." We are not dealing with the presumptions of a power but with the given fact of an actual existence. And this given fact is its own legitimation, because it is not a given object (in which case one would have to ask whether or not it is correctly produced), but rather the given fact of the existence of a legislation as the legislation of existence: reason exists as—or under—this law of freedom. That which exists (for example, reason as the given fact of existence, and not as the power of knowledge) is this self-legislation, and that which legislates is this existence. (One could say that with Kant begins the self-legitimation of existence, *and* existence as the *abyss* of this self-legitimation.)

Thus freedom is a "keystone" "to the extent that reality is proven by an apodictic law of practical reason." The logical modality of apodicticity corresponds to the categorial modality of necessity. The reality of freedom is a necessity, and necessarily gives itself as such. And it is freedom itself, as the *praxis* of reason that is first of all *praxis* of its own legislating factuality, which states this necessity. We will not depart from this apodicticity. No matter how considerable the displacements of concepts and contexts to which a historical elaboration of the motif of freedom (its effective destiny in thought) will lead, up until us, we will not depart from an apodicticity according to which freedom would be *in question*. (Here again, let us note in passing, Spinoza no doubt already preceded this apodicticity; but did it not always precede itself in all of philosophy?)

The proof of freedom—which will reveal itself to be more on the order of the test (or of *experience*) than of demonstration—is in its existence. More exactly, for this is assuredly not "freedom" as such, or as its concept, which does exist, this proof is found in existence as the existence of free being, and this proof or this experience finally proposes nothing other than the following: EXISTENCE AS ITS OWN ESSENCE IS NOTHING OTHER THAN THE FREEDOM OF BEING. On the subject of freedom, one can propose no other task of thought than to attempt to bring to light that which has already brought itself, in reason, before reason.

Accordingly, in other terms: *freedom cannot be the object of a question*, but is "only" the *putting into question of an affirmation*; and it cannot be the object of a question posed "about something," but only the putting into question of an affirmation *of itself* (of the "self" of free being, and likewise of the "self" of the thought on which the reaffirmation of this affirmation rests). (Reciprocally, is not affirmation itself essentially free, and questioning essentially constrained?) In its most developed Kantian form, this affirmation is that of §91 of the Third *Critique*:

> And, what is very remarkable, there is one rational idea (which is susceptible in itself of no presentation in intuition, and consequently of no theoretical proof of its possibility) which also comes under things of fact. This is the idea of *freedom*, whose reality, regarded as that of a particular kind of causality (of which the concept, theoretically considered to

be transcendent), may be exhibited by means of practical laws of pure reason, and conformably to this, in actual actions, and consequently, in experience. This is the only one of all the ideas of pure reason whose object is a thing of fact and to be reckoned under the *scibilia.*[3]

It is thus perfectly clear that the presentation of freedom, in experience, is not that of an object of knowing. Indeed the contrary is true—and it would appear to be necessary to alter the formula in order to speak of the presentation of a "subject of action." In properly Kantian logic (but that also means in the general logic of the metaphysics of subjectivity) it would still be necessary to specify, if one wanted to sustain this new formula, that if freedom is not "in itself" presentable, its particular causality does not present itself any the less to empirical perception as a "real action" in the course of the causality of phenomena. It is indeed possible that, in the passage quoted from the Third *Critique,* Kant is underhandedly alluding to the famous example of the thesis of the Third Antinomy: "If I at this moment arise from my chair, in complete freedom . . . " One would then have to say that the presented reality is the reality of the act of a subject, and not that of a signification of an object. But one would immediately have to add that this "subjective" (and "sovereign") reality only allows itself to be presented because it is objectivized—and that Kant thus gives himself room for a double violation of the most rigid critical principles: on the one hand the action of "arising," as a "completely free" action, would be subreptively withdrawn from the dialectical status that, from the interior of the "thesis" to which it belongs, it can never escape; and, on the other hand (this explaining that), the "particular causality" of freedom (whose nature can in no way be deduced from that of phenomenal causality) would also find itself subreptively slipping into the place of the general category of causality, thereby making possible, through its conjunction with the intuition of the gesture of arising, the quasi constitution of an object of experience: the free subject . . . Now, in all this, it can only be a matter of precisely a quasi constitution; in other words, this entire operation would come back to the *Schwärmerei.* It would definitively suppose this *schema* of freedom (permitting free causality to be united with an empirical act), all possibility of which is rigorously ex-

cluded by the Second *Critique*. This is, however, the only possible reconstitution, in Kantian terms, of the enigmatic logic of this passage
(and we have been able to see how this reconstitution, in spite of
everything, is discreetly named in Kant's text by the words "in itself,"
which seem to indicate that if the Idea is not "in itself" susceptible
to any presentation, it would however be susceptible to presentation
where it is not simply an "Idea in itself," where it overflows itself as
Idea . . . in an experience).

We have adhered to this analysis without conclusion in order to
show that the Kantian *fact* of freedom cannot receive, in a rigorous
Kantian logic, its status as fact. (And, in a more general way, it
cannot receive this status in a metaphysical logic if the means of the
demonstration can never be supplied except through a union of
the intelligible and the sensible where these are in principle posited
as irreconcilable.)

Strictly speaking, another analysis would be possible, one that
would no longer place on the side of intuition empirical action,
but rather the sentiment of respect for the law—which, incidentally,
properly constitutes the "intuitive," or at least receptive, element of
reason in its being-practical. Later on we will perhaps encounter the
significance of this respect. But here it is not helpful, because Kant
is referring to freedom's "particular type of causality," and respect does
not relate to freedom's causality but to its lawfulness. (Or rather, insofar as it is itself the sensible effect of the law, respect can only
summon an aporia comparable to the preceding one.) Thus the
recourse to causality, "particular" or not, hinders the elaboration
of the specific factuality of the fact of the experience of freedom; or
rather, and this amounts to the same thing, the "particularity" of free
causality conceals the following: freedom is not a type of causality.

This last proposition was the essential result of the course given
by Heidegger in 1930, "On the Essence of Human Freedom." The
categorial subordination of freedom to causality in the Kantian
problematic appeared to him as the limit of his eleutherological
enterprise, and he was able to say:

> *Causality*, in the sense of the traditional comprehension of the being of
> beings, in ordinary understanding as well as in traditional metaphysics,

is precisely *the fundamental category of being as presence-at-hand*. If *causality is a problem of freedom*, and not the inverse, then *the problem of being, taken absolutely*, is in itself *a problem of freedom*.[4]

Accordingly, by the same movement, the relation of freedom to causality had to be reversed, and the problem of freedom found itself promoted to the rank of the problem of ontology par excellence. In order to invert the relation between freedom and causality, it was necessary to engage in a determination of the *fact* of freedom other than the determination to which Kant seemed to deliver us. Heidegger had from the outset situated his inquiry into the reality of freedom—as such entirely taking up and reaffirming Kant's position—in the perspective of a specific "mode of reality" of *praxis*. Insofar as it is practical, reason is nothing other than will. Accordingly, *pure* practical reason is pure will. Pure will is the will that *wills* absolutely, which means the will that determines itself from nothing other than itself (or rather, if it is possible to paraphrase in this way, the will that simply *wills* and that thus does not will *anything* except will, or except willing). Now "the law of pure will . . . is the law determined for the existence of the will, which is to say that the will is willing itself." Therefore: "The *fundamental law of pure will*, of *pure practical reason*, is nothing other than the *form of legislation*." Pure will is thus the will of obligation that springs from the law (or that the law encloses by essence in its being-from-the-law, or in its being-the-law, which is identical to making-the-law), and from this form of the law that is the law of pure will. "The essence of willing . . . requires being willed," just as "*he who wills really wills nothing other than the duty of his being-there* [*das Sollen seines Daseins*]."

~

(Thus, the "will to will," in which Heidegger will later [in fact only slightly later] recognize the essence of metaphysical subjectivity, was first presented here in a very different manner: in accordance with the formally subjective structure of a "willing [for] oneself," certainly, but brought at once to an extremity where the "self" of "willing *oneself*" is immediately and only a "duty of being-there," which is to say immediately the abandonment of existence to an obligation, and the assignation of the injunction of this obligation into the having-to-exist. We will not attempt here to analyze the evolution and implications of Heidegger's thought on the will [but further on we shall see that it is implied by the analysis of the suspension of the motif of freedom in Heidegger]. We must content ourselves with noting how often, in this seminar of 1930, what is exposed in the name of *willing* tends more to represent the "self" or the identity of an irreducible *factuality* [we could also say: the "self" of a fact rather than the "fact" of a self], which is the factuality of the existence of the existent as being-given-over-to-the-law-of-being-free, and not the self-presence of a will which wills this very presence. Such a will, as self-presence, would instead lose the *ground*, and the *grounds*, of its subjective consistency and propriety, whereas the "self" of being-free in its fact would offer itself as the un-grounding [*dé-fondement*] of a self founded in itself by its desire-for-self [the will presenting itself here according to the element of a decision rather than according to the movement of a desire]. This also means that the text of this seminar could be annotated by saying that factuality unexpectedly happens to the "self" of the existent, and does not "found" it any more than factuality is for its part founded by the self or in the self. And this is why, as we will later come to see, this factuality is a specific factuality.)

   In this way we reach the proper factuality of *praxis*: this factuality cannot be exterior to the will's relation of obligation toward itself, which is equally the obligation's relation of will toward itself. This factuality cannot be that of an action (understood as empirical behavior), nor of anything consequent on willing (understood as representation and desire preliminary to action)—and this means that in the last instance nothing less than the essences of (free) action and of (free) willing are at stake in this factuality, which would no longer permit these essences to communicate with the determinations that metaphysics has given them. Neither can this factuality be that of an intuitive presentation of willing.[5] It is a factuality that does not depend on any insertion into a referential order of facts, nor on any constitution of an object. On the contrary, it is a self-referential and self-constitutive factuality (which does not necessarily mean a subjective factuality or the factuality of a subjectivity). Heidegger says, "*The reality of willing is only in the willing of that reality.*"

This reality itself does not depend on a positive decision being made in favor of obligation. We can "decide for pure obligated willing, that is, effectively willing, or against it, that is, not willing, or we can mix willing and nonwilling in turmoil and indecision": we are nonetheless always drawn into the fundamental structure according to which willing wills its reality of willing—even as indecision. Willing wills its own effectivity, and this, as we know, does not mean that it desires or decides it, but that it *resolves* [*se décide*], or even—at least in keeping with our questioning of Heidegger here—that the will of will presents nothing other than *effectivity insofar as it resolves to be effective*. More precisely, it is the effectivity of existence that here resolves to be effective, or to exist, and this decision does not amount to effecting *in actu* what should have been there *in potentia*, any more than it refers to a preexisting power of representation or to the energy of a power of realization, but it is the ex-istence of the effectivity that existence is of itself. It is the existence of the existent, its "essence" therefore, or: that the existent exists as the existent that it is.

This is the sense in which we must understand that the will is a will to obligate itself to its own effectivity. Obligation is the fact proceeding from the nonavailability, for the existent, of an essence (and/or power) of self that could be represented and intended. But if the essence of existence is existence itself, it is not available for representation or intentionality (nor, consequently, for the "will" in the sense of a voluntaristic will), and *it obligates itself, in its existence, only to exist*, that is, *to be exposed to the effectivity that it is*, because it "is" not in any mode of a property of existence. Here, "to will willing" therefore means to be effectively exposed to existing effectivity (which, moreover, is nothing other than exposing effectivity). *This* willing—this willing of willing that is the willing of its own duty—thus constitutes the very *fact of experience* of practical reason, or its practicity as the fact of experience. It is the fact of freedom. "*Freedom is, only insofar as it is the effective willing of pure obligation* [*des rein Gesollten* = of the pure ought]."

It is the practical fact *of reason*, but this does not mean that it would be a "fact of reason" in the same sense that one says "a rational being"; thus, it is not a theoretical "fact," ideal or unreal, ineffective and inexistent.[6] On the contrary, if one were to make explicit what Heidegger's text contains as indices, this fact is not only an existent fact—it is (as we have already seen) the fact of existence as such. It is the fact by which the existent (the *Dasein*) relates (to) itself as that which wants to be / obligates itself to be what it is. The existent is the being that in its being obligates itself / wants to be, and that obligates itself to / wants being. Or further: it is the being that is *decided for being*. In this way it transcends, that is, it ex-ists. The *fact* of freedom is the "right" of existence, or rather, the "fact" of existence is the *right* of freedom. This freedom is not the freedom *of* this or that comportment *in* existence: it is the freedom of existence to exist, to be "decided for being," that is, to come to itself according to its own transcendence (since, having no essence "to itself," it can only *be* "essentially" this transcendence "toward its being"). This freedom is, according to the formula employed in *Being and Time* (§40), "*the being-free for* the freedom of choosing-oneself-and-grasping-oneself."

The freedom of existence to exist is existence itself in its "essence," insofar as existence is itself essence. This "essence" consists in being brought directly to this limit where the existent is only what it is in its transcendence. "Transcendence" itself is nothing other than the passage to the limit, not its attainment: it is the being-exposed at, on, and as the limit. Here, the limit does not signify the arrested circumscription of a domain or figure, but signifies rather *that the essence of existence consists in this being-taken-to-the-edge resulting from what has no "essence" that is enclosed and reserved in any immanence present to the interior of the border.* That existence is its own essence means that it has no "interiority," without, however, being "entirely in exteriority" (for example, in the way that Hegel's inorganic thing is). *Existence keeps itself, "through its essence," on the undecidable limit of its own decision to exist.* In this way, freedom belongs to existence not as a property, but as its *fact*, its *factum rationis* which can also be understood as "the fact of its reason for existing," which is similarly "the reason for the fact of its existence." Freedom is the transcendence of the self toward the self, or from the self to the self—which in no way excludes, but on the contrary requires, as we can henceforth clearly see, that the "self" not be understood as subjectivity, if subjectivity designates the relation *of a substance* to itself; and which requires at the same time, as we will show later, that this "self" only takes place according to a being-in-common of singularities.

The *fact* of the existent's freedom consists in that, as soon as the existent exists, the very fact of this existence is indistinguishable from its transcendence, which means from the finite being's non-presence to itself or from its exposure on its limit—this infinite limit on which it must receive itself *as a law* of existing, that is, of willing its existence or resolving for it, a law *it gives to itself and which it is not.* In giving itself law, it gives itself over to the will to obey the law, but since it *is* not this law—yet, if we like, it ex-ists in it—it is to the same extent what can disobey, as well as obey, the law. (We could also say: "existence is law," but if law, in general, essentially traces a limit, the law of existence does not impose a limit *on* existence: it traces existence as the limit that it is and on which it resolves. Thus existence as "essence" withdraws into the law, but the law itself withdraws into the fact of existing. It is no longer a law that could be respected or transgressed: in a sense, it is impossible to transgress; in another sense, it is nothing other than the inscription of the transgressive/transcendent possibility of existence. Existence can only transgress itself.)

The existent's ex-istence *gives it over* [*livre*] to the possibility of *giving itself over* [*se livrer*] to its law, precisely because the law *has* neither essence nor law, but *is* its own essence and own law. When there is an existent, there is neither essence nor law, and it is in this an-archy that existence resolves. It renders itself [*se livre*] to itself, it de-livers [*dé-livre*] itself for itself or delivers itself from itself. *The fact of freedom is this de-liverance of existence from every law and from itself as law:* freedom there delivers itself as will, which is itself only the existent's being-delivered-and-decided.

~

Thus the fact of freedom is indistinguishable from the reality of existence inasmuch as this reality, for Kant, "signifies the setting into position of the thing in itself."[7] Existence in its reality is the thing in itself (of being). Freedom is the proper factuality of the "setting into position," of the *Setzung* of existence. (Thus, as we will better understand from what follows, freedom is the factuality of its birth and of its death.) Existence's thing in itself *is* not simply *posited*—already posed, positioned, *gesetzt*, as are all things that are nonexisting and placed *under* laws. It is, its reality is, in the *Setzung*, in the act, in the gesture or movement that puts it in the position of existence, that renders its being—or that, in it, renders being itself—to the *da* of *Da-sein*, in such a way that this "rendering" or "deliverance" delivers it for possibilities that are not posited. The fact of freedom is maintained in this movement, in this dynamic proper to the *Setzung*, which posits and *is* never *posited*—and reciprocally, the *Setzung* of existence as the "thing in itself," whose "in itself" is only a bringing-into-the-world, produces [*fait*] the reality of freedom.[8]

Consequently, the very factuality of freedom is the very factuality of *what is not done* [*fait*], but which will be done—not in the sense of a project or plan that remains to be executed, but in the sense of that which in its very reality does not yet have the presence of its reality, and which must—but infinitely—deliver itself for reality. In this way existence is actually in the world. What remains "to be done" is not situated on the register of *poiesis*, like a work whose schema would be given, but on the register of *praxis*, which "produces" only its own agent or actor and which would therefore more closely resemble the action of a schematization considered for itself.[9]

The fact of freedom, or the practical fact, thus absolutely and radically "established" without any establishing procedure being able to produce this fact as a theoretical object, is the fact of what is to be done in this sense, or rather, it is the fact *that there is* something to be done, or is even the fact that there is the *to be done* [*à faire*], or that there is the affair [*affaire*] of existence.[10] Freedom is factual in that it is the *affair* of existence. It is a fact, in that it is not an acquired fact any more than it is a "natural" right, since it is the law without law of an inessentiality. Human beings are not born free in the same way that they are born with a brain; yet they are born, infinitely, to freedom.

Thus Heidegger could say:

> The question: How is freedom possible? is absurd. From this, however, it does not follow that to a certain extent a problem of the irrational remains here. Rather, because freedom is not an object of theoretical apprehending but is instead an object of philosophizing, this can mean nothing other than the fact that freedom only is and can only be in the setting-free. The sole, adequate relation to freedom in man is the self-freeing of freedom in man.[11]

§4 The Space Left Free by Heidegger

Since Heidegger, philosophy has no longer viewed freedom thematically—at least not as its guiding theme, except in historical studies.[1] But in fact it was with Heidegger that an interruption occurred. Freedom was no longer thematized by him, after having been thematized on a par or with a rank *at least* comparable to that which Spinoza, Kant, Schelling, or Hegel conferred upon it— namely, as *"the fundamental question of philosophy, in which even the question of being has its root."*[2] We are the inheritors of this interruption. It offers [*livre*] us something, and it delivers [*délivre*] us for something else, or to something else.

In order for these assertions not to be gratuitous or merely formal, a lengthy work would obviously have to be undertaken here, devoted exclusively to the question of freedom and its interruption or withdrawal in the course of Heidegger's thought.[3] In a sense, this is the task that should now be performed. I will not undertake this task for several reasons. In the first place, for reasons of competence: I am far from being what one would call a Heidegger "specialist" (but, as can be seen, I do not refuse the freedoms that are given, not by a lack of competence as such, but by a certain distance, with its inevitable risks). Second, for reasons of mistrust: it is not certain that the work of reconstituting Heidegger's course could do anything more than simply lead us back to the suspension or interruption from which, on the contrary, we need to be able to depart. Finally, for reasons of decision: the decision to attempt, at least for the space of a brief programmatic essay, to take up the word "freedom" today, despite the Heideggerian interruption—in fact, because of it, and in the space of thought it opens.

There are some motivations for this decision. If the sense of the word "freedom" remains indeterminate, and if its philosophical concept is caught in the closure of the ontology of subjectivity, the word nonetheless preserves a burden of history, and a tradition—the transmission of an impulse that has never stopped throwing itself recklessly against necessity, or the transmission of a voice that has never stopped saying that it is necessary to assist *ananke* or even that destiny confronts nothing other than freedom—the tradition, therefore, of a force of appeal and joy that is difficult to ignore, even though it has been incessantly misused or abused. This has nothing to do with facile appeals to the self-sufficiency and self-satisfaction of a liberal, or even libertarian, individualism. It involves an appeal to existence, and consequently also an appeal to the finitude in which existence transcends—and by virtue of which existence also comports in itself, in its being, the structure and tonality of a call: the free call to freedom.[4] If metaphysical freedom, reduced to its simplest expression, has designated the infinite transcendence of the Subject's absolute self-presence, then the history of this freedom, and its tradition, which is also that of the problems forever put at stake by its thought, as well as of the struggles waged in its name, are *equally* the history and tradition of the transcendence that is henceforth recognizable as the exposure to its own limit, that is, as the finite exposure to the infinite separation of essence as existence. Let us recall briefly some testimonies (which speak for themselves) of what could be called the tradition of freedom's liberation *with respect* to its subjective appropriation:

> Yet this externalization [of the concept] is still incomplete; it expresses the connection of its self-certainty with the object which, just because it is thus connected, has not yet won its complete freedom. The self-knowing Spirit knows not only itself but also the negative of itself, or its limit: to know one's limit is to know how to sacrifice oneself. The

sacrifice is the externalization in which Spirit displays the process of its becoming Spirit in the form of *free contingent happening*. . . .

The truly free spirit will also think freely regarding spirit itself, and will not dissemble over certain dreadful elements in its origin and tendency.

Enlarge art? No. But go with the art in your ownmost narrowness. And set yourself free.[5]

Heidegger so little attended to the proper force of the word "freedom"—which is, in sum, the force of a resistance to the Concept or Idea of Freedom—that he used it until the end without retaining any of this force, or at least without any longer articulating any real notion of it. But if—on the other hand and in spite of everything, as it is legitimate to suppose since it is also true, as Adorno said, that freedom has "aged"—if it is a question of leaving a place for something other than "freedom" (let's say, once again, for a "generosity" that would be more "originary"), doesn't this transition have to be made visible as such? Isn't it therefore necessary to engage "freedom" itself, thematically, in order to be able finally to *free* the place of freedom?

∼

Without treating the question of freedom in Heidegger in a systematic manner, one can fix in outline the stages of its history, in order to try to discern the space left free by his thought.

After the freedom of *Dasein* "for its proper possibility" had furnished a repeated motif, though hardly developed for its own sake, of the analyses of *Being and Time* (1927), the course of 1928, *Metaphysische Anfangsgrunde der Logik* (volume 26 of the complete edition), proposed a circumstantial examination of the proposition according to which "the transcendence of *Dasein* and freedom are identical," and beginning in 1929, *The Essence of Reasons* thematically accounts for freedom as the "freedom to found." Freedom is then qualified as "*foundation of foundation*" and thus "because it is precisely this *Grund*, freedom is the *Abgrund* of human reality."[6] In

1930, the course that we have already cited above systematically analyzes the Kantian determination of freedom, both to establish the
question of freedom in the positing of the foundation of the ontological question itself, by means of a conversion of the ontological
dignity of causality, and to indicate in conclusion the necessity of
freeing freedom from its Kantian (but in fact more generally metaphysical) subordination to the category of causality.

From this point on, a program of work seemed to be sketched out:
on the one hand in the direction of freedom as "archi-foundation,"
and on the other, through a repetition of the philosophy of freedom
destined to displace freedom's relation to causality, in the direction
of a freeing of the resources of "foundation" at the core of the philosophical tradition itself.[7] The course of 1936, which was devoted
to Schelling's treatise "On the Essence of Human Freedom," was to
constitute the completion of the intended research.

In a sense, this course offered nothing other than a kind of continuous harmonic composition, where Heidegger's own discourse
would create an incessant counterpoint to Schelling's, without making the matter explicit on its own, and without the latter's discourse
being given a clear interpretation by that of the former (as was the
case with Kant or Leibniz). There would be here a singular interlacing of the concerns of metaphysics and those of the thinking of
being (up to the point, of course, where they end up separating)
analogous to what took place elsewhere with regard to Hegel and "experience." There would have been a period in which it seemed possible to Heidegger to rethink freedom at the surface of its philosophical tradition, or to replay its concept—since it seemed to him
impossible to proceed otherwise. In direct line with the course of
1930, Heidegger finds in Schelling a grasp of the proper factuality of
the fact of freedom, and this factuality refers to the theme, central
for Schelling, of freedom as the necessity of the essence of man.
In "seeking to formulate in a more originary way" this view of freedom, Heidegger ends up at this: "The necessity by which or as
which freedom is determined is that of its own essence" (p. 155). This
essence will be more precisely determined as "the overcoming of
self as grasping of self" in the "decidedness" and in the "resoluteness"

for "the openness of the truth of history" by which man can feel the
necessity of "his own being" (p. 155). However, having accompanied
or repeated Schelling up to this very advanced if not ultimate point
(a repetition completed by the subsequent analysis of the conjoined
possibility of good and evil), and having at the same time brought
him to a "more originary" thought, Heidegger abandons him. This
abandonment is essentially due to the fact that Schelling does not
manage to radically think the originary unity from which proceed
freedom as necessity as well as the correlative possibilities of good and
evil. He does not think this origin as "nothing," and he thus fails to
think that "the essence of all Being is finitude" (p. 162). Schelling thus
does not overcome Kant and the "incomprehensible" character of
freedom (p. 162). It must be understood that freedom remains incomprehensible as long as it exposes its necessity to the core of a
thought that orders it to an infinite necessity of being, and not as a
finitude for which being is not the foundation. (It is not so much
that freedom would become "comprehensible" in the "more originary thinking," but the question of freedom would certainly no
longer be posed in these terms—unless it were necessary, in order to
gain distance from a problematic of "comprehensibility," also to
gain distance from "freedom" itself.)

   If we interpret correctly the last pages of this course, two things
are signified at once:

   1. The essential character of freedom has been attained in the
necessity for man to assume his proper essence as that of a decision
relative to "essence and deformation of essence" (p. 156), which
means to good and evil as the realization of this couple of essences
in a "history" (ibid.) that involves "encountering a destiny" (p. 162),
insofar as destiny consists precisely in man's exposure to his own necessity.

   2. But this thought has not yet penetrated to the "nothing" of the
origin of this necessity; it has therefore not thought the essential finitude of essence itself (of existence) in the essence of freedom—
which consequently, in its decision and in its perdurance, does not
match up with the necessity of an essentiality (that of *man*, whence
the distance Heidegger takes *in fine* from Schelling's "anthropo-

morphism"), but matches up with what we would call, condensing the terms and tone of these pages, *the pain of the historiality of the nothing*, in which finite freedom heroically maintains itself.

Up to this point, but just short of it, and also in the seminars between 1941 and 1943, Schelling will have taken the relay from Kant as Heidegger's essential reference on freedom, and he will have played, on this register, a role parallel to the Kant of the *Kantbuch*: a "repetition of the foundation of metaphysics" will have *almost* been performed on his doctrine of freedom. But the parallel stops there—for if the Kantian resource offered itself expressly for a repetition, and if it was destined to come back, in other ways, to Heidegger (and even later, for example with *Kant's Thesis on Being* in 1963), even if it had nothing to do with the same repetition (and one could say the same, *mutatis mutandis*, of the Hegelian resource), the *entire* enterprise of accompanying and reproducing Schellingian freedom according to a more authentic origin will, for its part, at a certain moment be abandoned without return. And this abandonment will give way to very little explanation. A note from the seminar of 1943, in the context of which the reference to Schelling is present, declares the following:

> Freedom: metaphysically as the name for capacity by itself (spontaneity, cause). As soon as it moves metaphysically into the center (into true metaphysics) it intrinsically unifies the determinations of cause [*Ursache*] and selfhood (of the ground as what underlies and of the toward-itself, for-itself), that is, of *subjectivity*. Thus ultimately we have freedom as the resolve to the inevitable (affirmation of "time"!), as essential self-deception. *Freedom forfeited its role originally in the history of Being*, for *Being* is more original than beingness and subjectivity.[8]

In this note (which we will eventually have to comment on again in several ways, directly or indirectly), the principal argument is clear: metaphysical freedom designates the capacity to be a cause by and of oneself. Now causality belongs to beingness [*étantité*], not to existence, as does subjectivity insofar as it is the for-itself of the foundation. The two concepts are reunited in the idea of a foundation-being [*fondation-étant*], which causes. But being [*être*] has nothing to do with beings [*étants*]. If being is foundation, it cannot be so in the mode of this freedom. Yet no other kind of freedom is proposed. The concept and the word are abandoned to "metaphysics in the proper sense of the word" (though Heidegger's reading was not oblivious to the role played by subjectivity in Schelling's text, even while it appeared to constitute itself as a "repetition"). We must therefore conclude that what could have been, in 1936, "a more originary thinking" of freedom becomes six years later the letting go of this motif. If Heidegger firmly demotes freedom to non-"originary" thought, this is because at every point metaphysics presents him definitively (but this is nothing new since *Being and Time*) with the closure of a beingness of being (corollary to the subjective closure of the will that he recognized at that time, after having used up, as we've indicated, a motif of free will). In this closure, freedom can only appear as the *causa sui et mundi* of a supreme being (or of a subject being, which amounts to the same thing) who then binds up the totality of beings into the "inevitable," and freedom into "self-deception."

Would not Heidegger then have recognized both his own course of 1930 and his own reading of Schelling in §27 of Hegel's *Philosophy of Right*?

> The absolute goal, or, if you like, the absolute impulse, of free Spirit is to make its freedom its object, i.e. to make freedom objective as much in the sense that freedom shall be the rational system of Spirit, as in the sense that this system shall be the world of immediate actuality. In making freedom its object, Spirit's purpose is to be explicitly, as Idea, what the will is implicitly. The definition of the concept of the will in abstraction from the Idea of the will is "the free will which wills the free will."⁹

Thus in Hegel too, or in relation to Hegel, Heidegger would have intended to separate himself from the metaphysics of freedom. But if the gesture of repetition in which he had previously engaged no doubt remained insufficiently articulated for him, was not this gesture of separation in turn too easily executed? This question, or this suspicion, forms at least the first motivation for an essay of repetition, after Heidegger, of the theme of freedom. For the moment, we will simply add the following remark: the note of 1943 also shows very clearly that the abandonment of this "freedom," which Heidegger himself takes care to name between quotation marks, is here made in the name of an other and more authentic "freedom." We could say that the freedom of man, and of the subject, is abandoned in favor of a freedom of being. Doubtless this will perhaps have to be no longer named "freedom," but it still retains the possibility, if not the necessity, of *hearing* this name differently.

From this moment until the end of his work, Heidegger will have stopped seeking thematically an essence of freedom, and he will make no more than an episodic use of this word, which can now appear as accidental (*at least* in view of the immediate contexts in which it most often appears) and stripped of any specific problematic.[10] Succeeding it, however (if one can call it a succession—and in what sense? Here the analysis would have to be extremely long and delicate), is the use of the theme of the "free" (*das Freie*) and of "free space," of which we will again have to speak.

The situation is thus quite strange: a concept is rejected, a word loses the privileges of questioning that it seemed until then to enjoy, and yet a semantic root is kept, it is even, dare we say, concentrated, and it is used for ends that, as we will see, are essential ends of thought. In a certain sense, something of "freedom" will never have ceased to be found at the heart of the thinking of being: but in this heart, this "something," exempted in principle from identification, has been submitted to transformations that have not been posited or made explicit as such.

Contemporaneous with the note of 1943 (but its first version already dates from 1930), the text *On the Essence of Truth* presents at least the principle of this transformation. There Heidegger relates truth—understood as the conformity of the utterance—to freedom as to its essence. Freedom then designates the "resistance" thanks to which beings are allowed to be what they are. Accordingly, freedom is neither the "caprice of free will nor the mere readiness for what is required and necessary (and so somehow a being)." The step taken by Schelling (and by idealism in general, including transcendental idealism) out of free will and toward a necessity of essence is thus given a merely ontic cast, even if this is not the intention of the text. On the contrary, freedom henceforth affirms its ontological character or stake in what is called "the exposure to the disclosedness of beings." It is this exposure, this possibility of openness *to* the open in which beings are offered as such, which makes the enunciation of truth possible.

But the hierarchy thus posited is in turn inverted. For freedom "receives its own essence from the more original essence of uniquely essential truth."[11] Ontological primacy then amounts, in the final analysis, to truth. This is so because truth carries in its essence and as its essence concealment and errancy. In effect, the concealment of beings—"mystery"—precedes every exposure to disclosedness: letting beings disclose themselves indicates and preserves a more original concealment or mystery of beings as such. The errancy that is correlative of this mystery is the "free space" to which ex-istence is constitutively exposed, and which founds the possibility of error. Thus the question of the essence of truth is itself revealed to be the question "of the truth of essence." If essence must in fact designate being, then the "meaning" of being can be discerned as the errant exposure of existence to the mystery of the concealment of the being of beings. In this way, history takes place, beginning with its "concealed uniqueness."

The reversal of ontological precedence between freedom and truth amounts, at the same time, to burying freedom more deeply in being, which, as being, is revealed to be abstracted from every necessity endowed with presence and signification. Being is the "freedom" of the withdrawal of presence and meaning that accompanies every disclosure, or more exactly, that permits disclosure as such, in its principial relation to concealment and errancy. This interpretation would allow us to understand that Heideggerian ontology remains finally and fundamentally an "eleutherology." But Heidegger does not want to be understood in this way. We hear instead that *freedom is the withdrawal of being*, but that for this very reason *being is the withdrawal of freedom*; in other words, being withdraws freedom short of freedom itself, in its qualities of decision and opening, in order to give it back to truth, that is, to the condition of being's (non)-manifestation.

In sum, it is only a question of a difference of emphasis. But up to what point can—or must—this difference of emphasis be understood as a sort of recoil of the "practical" into the "theoretical"? More precisely, how can it be understood as the *maintenance* of a distinction (if not of a certain opposition) between freedom and truth, which the text tends to undo, but which would invincibly reconstitute itself, as if it reconstituted with it at least one part of the traditional philosophical prevalence of the "theoretical" over the "practical"? (This prevalence, however, would not be simply recognizable at all points of the philosophical tradition: not with Aristotle, for example, or Spinoza, or Kant, or even Hegel.) Up to what point does the specific factuality of freedom not risk dropping out of sight (which does not mean suppressed)? Such is the question that we are here led to ask. Or further: out of a more profound fidelity to at least one of the directions of Heidegger's thought, would it not be necessary to try to preserve and expose, *together* and *in the same originarity*, the withdrawal of freedom's being and its singular factuality? Obviously this is not a simple question, and, as we can see, it is one that can only be posed on the basis of Heidegger himself. But the important thing for us is that it seems necessary to pose it, and this question, under these conditions, ought to provide the regulative indication of the relation with Heidegger's thought that we are here undertaking.

～

This question is much less simple than the one posed in *The Principle of Reason* (1956)—one of Heidegger's most important works at the time—which in spite of everything opened a new space of play for freedom. The examination of the "principle of reason" in effect leads thought to a "leap." This leap allows one to pass from the interrogation of being as ground or as reason (*Grund*) to the thinking of being as "without reason" in the "groundlessness" of its play. Heidegger writes:

> The leap remains a free and open possibility of thinking; this so decisively so that in fact the essential province of freedom and openness first opens up with the realm of the leap.[12]

It is doubtless necessary to have the leap, which is the leap of thinking in its "theoretical" consideration of being, *in order* for thinking
to put itself in the state of perceiving the region of freedom. Yet the
leap is nothing other than the leap of theoretical consideration outside of or beyond itself; the leap is transcendence and transgression of theoretical reason in its examination of "reason" as *Grund.*
Therefore, the leap may not accede to a "vision" of freedom except
to the extent that it has "leapt" outside of or away from theoretical
"vision" in general. Yet this is precisely what is not made explicit.

In any case, the "region" in question designates nothing other
than what the "Letter on Humanism" (1946) already designated,
with no other real explication, as "the free dimension in which freedom conserves its essence."[13] On the subject of the "free dimension"
or "the free," other texts will provide us with further examples. For
the moment, let us simply remark that it is no longer a question here
of *freedom* as a property or as a power in whatever sense, but of a specific element, "the free," which appears as a quality attributed to a
substratum, "the dimension," only through a banal constraint of language, but which in reality is indistinguishable from this "dimension." What will also be, in *Being and Time,* the "free space of time"
is determined through this proper spatiality that holds in reserve the
essence of a freedom henceforth only named. The quality proper to
this space, its *libertas,* will not otherwise be determined, and above
all not through a new analysis of the notion of freedom. Therefore,
it must also be concluded that Heidegger intended to set aside a
space for freedom—by keeping the semantic kernel, or index, of the
word "free"—but a space in which "freedom," in each of its philosophical determinations, appeared to him as an obstruction or obstacle, rather than as an opening and release into the open air.

Keeping a space free for freedom: does this free (and if so, how?)
what *truth* seemed to withhold from us? Does it let this call to freedom happen with its proper force, this call that—in one way or
another—the thinking of being (or the thoughts that follow it)
clearly cannot refuse?

§5 The Free Thinking of Freedom

Keeping a space free for freedom might amount to keeping one-self from wanting to understand freedom, in order to keep oneself from destroying it by grasping it in the unavoidable determina-tions of an understanding. Thus the thought of freedom's incom-prehensibility, or its unpresentability, might seem to heed not only the constraint of a limitation of the power of thought but also, positively, a respect for and a preservation of the free domain of freedom. This consideration is doubtless imposed from the very interior of the metaphysics of freedom, to the extent that this meta-physics often finds itself exposed to the danger of having surrepti-tiously "comprehended" freedom—somehow even before it has *reached* it—by having assigned freedom a residence in knowledge and, above all, in the self-knowledge of a subjectively determined freedom.

Rousseau's *Social Contract* offers unquestionably the clearest ma-trix of the schema according to which freedom, as it becomes con-scious of itself (and becomes in fact self-consciousness) in the con-tract, simultaneously produces objective self-knowledge in the sov-ereign, thereby constituting the sovereignty of the sovereign both in absolute comprehension of his own freedom and in absolute con-straint over himself and over every member of the sovereign body ("We will force him to be free . . . "). The transcendental treatment of this matrix produces, in Kant, the identity of freedom and law, or more exactly, the identity of freedom and rational legislation. This legislation is assuredly nothing other than a legislation of freedom: but this means that freedom has to be projected and proposed to itself as the lawfulness of a moral nature, necessary in itself in the same way that the lawfulness of a physical nature is necessary in itself.

Freedom is thus understood not only as a particular type of causality in the production of its effects; it is also understood, on the model of physical causality, as lawful succession. The specific mode of freedom's causality remains incomprehensible, or rather, *it is the incomprehensible* (which is why there can be no "schema" of moral law, but only a "type," that is, an analogical schema, and this "type" is provided by nature in the lawfulness of its phenomena). In contrast, however, the idea of the legislation of a "nature" or "second nature" regulated by freedom is perfectly comprehensible by means of the *type*, which provides, in the mode of the physical world, the general model of a lawful necessity or necessitation. Now if this idea is quite easily understood (despite the *ideal* character of a world ruled by morality), that is because it can be analyzed definitively in the following terms (which Kant certainly would not have accepted, despite the conformity of their logic to his own, particularly in the context of the idea of a creating God): ultimately, *freedom encloses the secret of causality because it is in itself (un)comprehended as the very power of causation.* Freedom is a particular kind of causality in that it holds and presents (at least in Idea) the *power of effectuation* that theoretical causality lacks. The principle of theoretical causality states in effect *that* such is the law of the succession of phenomena for our understanding, but it cannot present *what* enables the production, one after another, of the successive linkages of these phenomena. Freedom holds the secret of causality since it is defined as the power *of being by itself a cause,* or as the power of causing, absolutely. Fundamentally, freedom is causality that has achieved self-knowledge. In this respect, the "incomprehensible" encloses in itself the self-comprehension of being as Subject.

A world in freedom would be a world of causality transparent to itself. The secret is contained in the formula of the will: "the power to be *by means of one's representations* the cause of the reality of these same representations." This is the power of the (pre)formative Idea of reality. Philosophical understanding of freedom culminates in the "incomprehensible" self-comprehension of the self-productive self-knowledge of the Idea. Henceforth, law is the representation of the necessity of the Idea. Now, the Idea is through itself a (re)presentation of necessity; the law of freedom represents the necessity of necessity.

From Kant to Hegel, certainly to Nietzsche, and probably even to the Heidegger of "the will to will as the will of its own duty," the thought of freedom is fulfilled as if irresistibly, at least through one of its aspects, in a comprehension of the necessity of necessity. The point of incomprehensibility is the ultimate point of the comprehension that grasps that necessity necessitates itself. Because of this, human freedom is always susceptible to being understood as the repetition and appropriation of this subjective structure. To be free is to assume necessity. The "assumption of necessity," or the "liberation through law," or even the "inner freedom" that "takes charge of" external constraints become from this point on the formulas of a world that perceives itself to be overburdened with irreversible and weighty processes, with coercions of all kinds (naturally, this freedom of subjective assumption has as its symmetrical counterpart the acceptance of pure libertarian anarchy, of freedom reduced to arbitrariness). These formulas represent what we could call the major philosophical ideology of freedom that has developed from the philosophy of the Idea and of subjectivity.[1] Yet it is entirely clear that they constitute just so many admissions of a theoretical and practical powerlessness, and that this comprehension of freedom is equivalent to the resignation that Heidegger designated as the illusory "resolve" toward the "inevitable." (In this sense, Heidegger's abandonment of the theme of freedom signifies primarily the refusal of this resignation.)

Thus it would be possible to say: if the Idea of freedom—and consequently a determination of its necessity, since the idea of Idea contains in principle necessity and self-necessitation—precedes freedom and in sum envelops it beforehand in its intellection, its intellection will remain negative with respect to the "nature" of free ne-

cessity, so that freedom is noticeably absent. It is absent here because
it is in principle subjected to a thinking that fundamentally thinks
being as necessity and as the causality of self-necessitation. This
thought does not even think of itself as free; it considers itself to be
the self-(un)comprehension of this being. Freedom is absent because in this thinking it is *assured* in advance (founded, guaranteed, and self-assured): "the Idea *freely releases* itself in its absolute self-
assurance and inner poise."[2]

If the factuality of freedom is the factuality of "what is not yet *done*
[*fait*], or made into a fact," as we have claimed, it must also and perhaps above all be understood as the factuality of what has no *Idea*,
not even an idea determined to be "incomprehensible" or "unpresentable." This must mean, in one way or another, that this factuality escapes philosophy and even thought if, in whatever way we
take the word "thought," it is oriented toward a "thought of freedom," and not primarily (or even exclusively) toward a freedom
or liberation of thinking. We gain a sharper perception of the way
Heidegger, at Davos, was driven to withdraw freedom from the jurisdiction of "theory" in order to restore it to the practice of "philosophizing," a practice designated a "liberation," or at least as cor-
responding to the liberation of freedom. But this in no way allows
us to forgo interrogating the exact nature and stakes of this "philosophizing" (which Heidegger, at a later date, would replace with
"thinking").

Such "philosophizing" can actually be presented as the decon-
structive penetration that reaches the heart of metaphysical idealism
at the point where the Idea binds [*enchaîne*] freedom, in order to
show that at this same point something different "unleashes itself"
[*se "déchaîne"*]; for example (and this underlies Heidegger's text), a
praxical factuality irreducible to the theoretical. Another example
would be the structure that obliges the jurisdiction of reason to
fall, literally, over its own case, the case of the instauration or enunciation of law, as over that which, contrary to the logic of the "case"
in general, cannot but escape law and thereby reveal that the essence
of jurisdiction is to pronounce "the right of what is by right without
rights." We can also state that, in the imperative, "law is separated

from itself as fact."³ This links up in a number of ways with a mode that would no longer be that of the "necessity of necessity," but which would be precisely the mode of its liberation. Here we rejoin the Kantian inconceivability of freedom and its commentary by Heidegger:

> The only thing that we comprehend is its incomprehensibility. And freedom's incomprehensibility consists in the fact that it resists com-prehension since it is freedom that transposes us into the realization of Being, not in the mere representation of it.⁴

But what does "comprehending incomprehensibility" mean, and, consequently, what is meant by the "philosophizing"—or whatever it will be called—that manages to reach the furthest border of its own possibility in order there to designate and free, through this very designation, precisely what it does not comprehend? Or, perhaps more exactly, what does this gesture or activity which is neither "theoretical" nor "practical" represent, a gesture that brings to light the division of these two concepts limiting metaphysics, and that would accordingly reserve for freedom a space that is truly free?

Comprehending that something is incomprehensible cannot signify simply that comprehension would come to a halt with the discovery of one of its limits. For the limit, once it is recognized as such, is not only "comprehended" as an obstruction or screen: the *pure* encountering of an obstacle is impossible if we understand by this that we would therefore have no knowledge other than knowledge of the obstacle (or this is death—perhaps). Yet the obstacle—by virtue of this law of presentation to which Heidegger was so attentive—necessarily presents with itself, as if through itself, the free passage to which it is an obstacle. Such is the logic of the limit in general: the limit has two borders, whose duality can neither be dissociated nor reabsorbed, such that touching the internal border amounts *also* to touching the external border ("from the interior," one could add—which would render the description of the operation infinite and vertiginous). Comprehending that something is incomprehensible is certainly not comprehending the incomprehensible as such, but neither is it, if one can say this, purely and simply comprehending nothing about it. We comprehend that there is the incomprehensible because we comprehend, in the present example, that "the realization of being" escapes its "representation" (don't these formulas recall something of the "theoria/praxis" couple?). We therefore comprehend the *in*-comprehensibility of the incomprehensible. With this privative "*in*," we comprehend that the incomprehensible—freedom—is not, properly speaking, "beyond" our capacity of comprehension, but it does not simply arise from this capacity. Freedom is not exactly out of comprehension's reach; for example, it is not located higher up on a ladder of intelligibility, on a rung accessible, for instance, only to an intelligence other than our own. Even less is freedom opposed to comprehending: it makes itself understood, at the limit of comprehension, as what does not originate in comprehension. The "realization of being" (or *praxis*?) has no *object*, or *theme*, except itself, in its independence with respect to objectality and thematicity. Thus, incomprehensible freedom makes itself understood *at the limit* [*à la limite*], in a very precise sense of this expression, as a self-comprehension independent of the comprehension of understanding [*entendement*].[5] What we comprehend, at the limit, is that there is this autonomous comprehension, which is the realizing [*accomplissante*] comprehension of realization. We comprehend that realization *comprehends itself* [*se comprend*] (even if it does not *understand* itself [*s'entend*] and even if we do not understand it), in its specific mode. Yet we see that this specific mode strangely resembles that of the self-comprehension— and of the self-realization—of "reason," "thinking," or "theory" as such. . . .

Our comprehension, then, is not meaningless, and it even forms one of the summits of philosophical comprehension: for it has also come to be formulated, not accidentally, as the comprehension of the philosophical necessity of superseding philosophy in the realization of philosophy (in the realization of being). Hegel offers a formula for this, and its displaced or transformed meaning could hold for Heidegger as well:

Ethical life is the Idea of freedom in that on the one hand it is the good become *alive*—the good *endowed* in self-consciousness with knowing and willing and *actualized* self-conscious *action*—while on the other hand self-consciousness has in the ethical realm its absolute foundation and the end which actuates its effort. Thus ethical life is the concept of freedom *developed into the existing world and the nature of self-consciousness.*[6]

Thus, at the self-realizing end of this ethical life:

The state is the actuality of the ethical Idea. It is ethical spirit *qua* the substantial will manifest and revealed to itself, knowing and thinking itself, accomplishing what it knows and in so far as it knows it.[7]

What above all must not be underestimated is the power of this philosophical comprehension of the overstepping of the theoretical limit and, on the reverse side of this limit, of the expansion of praxical self-comprehension. We must not even stop at Hegel's exterior and banal comprehension that would have us admit that philosophy here perfectly comprehends a concept of practice which philosophy itself elaborated, and from which it does not escape. For the demand of Hegelian Spirit is precisely the demand to be actualized in an actuality that *frees* it from its simple being-in-itself, and for Hegel it is indeed only practically and outside of itself that Spirit can comprehend itself in its freedom and as freedom. What discourse (un)comprehends—such is the entire theme of the dialectical sublation of predicative judgment in speculative thinking—is that practical actuality constitutes the *real* (material, historical, etc.) self-realization and self-comprehension of what discursive comprehension comprehends without, however, being able to penetrate the sphere of authentic self-comprehension. This is also why philosophy, with Hegel, having reached the limit where it is actualized, no longer "comprehends," but "contemplates"—it contemplates, for example, the majesty of the monarch in whose individuality of body and spirit the actuality of the State is concentrated. This contemplation is the comprehension that surmounts, surpasses, and sublates itself in the act of its finally deployed freedom.

Clearly, we must conclude nothing less than that (un)comprehension is in reality the supreme stage of the comprehension that attains knowledge of self-comprehension as self-realization. Not only is comprehension grasped, at its limit, outside of itself as in its innermost truth, but more profoundly, it grasps itself in this apprehension entirely stretched out of itself, as its own *passage into action*: it comprehends itself as its own becoming-practical. It *knows* that such is its truth, and moreover, it *puts itself to the test*, at its limit, as already actualizing, before it is actual, this free *act* that it would not be able rigorously to comprehend. There is thus a self-comprehension *of* the comprehension of incomprehensibility. In this self-comprehension, "theory" comprehends "praxis" as its truth, *and* it comprehends itself as practical, which also means that in it practice is theoretically comprehended as the realization of the freedom (un)comprehended by theory. Freedom is therefore, despite everything, comprehended. Yet once again necessity is comprehended as freedom, and freedom has been earmarked as necessity. This may take many forms, from Rousseau's or Kant's enthusiasm to Marx's reversal of the dialectic's reversals,[8] to the weight conferred by Heidegger on the word "thinking" (thinking being itself thought of as an "acting"): it should be said, always, that *freedom will take itself up in the necessity of its practical self-comprehension.*

～

Of course, this is not all. This is not the totality of what there is to decipher in this series of gestures made by philosophical texts. Yet we cannot avoid going by way of the preceding analysis if we are unwilling to reserve for freedom a space that risks being revealed as already enclosed by necessity—even if this should be by the necessity of this very reserving. Must anything be *reserved for* freedom? Must its space be *kept* free? We should ask instead if this is even possible. Is not freedom the only thing that can "reserve" its own space?

Would not what is at stake in freedom be the fact that, according to a logic resolutely separate from every dialectic of (in)comprehensibility, freedom in any case precedes the thinking that can or cannot comprehend it? Freedom precedes thinking, because thinking proceeds from freedom and because it is freedom that gives thinking.

The thinking whose thoughts not only do not calculate but are absolutely determined by what is "other" than beings might be called essential thinking. Instead of calculating beings by means of beings, it expends itself in Being for the truth of Being. This thinking answers to the demands of Being in that man surrenders his historical essence to the simple reality of the sole necessity whose constraints do not so much necessitate as create the need [*Not*] which is realized in the freedom of sacrifice. . . . Freed from all constraint, because born of the abyss of freedom, this sacrifice is the expenditure of the essence of the human being for the preservation of the truth of Being in respect of beings.⁹

In a sense, this declaration is perhaps less novel than it seems. It gathers something that undoubtedly traverses, more or less visibly, the entire tradition in which philosophy has always considered freedom to be the source, element, and even ultimate content of thinking. "Philosophy is an immanent, contemporary, and present thought and contains in its subjects the presence of freedom. What is thought and recognized comes from human freedom."¹⁰

But how is the co-belonging of freedom and thinking determined when, in Heidegger's terms, thinking is "born of the abyss of freedom" and thus engages "sacrifice" or engages itself as "the sacrifice of the essence of the human being"? Let us leave aside the implication of sacrifice, which is certainly not insignificant from the point of view of a consideration of the whole of Heideggerian philosophy (this sacrifice at the altar of truth, in which one could easily detect, as Bataille might have, the comedy of the simulacrum where nothing essential is lost, or the model of dialectical tragedy that would destroy human beings only in order to find them again elevated to the posture of the contemplators and celebrators of truth, of philosophers as theoreticians). In spite of all this, there is another facet of sacrifice (one through which, after all, there is perhaps no longer "sacrifice" in any sense): prodigality. Thinking expends what it thinks, free of "calculation," in such a way that in spite of all the benefits that cannot help but return, whether to the thinking subject or to the economy of its discourse, what is truly *thought* can only be what is expended (which also means: that of which "thinking" is or has "experience," and not that of which it elaborates a conception or theory). Thinking expends, since it comes from "the abyss of freedom." Above all, freedom is what expends: freedom is primarily prodigal liberality that endlessly expends and dispenses thinking. And it dispenses thinking primarily as prodigality. In this way, freedom gives without counting (or the measure of its account would be none other than its very self as gift; I must speak further of this); it gives thinking, it gives something to be thought about, yet it also simultaneously gives itself to be thought about in every thinking.

This simply means that there might not be thinking. This also means that there might not be human beings. Which means in turn that there might not be *existence*—and it is in this that existence can be recognized: in that its singularity might or might not be given, in that its thing-in-itself might or might not be posited. Phenomena are necessary, the very existence of the thing is free. That there is existence (human beings, thought), that there is that which is its own essence, cannot derive from a necessity for essence, and can only be given, freely given (which is a tautology). Reciprocally: if there were no existence (but this hypothesis is absurd—since we are speaking here of "existence" and since this very fact, "speaking of something," implies existence—and yet never entirely deniable, if existence, existents, speech, and thought are also always susceptible to renouncing themselves, to becoming essences . . .) . . . if there were no existence, then there would not be nothing and yet there would not be "something": for the "thing," and the indetermination of the "some" that assembles each of its possible singularities as presences in or of the world, already completes the program, so to speak, of a thought. If there is "something," this is because it is possible to keep "the thing" and its "being some (thing)" in sight. If this were *necessary*, there would be no "there is," no "some," and no "thing." There would be only—and this would not be "there is"—the repletion, always already realized and drawn back to itself, of the general and immanent being of what, even as it is *all*, cannot be *something*. We would only have: "*it is*" and no thought. If it is possible that the "there is something" arises as such (as thinking, as existence), this is because this arising is the gift of a freedom or a freedom that is given.

Every thinking is therefore a thinking about freedom at the same time that it thinks *by* freedom and thinks *in* freedom. It is no longer exactly a question here of the limit between the comprehensible and the incomprehensible. Or rather, what happens here, in the free arising of thought, happens precisely on this limit, as the play or very operation of this limit. Thinking is always thinking on the limit. The limit of comprehending defines thinking. Thus thinking is always thinking about the incomprehensible—about this incomprehensible that "belongs" to every comprehending, as its own limit.[11] Yet this does not mean that thought is a kind of "supra-comprehension" (regardless of how we would like to see it, the mystics' impasse—including what remains of the mystical in Heidegger—is always presented in this way) and this also does not mean that it is a *Schwärmerei* (the entirely rationalist definition of this notion produces in Kant an impasse symmetrical to that of the mystics). Thinking does not push comprehension beyond what it comprehends, and neither does it prophesy. Thinking thinks the limit, which means there is no thought unless it is carried to the limit of thought. Insofar as it "comprehends," it does not comprehend its own limit, and it comprehends *nothing* insofar as it does not comprehend; neither is it mediated in a "comprehension of incomprehensibility." Yet it is no longer a question of comprehensibility and incomprehensibility. Both emerge from necessity, and thinking is delivered to freedom. It is not subjected to comprehension and its opposite. If we must say that thinking is subjected to a necessity, this will be in such a way that the necessity of freedom *would not be* the freedom of necessity. The freedom of necessity is realized in the Hegelian concept to the extent that the Hegelian concept is itself realized. The necessity of freedom is "necessary" only in the sense that it unleashes itself in its abyss and from its abyss.

Now, the "abyss" (whatever Heidegger, for his part, means by this) does not "open" under the pressure of some necessity in order to give or deliver something. The abyss is not the essential reserve *from* which would be produced—by some necessity of trial, extraction, or engendering—what comes into thought. The "abyss" (of freedom) *is* that there is something, and it is nothing else. It "is" therefore, as abyss, only the unleashing that emerges "out of it," or more exactly and because there is no substantiality or interiority to the abyss, the "abyss" itself—a term still too evocative of depths—is only the unleashing, prodigality, or generosity of the being-in-the-world of something. It is what gives thinking, in the sense that thinking is nothing other than the being-delivered to this generosity. Freedom is not the vertiginous ground of the abyss, opened and revealed to comprehension. Freedom arises *from nothing*, with thinking and like thinking, which is existence delivered to the "there is" of a world. It is from the outset the limit of thinking—thinking as limit, which is not the limit of comprehension, but which, according to the logic of the limit, is the il-limitation of the prodigality of being. Thinking is *at the surface of* this il-limitation of the "there is," it is in itself the unleashed freedom in accordance with which things in general are given and happen. This is why thinking does not have freedom as something to be comprehended or to be renounced from comprehension: yet freedom offers itself in thinking as what is more intimate and originary to it than every object of thought and every faculty of thinking.

To be sure, here there is no longer even "freedom," as a defined substance. There is, so to speak, only the "freely" or the "generously" with which things in general are given and give themselves to be thought about. No doubt "freedom itself" unleashes "itself" both in the sense that it would be the subject of this act and in the sense that it would expend its own substance. Yet what unleashes "itself" was not previously attached to a substantial unity: on the contrary, the subject follows only from freedom, or is born in her. What is expended was not previously reserved in a pregnant enclosure, nor even contained in itself like an abyss. Generosity precedes the possibility of any kind of possession. The secret of this generosity is that it does not have to do with giving what one has (one has nothing, freedom has nothing of its own), but with giving oneself—and that the *self* of this reflected form is nothing other than generosity, or the generousness of generosity. The generousness of generosity is neither its subject nor its essence. Rather, it remains its singularity, which is at the same time its event:[12] generosity happens, it gives and is given in giving, always singular and never held back in the generality of its own quality—and its unique manner of not "taking place" in the sense of a simple positing, but of always preceding itself by always succeeding itself. It unleashes itself, without "being unleashed," before being, but also well after it—already hurled, sent, expended, without having had the time to know that it is "generous," without having been subjected to the time of such a qualification. What is generous abandons itself to generosity, which is not its "own," without having or mastering what it does. It is like hitting one's head (thinking as hitting one's head . . .), it is having been delivered or abandoned not only without calculation and without having been able to calculate, but even without an *idea* of generosity. This is not an unconscious, but on the contrary—if these terms can be used—the most pure and simple consciousness: that of expended existence. Thought that is given in this way is the most simple thought: the thought of the freedom of being, the thought of the possibility of the "there is," that is, thought *itself*, or the thought of thought. It does not have to "comprehend" or "comprehend itself"—or uncomprehend. It is expended to itself, in existence and as the ex-istence of the existent, as its own inessential essence, well before the conditions and operations of all intellection and (re)presentation: it is expended as the very freedom of eventually being able to comprehend or not comprehend something. This freedom is not a question or problem for thinking: in thinking, freedom remains its own opening.

～

"Freedom" cannot avoid combining, in a unity that has only its own generosity as an index, the values of impulse, chance, luck, the unforeseen, the decided, the game, the discovery, conclusion, dazzlement, syncope, courage, reflection, rupture, terror, suture, abandonment, hope, caprice, rigor, the arbitrary.[13] Also: laughter, tears, scream, word, rapture, chill, shock, energy, sweetness. . . . Freedom is also wild freedom, the freedom of indifference, the freedom of choice, availability, the free game, freedom of comportment, of air, of love, or of a free time where time begins again. It frees each of these possibilities, each of these notions of freedom, like so many freedoms of freedom—and it is freed from these.

In effect, it is not a dialectical montage—and even less an eclectic recapitulation; it is a heterogeneous dissemination of states, concepts, motivations, or affects, which could compose, so to speak, an infinity of figures or modes of a unique freedom, but which in reality are offered as a prodigality of *bursts* whose "freedom" is not their common *substance* but rather . . . their bursting. Nor is freedom their transcendent condition, and they are not its transcendentals. In sum, these bursts are all the possible determinants of freedom to the extent that freedom expends itself in the withdrawal from every determination. Each of them, or the figures that can be composed from them, would no doubt call its own elaboration phenomenological, but above all, their long list—unfinished and unfinishable—signifies its own proliferation (and we do not want to be misunderstood as seeing an anthropological bricolage here), which itself definitively means that freedom *essentially bursts*. Nonetheless, it is not necessarily "the Bacchanalia in which every member is drunk," but there is no freedom without some drunkenness or dizziness, however slight.

Therefore it is the "abyss" of freedom in the sense that *freedom does not belong to itself.* In this way, the freedom of being is not a fundamental property that would be above all else posited as an essence, but is immediately being in freedom, or the *being-free of being*, where its being is expended. It is its very life, if life is understood as originary auto-affection. But being is not a living being and is not "affected" by its freedom: being is only what it is insofar as it is in freedom and as freedom, the being of a bursting of being that delivers being to existence.

What *is* in this way is never at first on the order of action, nor is it on the order of volition or representation. It is a bursting or a singularity of existence, which means existence as deprived of essence and delivered to this inessentiality, to its own surprise as well as to its own decision, to its own indecision as well as to its own generosity. But this "own" of freedom is nothing subjective: it is the inappropriable burst from which the very existence of the subject comes to the subject, with no support in existence, and even without a relation to it, being "itself" more singularly than any ipseity, "itself" in the burst of a "there exists" that nothing founds or necessitates, that happens unexpectedly and only surprises, vertiginous to the point that it is no longer even a question of assigning an "abyss" to its vertigo: this very vertigo, its existence and its thought *are* the vertigo of the prodigality that makes it exist *without allotting it any essence* and that is therefore not an essence, but rather the free burst of being.

～

Freedom, in the existent, thus also immediately forms its immanence (we could say, in terms taken from a register that is no longer applicable: the necessity of its chance, of its contingency, the legitimacy of its caprice) as well as its transcendence. That the existent transcends means: it has no immanence in the freedom with which it exists. But its freedom, with which it is more intimate than any property of essence, is in this very intimacy only the "strike" or "cut" of its existence: the archi-originary bursting of pure being. This transcendence therefore should not be understood as an "opening to" or as a "passage out of"—in a sense, it is not ek-static, and existent freedom is not ek-sistent, but it is the insistence of a burst; transcendence takes place on the spot, here and now, as a presence that would be the singular presence of a strike, of a spring, of a free leap in existence and of existence.

Thus it is freedom that definitively "leaps," or rather it is freedom that is the "leap," whereas Heidegger would have the leap provide access to freedom. The leap is therefore not a free decision of thinking. It is freedom and freedom gives thinking, because thinking is what "holds itself" in the leap. Freedom is the leap into existence in which existence is discovered as such, and this discovery is thinking. Well before being or seeking to be "the thought of freedom," thinking is thus *in* freedom. Thinking is in this leap, from Pascal's "chance which gives thoughts and takes them away" to this other extremity where thinking can no longer even have "thoughts" (ideas, concepts, representations), not because it would be limited with re-

spect to a mightier power of (re)presentation, but because it touches, in and of itself, *this limit that is its very freedom*. On this limit,
thinking neither comprehends nor uncomprehends. It is supported
by nothing, and it is not thrown into the Kantian dove's empty
space—it leaps into and over nothing. It is but the leap of a start, a
burst of existence, an unleashing that unleashes nothing more than
the trembling of the existent at the border of its existence. Thinking
trembles with freedom: fear and impatience, luck, the experience that
there is no thinking that would not always be given in freedom
and to freedom. As soon as it thinks, thinking knows itself to be free
as thinking, and not only—or even necessarily—as the possibility of
choosing or inventing its ideas or representations. It knows itself to
be free because it knows that it already is, as thinking, the experience
of freedom: simply from the fact that "thinking" means *not being necessity by way of an essence, foundation, or cause*, or *at least* not being
so without immediately having to relate itself to this necessity *as* necessity (which amounts to saying: as a *thought* necessity). Thinking
cannot think without knowing itself as thought, and knowing itself
as such, it cannot not know itself as freedom—if only as this feeblest
infinite trembling *at the limit* of every necessity, or even as this feeblest infinite surprise of the existent in the face of the "there is—of
being."

But this experience of freedom (which is not experience "in
thought," but which is thought, or thinking, *as* experience) is only
the knowledge that in every thought there is *an other* thought, a
"thought" which is no longer thought by thought, but which thinks
thought itself (which gives it, expends it, and *weighs* it—which is
what "thinking" means): a thought other than understanding, reason, knowledge, contemplation, philosophy, other finally than
thought itself. The *other* thought of all thought—which is not the
Other of thought, nor the thought of the Other, but that by which
thought thinks—is the burst of freedom.

§6 Philosophy: Logic of Freedom

Who is in charge of this other thinking? No one is its operator, official, or "specialist." This other thinking thinks in all thought—and it thinks this thought, which means that it weighs it, tries it, and puts it to the test of freedom. It thinks "in all thought": it might be at stake in a thinking of mathematics, of politics, of technology, of everyday life, and so on. This might be when one is thinking about somebody, when one "isn't thinking about anything," when one is concerned about making a decision, or is under the pressures of suffering, or even under the hardship or insipidity of necessities, as well as when one forms concepts, meditates, or organizes a discourse. We have said before that this other thinking, which frees all thought as such, is not restricted to any definite form of thought—it is perhaps the form-lessness of all thought—and is accordingly not restricted by that which goes by the name of "philosophy." Moreover, it should be said that we are done with "philosophy" because it has enclosed freedom in the empire of its necessity and thus stripped itself of this other thinking, of the freedom in thinking. In this way, philosophy has constituted freedom as a *problem*, whereas freedom is, of course, anything but a "problem." In thought, that which addresses itself to thought and addresses thought to itself cannot constitute a "problem": it is a "fact," or a "gift," or a "task."

Why then philosophy, or whatever one chooses to call it?

(Heidegger tried to substitute "thinking" for this word—for excellent reasons that here guide even my own discourse—nevertheless, here he remains a *philosopher* who determines the necessity and stake of this substitution on the basis of philosophy, and "philosophy" always makes reference, at least technically or practically, and, for example, institutionally, to the possibility of putting at stake the most unapproachable freedom of thinking, and freedom as thinking.) Should there be a philosophy of freedom? It has already taken place: it has taken place in all of philosophy and *as* all of philosophy. One could say that "freedom" appeared in philosophy—and remained a prisoner of its closure—as philosophy's very Idea folded back onto its own ideality, even where philosophy wanted to go beyond itself or realize itself. This is why, whenever there has not been the abandonment of philosophy, there has been, in philosophy, the abandonment of freedom—to the point that today the undertaking of a philosophical discourse on freedom has something of the ridiculous or indecent about it. Indeed, "philosophy" matters little if it has nothing to do with freedom, or rather "philosophy" matters little if it is not the inscription of the *fact* of freedom, instead of being the (in)comprehension of its Idea. Freedom— "she" matters to us. Not because she would be a *good* that we desire and have the right to enjoy, but because we have always been defined and destined in her. Always: since the foundation of the Occident, which also means since the foundation of philosophy. Our Occidental-philosophical foundation is also our foundation in freedom—even if (and perhaps precisely because) the foundation of freedom and freedom as foundation slip away from philosophical grasp. Now philosophy has always meant—or at least always indicated—more and something other than "philosophy," other than, as it were, the pure discipline of concepts that is by itself the discipline of foundation in general. (Even the privileged "thinking of being" designates *first* the study of a concept and the systematic interrogation of its relation to foundation). Indeed, there is an idea of something as a pure discipline of concepts *only* because there is—by a kind of absolute preliminary of philosophy, where philosophy necessarily precedes itself and exceeds itself—the pre-understanding that the order of the concept itself pertains, in origin and essence, to the element of freedom. The concept itself can easily appear as a representational abstraction; but the concept of the concept, if we can say this, cannot be anything other than the freedom through which the access to representation occurs—and the access to the representation of foundation, as well as to the foundation of representation: that is, the mode of being according to *existence*, or even *thinking* as the free possibility of having a *world*, or as the availability *to* a world (even if this is, as it comes into philosophy, only a world of representation). The factuality of freedom *is* also the fact of thinking. It is thus also present in the fact—which opens philosophy, and hence also precedes it—that we define "man" by thought: we do not define him as a part of a universal order, or as a creature of God, or as the inheritor and transmitter of his own lineage, but as *zōon logon ekhōn*. Thought is specified as *logos*, and *logos*, before designating any arrangement of concepts and any foundation of representation, essentially designates—within this order of the "concept of concept" and "foundation of foundation" to which its dialogic and dialectic are devoted—*the freedom of the access to its own essence*. *Logos* is not first the production, reception, or assignation of a "reason," but is before all the freedom in which is presented or by which is offered the "reason" of every "reason": for this freedom only depends on the *logos*, which itself depends not on any "order of reasons" but on an "order of matters" whose first matter is nothing other than freedom, or the liberation of thought for a world. The *logos* would never, for lack of this freedom, pose any question of the concept as concept, of the foundation as foundation, or of representation as representation (or any question of the *logos* as *logos*). Thus the *logos*, before any "logic," but in the very inauguration of its own logic, freely accedes to its own essence—even if this is in the mode of not properly *acceding* to any *essence*. This access, which also produces its source, never stops being put at stake, as much when the *logos* attempts to master "freedom" in a "logic" as when it renounces assigning any "reason" to this freedom. But whether it masters (itself) or renounces (itself), the *logos* is already seized by freedom, which undoes *on the surface of the logos* its mastery or its abdication. This amounts to saying that freedom offers or casts thought, in philosophy, always beyond "philosophy" *conceived as* the Concept or Foundation of the *logos*. That is why there is no philosophical conclusion or closure that does not once again require and provoke, if not exactly "philosophy," then at least a philosophical freedom always more ancient and always more recent than every philosophy. We are therefore not saying that philosophy *is* thinking in its freedom; we are, however, saying that for the entire tradition of the Occident, to which the idea of freedom inevitably belongs, since it founds this tradition (or since it is [un]comprehended as its foundation), it is only *on the surface of* philosophy (if not *in* it as a doctrine, a body of thought, or a construction of concepts) that the *logic* of freedom passes, for it answers to nothing other than the existing opening of thought. Thought and freedom are correlatively determined and destined in philosophy. Even if we have to free ourselves from this determination, we cannot do so, by definition, in any simple "outside" of philosophy (which does not mean that outside of philosophy there is neither thought nor freedom, but that there is in effect neither the one nor the other in the sense of their reciprocal determination in the *logos*).

There is thus no pure discipline of concepts in the sense that there would be a discipline of unverifiable ideas, of great ideas freely produced outside the constraints of objectivity and practice, or of visions of the world whose free market would occupy the poverty zone of our knowledge—this is how we too often understand philosophy and philosophical freedom (the idea of freedom itself being one of the very first products put into circulation in this philosophical free-exchange. But "truth," "objectivity," and "knowledge" in general, being (un)founded in the *logos*, are (un)founded in freedom. Philosophy is the thought that guides the discipline of concepts back to the experience of this foundation, or rather, it is only the forgetting or obliteration of its *own* constitution.

Philosophy is not at all a founding discipline (there precisely can be no such thing), but is the very folding, in discourse, of the freedom that defines the *logos* in its access to its own essence. Philosophy

= the fact that thinking, in its essence, should be the liberation of existence for a world, and that *the freedom of this liberation cannot be
appropriated as an "object of thought," but that this freedom marks
with an ineffaceable fold the exercise of thinking.* This is the fold
along which thought touches itself, tests itself, or accedes to its
own essence following the experience of freedom, without which it
would not be "thought" and even less *logos* as free access to its own
essence.

Thus philosophy does not produce or construct any "freedom,"
it does not guarantee any freedom, and it would not as such be
able to defend any freedom (regardless of the mediating role it can
play, like every other discipline, in actual struggles). But it *keeps
open the access to the essence of the logos* through its history and all its
avatars. In this way it must henceforth keep the access open—freedom—beyond the philosophical or metaphysical closure of freedom. Philosophy is incessantly beyond itself—it now has a thematic knowledge of this from the interrogation of the very concept of philosophy—not because it is the Phoenix of knowledges, but
because "philosophizing" consists in keeping open the vertiginous access to the essence of the *logos,* without which we would not have any
idea of even the slightest "logic" (discursive, narrative, mathemati-
cal, metaphysical, etc.). But this maintenance is not an operation of
force or even one of preservation: it consists in testing in thought
(which means: inscribing in language) this fold of freedom that articulates thought itself (which means: inscribing in language the
freedom that articulates it and that never appropriates it).

Accordingly, when it is said that true philosophy is where "in
such knowledge the whole of existence is seized by the root after
which philosophy searches—in and by *freedom*,"[1] or even that philosophy is "rigorous conceptual knowledge of being. It is this, however, only if this conceptual grasp (*Begreifen*) is in itself the philosophical apprehension (*Ergreifen*) of *Dasein* in freedom," it is not said
that the philosophical concept would comprehend existence in its
freedom, but rather that it is freedom which grasps the concept itself in its "conceiving." This is not a "conception of existence" and
still less, if that is possible, a "conception of freedom," but it is ex-

istence in the exercise of the freedom of the concept, it is existence as thinking, which is not a thinking *about* anything unless it is a thinking *for* the freedom of being-in-the-world. In short, it is the *praxis* of the *logos* (or "practical reason"), which is not so much a "theoretical practice" as that which brings the *logos* to its limit, on the very limit of existence, which the logos "grasps" not by absorbing or subsuming, but instead by assuming the *fact* that the freedom of existence is what gives it—and strips it of—its own essence of *logos*.

Philosophy is not the free sphere of thinking in general, nor is it the theoretical relay between moral, political, or aesthetic practices of freedom, and it does not supplement the material deprivations of freedom by way of an independence of spirit. In philosophy the logic of freedom merely rejoins incessantly the practical axiom that inaugurates it: thinking receives itself from the freedom of existence.

§7 Sharing Freedom: Equality, Fraternity, Justice

Freedom cannot be presented as the autonomy of a subjectivity in charge of itself and of its decisions, evolving freely and in perfect independence from every obstacle. What would such an independence mean, if not the impossibility in principle of entering into the slightest relation—and therefore of exercising the slightest freedom? The linking or interlacing of relations doubtless does not precede freedom, but is contemporaneous and coextensive with it, in the same way that being-in-common is contemporaneous with singular existence and coextensive with its own spatiality. The *singular* being is in relation, or according to relation, to the same extent that its singularity can consist (and in a sense always consists) in exempting itself or in cutting itself off from every relation. Singularity consists in the "just once, this time" [*une seule fois, celle-ci*], whose mere enunciation—similar to the infant's cry at birth, and it is necessarily *each time* a question of birth—establishes a relation at the same time that it infinitely hollows out the time and space that are supposed to be "common" around the point of enunciation. At this point, it is each time freedom that is singularly *born*. (And it is birth that *frees*.)

Ontology has only two formal possibilities (but these are equally material possibilities: it is always a question of the body . . .). Either Being *is* singular (there is only Being, it is unique and absorbs all the common substance of the beingness [*étantité*] of beings—but from that moment it is clear that it *is not* singular: if there is *just one* time, there is never "once"); or, *there is no* being *apart from* singularity: each time just this once, and there would be nothing general or common except the "each time just this once" [*chaque fois cette seule fois*]. This is how we must understand Heidegger's *Jemeinigkeit*, *Dasein's* "each time as my own," which does not define the subjectivity of a substantial presence of the *ego* to *itself* (and which is therefore not comparable to the "empty form" of the Kantian "I" that accompanies representations), but which on the contrary defines "mineness" on the basis of the "each time." Each time there is the singularity of a "time," in this German *je-* which so strangely mimes the French *je*, at every strike of existence, leap of freedom, or leap into freedom, at every birth-into-the-world, there is "mineness," which does not imply the substantial permanence, identity, or autonomy of the "ego," but rather implies the withdrawal of all substance, in which is hollowed out the infinity of the relation according to which "mineness" *identically means the nonidentity* of "yourness" and "his/her/its-ness." The "each time" is an interval structure and defines a spacing of space and time. There is nothing *between* each time: there being withdraws. Moreover, being is not a continuum-being of beings. This is why, in all rigor, it *is not*, and has no being except in the discreteness of singularities.

The continuum would be the absence of relation, or rather it would be the relation dissolved in the continuity of substance. The singularity, on the other hand, is immediately in relation, that is, in the discreteness of the "each time just this once": each time, it cuts itself off from everything, but each *time* [*fois*] as a *time* [*fois*] (the strike and cut [*coup et coupe*] of existence) opens itself as a relation to other times, to the extent that continuous relation is withdrawn from them. Thus *Mitsein*, being-with, is rigorously contemporaneous with *Dasein* and inscribed in it, because the essence of *Dasein* is to exist "each time just this once" as "mine." One could say: the singular of "mine" is by itself a plural. Each *time* is, as such, *another* time, *at once* other than the other occurrences of "mineness" (which makes the relation also a discrete relation of "me" to "me," in "my" time and "my" space), and other than the occurrences of "minenesses" other than "mine." Singularity—for this reason distinct from individuality—takes place according to this double alterity of the "one time," which installs relation as the withdrawal of identity, and communication as the withdrawal of communion. Singularities have no *common being*, but they *com-pear* [*com-paraissent*] each time *in* common in the face of the withdrawal of their common being, spaced apart by the infinity of this withdrawal—in this sense, without any relation, and therefore thrown into relation.[1]

The existence of the existent only takes place singularly, in this *sharing* of singularity, and freedom is *each time* at stake, for freedom is what is at stake in the "each time." There would be no "each time" if there were not birth each time, unpredictably arising and as such unassignable, the surprise of the freedom of an existence. On the one hand, in effect, the originary setting into relation is contemporaneous and coextensive with freedom insofar as freedom is the discrete play of the interval, offering the space of play wherein the "each time" takes place: the possibility of an irreducible singularity occurring, one that is not free in the sense of being endowed with a power of autonomy (it is immediately *at once* in the heteronomy of the relation—or rather, it happens on this side of autonomy and heteronomy), but that is already free in the sense that it occurs in the free space and spacing of time where only the singular *one time* is possible. But on the other hand, and consequently, freedom precedes singularity, though it does not found or contain it (singularity is unfoundable, unholdable). Freedom is that which spaces and singularizes—or which singularizes *itself*—because it is the freedom of being in its withdrawal. Freedom "precedes" in the sense that being *cedes* before every birth to existence: it withdraws. Freedom *is* the withdrawal of being, but the withdrawal of being is the nothingness of this being, which is the being of freedom. This is why freedom *is not, but it frees being and frees from being*, all of which can be rewritten here as: *freedom withdraws being and gives relation*.

This does not mean that my freedom is measured in relation to others in the sense of two courses of action or legitimacy whose circles must remain tangential in order not to encroach upon one another (as we have said, the spacing of singularities is infinite and cannot include tangency—which does not prevent it from being at the same time infinitely intimate). Instead, this means that freedom is relation, or at least in the relation, or like the relation: it is, or effects, the singular step [*pas*] of my existence in the free space of existence, the step of my com-pearance which is *our* com-pearance. Freedom is properly the mode of the discrete and insistent existence of others in my existence, as originary for my existence.[2] But at the same time, it is also the mode of the other existence insisting in my identity and constituting (or deconstituting) it as *this* identity: for relation is also, as I have said, relation to "me," and it is *also* in relation to "me" that "I" am free, or that I "is" free. Furthermore, this means, symmetrically, that relation is freedom: relation happens only in the withdrawal of what would unite or necessarily communicate me to others and to myself, in the withdrawal of the continuity of the being of existence, without which there would be no singularity but only being's immanence to itself. (In this case, we could not even say that "there is" immanence, and there would not even be anyone to say that we could not say it. . . . Being would immediately be its own thought, language, and freedom. It would be its own other, a pure essence that would indeed be the essence *of* existence, but which for this very reason would exist in no other way.)

Being-*in*-common means that being is nothing that we would have as common property, even though we *are*, or even though being is not common to us except in the mode of *being shared*. Not that a common and general substance would be distributed to us, but rather, being is *only* shared *between* existents and *in* existents (or between beings in general and in beings—compare note 2 above—but it is always according to existence as such that being is at stake as being). Consequently, on the one hand, there is no being between existents—the space of existences is their spacing and is not a tissue or a support belonging to everyone and no one and which would therefore belong to itself—and on the other hand, the being of each existence, that which it shares of being and by which it *is*, is nothing other—which is not "a thing"—than this very sharing.

Thus what divides us is shared out to us: the withdrawal of being, which is the withdrawal of the properness of self and the opening of existence as existence. This is why, if it is true in some sense that solitude is total, as our entire tradition keeps claiming, and if it is also true in some sense that freedom is the capricious, unapproachable independence of a singular being unbound to anything, it is also true, in an equally reducible fashion, that in solitude and even in solipsism—at least understood as a *sola ipsa* of singularity—ipseity is constituted by and as sharing. This means that *the ipseity of singularity has as its essence the withdrawal of the aseity of being.* Also, the being of its "self" is what remains of "self" when nothing comes back to itself.[3]

If existence transcends, if it is the being-outside-of-itself of the being-shared, it is therefore *what it is* by being outside of itself: which amounts to saying that it has its essence in the *existence* it is, essentially in-essential. This fundamental structure (or: this opening with no return . . .) does not answer to a dialectic of immediatizing mediation (which recuperates the essence beyond its negation), nor to an "ec-stasy" sublimated in reappropriation. Outside of itself, it is freedom, not property: neither the freedom of representation, nor of will, nor of the possessed object. *Freedom as the "self" of the being-outside-of-itself does not return to or belong to itself.* Generally speaking, freedom can in no way take the form of a property, since it is only from freedom that there can be appropriation of anything—even of "oneself," if this has any meaning.

Freedom is here precisely what must be substituted for every dialectic (and for every "ecstatic," understood in the sense suggested above), since it is not the struggle for recognition and self-mastery of a subjectivity. It is, from birth until death—the last birth of singularity—what throws the subject into the space of the sharing of being. Freedom is the specific logic of the access to the self outside of itself in a spacing, each time singular, of being. It is in *logos*: "reason," "speech," and "sharing." Freedom is *logos*, not alogical, but open at the heart of *logos* itself, of shared being. Ontological sharing, or the singularity of being, opens the space that only freedom is able, not to "fill," but properly to space. "Spacing space" would mean

keeping it as space and as the sharing of being, in order *indefinitely to share the sharing* of singularities.

This is also why, as this *logos* of sharing, freedom is immediately
linked to equality, or, better still, it is immediately *equal to equality*.
Equality does not consist in a commensurability of subjects in relation to some unit of measure. It is the equality of singularities in
the incommensurable of freedom (which does not impede the necessity of having a technical measure of equality, and consequently
also of justice, which actually makes possible, under given conditions,
access to the incommensurable). For its part, this incommensurability
does not mean that each individual possesses an unlimited right
to exercise his will (moreover, if "each" designates the individual, how
could such a right be constructed in relation to the singularities
that divide the individual himself and in accordance with which
he exists? One would first need to learn how to think the "each" on
the basis of the series or networks of singular "each times"). Nor does
this incommensurability mean that freedom is measured only
against itself, as if "it" could provide a measure, a standard of freedom. Rather, it means that freedom *measures itself against nothing*:
it "measures" itself against existence's transcending in nothing and
"for nothing." Freedom: to measure oneself against the nothing.

Measuring oneself against the nothing does not mean heroically
affronting or ecstatically confronting an abyss which is conceived of
as the *plenitude* of the nothingness and which would seal itself
around the sinking of the subject of heroism or of ecstasy.
Measuring oneself against the nothing is *measuring oneself* absolutely,
or measuring oneself against the very "measure" of "measuring oneself": placing the "self" in the position of taking the measure of its
existence. This is perhaps, and even certainly, an excess [*démesure*].
In no way and on no register of analysis will one avoid the excess of
freedom—for which heroism and ecstasy are in fact also figures
and names, but these must not obscure other examples, such as
serenity, grace, forgiveness, or the surprises of language, and others
still.

Essentially, this excess of freedom, as the very measure of existence, is common. It is of the essence of a measure—and therefore of an excess—to be common. The community shares freedom's excess. Because this excess consists in nothing other than the fact or gesture of measuring itself against nothing, against the nothing, the community's sharing is itself the common excessive measure [(*dé)mesure*] of freedom. Thus, it has a common measure, but not in the sense of a given measure to which everything is referred: it is common in the sense that it is the excess of the sharing of existence. It is the essence of equality and relation. It is also fraternity, if fraternity, it must be said, aside from every sentimental connotation (but not aside from the possibilities of passion it conceals, from hatred to glory by way of honor, love, competition for excellence, etc.), is not the relation of those who unify a common family, but the relation of those whose *Parent,* or common substance, *has disappeared,* delivering them to their freedom and equality. Such are, in Freud, the sons of the inhuman Father of the horde: becoming brothers in the *sharing* of his *dismembered* body. Fraternity is equality in the sharing of the incommensurable.

What we have as our own, each one of "us" (but there is only a singular "us," there again, in the "each time, only this time" [*à chaque fois, une seule fois*] of a singular voice, unique/multiple, which can say "us"), is what we have in common: we share being. It gives itself as such in the very possibility of saying "us," that is, of pronouncing the plural of singularity, and the singularity of plurals, themselves multiple. The "us" is anterior to the "I," not as a first subject, but as the sharing or partition that permits one to inscribe "I." It is because Descartes can say *we* know, each and every one of us, that *we* exist—as each one of us—that he can pronounce *ego sum.* (This does not, however, imply that the "we," at this level, functions simply as the "shifter" [*embrayeur*] of the enunciation over its enunciating subject. "We" makes a blocked shifter, distanced from itself, function. One cannot say who enunciates "we." What would have to be said is this: "one" evidently knows one exists,[4] and it is thus that *we* exist, sharing the possibility that *I* say it at every moment.)

If being is sharing, *our* sharing, then "to be" (to exist) is to share. This is relation: not a tendential relation, need, or drive of portions of being that are oriented toward their own re-union (this would not be relation, but a self-presence mediated by desire or will), but existence delivered to the incommensurability of being-in-common. What measures itself against the incommensurable is freedom. We could even say that to be in relation is to measure oneself with being as sharing, that is, with the birth or de-liverance of existence as such (as what through essence de-livers itself), and it is here that we have already recognized freedom.

⁓

If it is indeed true that freedom belongs in this way to the "essence" of human beings, it does so to the extent that this essence of human beings itself belongs to being-in-common. Now, being-in-common arises from sharing, which is the sharing of being. On the archi-originary register of sharing, which is also that of singularity's "at every moment," there are no "human beings." This means that the relation is not one between human beings, as we might speak of a relation established between two subjects constituted as subjects and as "securing," secondarily, this relation. In this relation, "human beings" are not given—but it is relation alone that can give them "humanity." It is freedom that gives relation by withdrawing being. It is then freedom that gives humanity, and not the inverse. But the gift that freedom gives is never, insofar as it is the gift of *freedom*, a quality, property, or essence on the order of "*humanitas*." Even though freedom gives its gift under the form of a "*humanitas*," as it has done in modern times, in fact it gives a transcendence: a gift which, as gift, transcends the giving, which does not establish itself as a giving, but which before all gives *itself* as gift, and as a gift of freedom which gives essentially and gives itself, in the withdrawal of being. This is why "man" is also, as we know, a figure that is susceptible to being effaced. *Freedom gives—freedom.* It only pertains to the "essence of man" insofar as it withdraws this essence away from itself, into existence. And in existence, freedom gives itself as the possibility for the existent of a "*deitas*" or "*animalitas*," as much as of a "*humanitas*" or "*reitas*." But above all, before every determination of essence (which belongs no less to the decision in which freedom is at stake and which

we will discuss further), freedom shares out existence in accordance
with relation, and is shared therein: it *is* freedom (and therefore, in
this sense, nothing other than a "*libertas*") *only* in the singular/com-
mon occurrence of singularities.

Freedom is therefore singular/common before being in any way
individual or collective. Existence in accordance with relation would
then be the ontological determination of what Hannah Arendt
tried to represent as the anteriority of public freedom to private or
interior freedom, an anteriority which, for her, allowed one to think
the true origin and nature of the very idea of freedom.[5]

> Before it became an attribute of thought or a quality of the will, free-
> dom was understood to be the free man's status, which enabled him to
> move . . . and meet other people in deed and word.

It matters little that the historical accuracy of the representation
of an ancient city with a spontaneous sense of free public space
would have been degraded or lost in later history. We simply want
to note that it is possible, perhaps even necessary, from the interior
of our tradition, to represent the originary form of freedom as a
free space of movements and meetings: freedom as the external
composition of trajectories and outward aspects, before being an internal disposition. No doubt something like an individual autonomy seems to be implied in an identical way in both cases. However,
the "automobility" of the first case does not precisely designate the
autolegislation of the second. The first "autonomy" depends on
the opening of a space in which only the closing of the second can
take place. Now, by definition, free space cannot be opened through
any subjective freedom. Free space is opened, freed, by the very
fact that it is constituted or instituted as space *by* the trajectories and
outward aspects of singularities that are thrown into existence.
There is no space previously provided for displacement (which is why
the images of the *agora* or *forum* could be misleading), but there is
a sharing and partitioning of origin in which singularities space
apart and space their being-in-common (points and vectors of the
"at every moment," shocks and encounters, an entire link without
link, an entire link of unlinking, a fabric without weave or weaver,

contrary to Plato's conception). Freedom does not appear here as an internal rule of community, nor as an external condition imposed on the community, but it appears as precisely the internal exteriority of the community: existence as the sharing of being.

Provided the assets or rearticulations of these notions outweigh their liabilities, we will call this space the public or political space, as does Hannah Arendt, though ours may not be exactly in accordance with her perspective. That the political space is the originary space of freedom does not therefore mean that the political is destined primarily to guarantee "freedom" or "freedoms" (in this regard it is not space that must be spoken of, but only the apparatus) but that the political is the "spaciosity" (itself spatiotemporal) of freedom. It gives place and time to what we have called "measuring oneself with sharing." It gives space and time to the taking measure of this "measuring oneself" in its various forms, an archi-politics from which it is possible to consider politics as well as to distinguish political orders from other orders of existence.

The *justice* necessarily in question here—because it is a question of sharing and of measure—is not that of a just mean, which presupposes a given measure, but concerns a just measure of the incommensurable. For this reason—regardless of the negotiations that at the same time must be conducted with the expectations and reasonable hopes for a just mean—*justice* can only reside in the renewed decision to challenge the validity of an established or prevailing "just measure" *in the name of the incommensurable*. The political space, or the political as spacing, is given from the outset in the form—always paradoxical and crucial for what is neither the political nor the community, but the management of society—of the common (absence of) measure of an incommensurable. Such is, we could say, the first thrust of freedom.

It is in this sense that propositions such as this one from Lacoue-Labarthe—all differences and disputes aside—should be taken:

> The contours of the political are traced or retraced only on the measure of the withdrawal, in the political and from the political, of its essence.[6]

Or from Lyotard:

Politics . . . bears witness to the nothingness which opens up with each occurring phase and on the occasion of which the differend between genres of discourse is born.[7]

Or from Badiou:

The event . . . , through its potential for interruption, amounts to supposing that what is admissible ceases to have value. The inadmissible is the major referent of any politics worthy of its name.[8]

However, while these propositions—like the formula of a "just measure of the incommensurable," which I am freely taking the right to impose on them as a kind of common factor—rightfully open, so it seems, directly onto another proposition that could be represented, at least for the moment, by this one from Badiou—

Revolutionary politics, if we want to keep this adjective, is essentially interminable.

—they still do not indicate, or at least not explicitly enough, *what* is properly "intèrminable" in a "revolutionary politics" (whose appellation would accordingly refer to the relation of the political to its own spacing, the opening and reopening of its own space as such). This is not the infinite readjustment of the aim of a correctness [*justesse*] or justice which, posited as regulative Idea, is interminable. This aim would be that of a "bad infinity" in the Hegelian sense (and whatever the actual services it has rendered since its Kantian inception, it can equally accompany the resignations familiar to us today in the thinking of the left, up to the point of resignation where one no longer knows what "left" and "right" mean). What is bad in this regulating infinity is that freedom in its fact—the reality constituting the space of sharing, which we are designating here as the political—and, consequently, along with this freedom, equality, not to mention fraternity, are guaranteed beforehand in the Idea *and* at the same time delivered to the infinite distance of a representation (or of the representation of an impossibility of representation) in whose element the *right* to these Ideas is by definition contained. By interminably invalidating history's records in the name of this right, we blend in equal parts the will and the despair of the will—which threatens to define subjectivity's will, and freedom, as "self-deception," with an unavoidable counterpart of disillusionment . . .

But if freedom is on the order of fact, not right, or if it is on the order in which fact and right are indistinguishable, that is, if it is truly existence as its own essence, it must be understood differently. It must be understood that what is interminable is not the end, but the beginning. In other words: the political act of freedom *is* freedom (equality, fraternity, justice) in action, and not the aim of a regulative ideal of freedom. That such an aim could or should belong to this or that pragmatic of political discourse (it remains less and less certain that this would be a pragmatically desirable and efficient mediation or negotiation with the discourses of Ideas) does not impede the political act—as well as the act that would decide to have a discourse of this sort—from being *at the outset* freedom's singular arising or re-arising, or its unleashing.

Perhaps the political should be measured against the fact that freedom does not wait for it (if ever freedom waits, anywhere . . .). It is initial and must be so in order to be freedom. Kant wrote:

> I grant that I cannot really reconcile myself to the following expressions made use of by clever men: "A certain people (engaged in a struggle for civil freedom) is not yet ripe for freedom"; "The bondmen of a landed proprietor are not yet ready for freedom," and hence, likewise: "Mankind in general is not yet ripe for freedom of belief." For according to such a presupposition, freedom will never arise, since we cannot *ripen* to this freedom if we are not first of all placed therein (we must be free in order to be able to make purposive use of our powers in freedom).[9]

Freedom cannot be awarded, granted, or conceded according to a degree of maturity or some prior aptitude that would receive it. Freedom can only be *taken*: this is what the *revolutionary* tradition represents. Yet taking freedom means that freedom *takes* itself, that it has already received itself, from itself. No one begins *to be* free, but freedom *is* the beginning and endlessly remains the beginning.

(The beginning as the beginning of history is found only where there is freedom, that is, where a human group comports itself resolutely toward beings and their truth.)[10]

If it is not possible here to attempt to go further in this determination of the political, we will at least posit that the political does not primarily consist in the composition and dynamic of powers (with which it has been identified in the modern age to the point of slipping to a pure mechanics of forces that would be alien even to power as such, or to the point of a "political technology," according to Foucault's expression),[11] but in the opening of a space. This space is opened by freedom—initial, inaugural, arising—and freedom there presents itself in action. Freedom does not come to produce anything, but only comes to produce itself there (it is not *poiesis*, but *praxis*), in the sense that an actor, in order to be the actor he is, produces himself on stage.[12] Freedom (equality, fraternity, justice) thus produces itself as existence in accordance with relation. The opening of this scene (and the dis-tension of this relation) supposes a breaking open, a strike, a decision: it is also as the political that freedom *is* the leap. It supposes the strike, the cut, the decision, and the leap onto the scene (but the leap itself is what opens the scene) of that which cannot be received from elsewhere or reproduced from any model, since it is always beginning, "each time."

Or more exactly, if this is the reproduction of a model—which is at any rate not a model of production—it is simply the model of the beginning or of initiality. The beginning is not the origin. Correcting the general use of this term that we have made up until now, we will say that the origin is the origin of a production, or at any rate, in the Platonic sense of *poiesis*, it is the principle of a coming into being. Power has an origin, freedom is a beginning. Freedom does not cause coming-to-being, it is *an initiality of being*. Freedom is what is initially, or (singularly) *self-initiating* being. Freedom is the existence of the existent as such, which means that it is the initiality of its "setting into position."[13] It "postures" existence, according to sharing, in the space of relation. Freedom: event and advent of existence as the being-in-common of singularity. It is the simultaneous breaking into the interior of the individual and of the community, which opens the specific space-time of initiality. What is lacking today, and lacking up until now in the philosophy of democracy, is the thought of this initiality, before or beyond the safeguarding of freedoms considered to be established freedoms (from nature or by right). It is possible that for this reason it may no longer even be possible, in the future, to think in terms of "democracy," and it is possible that this also signifies a general displacement of "the political," a word we have provisionally mobilized here: perhaps a liberation of the political itself. All things considered, what is lacking is a thinking of the freedom that is not established, but that *takes itself* in the act of its beginning and its recommencement. This remains for us to consider, perhaps beyond our entire political tradition—and yet in some ways the direction of this imperative has already been thought by at least one part of the revolutionary tradition. In at least one of its aspects, revolutionary thinking has always acceded—and not without risks that cannot be overlooked—not so much to the overturning of power relations as to the arising of a freedom untainted by any power, though all powers conceal it. What must also be understood along these lines is the radical demand in Marx for a freedom that would not guarantee political, religious, and other freedoms, but an *inaugural liberation* with respect to these freedoms, insofar as they would be nothing other than the freedoms of choice at the interior of a closed and preconstrained space.

It is not a question of substituting for the framework of these established rights the coercion of a "liberation" whose principle and end would themselves be established (which is not necessarily the case in Marx). We know what this means: the material destruction of all freedom. Rather, it is a question of permitting the reopening of the framework and the liberation from every establishment, or its overflowing, by freedom in its *each time* irreducible (re)beginning: this is the task of politics as the liberation of freedom, as the (re)opening of the space of its inaugural sharing.

To reach even further back into the revolutionary tradition, toward a beginning whose naiveté and danger we are well aware of, and of which something doubtless still remains to be thought, if the political itself still remains to be thought, let us cite Saint-Just: "Although France has established judges and armies, it must see to it that the public is just and courageous."[14] This meant that France was to free itself for its own being-free and not merely to preserve its instituted freedoms.

But "seeing to it" should not be an operation, nor should the "public" be a work, its "justice" and "courage" a production. A politics—if it still is one—of initial freedom would be a politics putting freedom at the surface of beginning, of allowing to arise, in the sense of allowing to be realized—since it is realized in arising and in its breaking open—*what cannot be finished.* Like sharing, freedom cannot be finished.

§ 8 Experience of Freedom: And Once Again of the Community, Which It Resists

In its highest form of explication nothingness would be *freedom*. But this highest form is negativity insofar as it inwardly deepens itself to its highest intensity; and in this way it is itself affirmation—indeed absolute affirmation.[1]

Thus, in Hegel himself, at least at the literal level of this text, freedom is not primitively the dialectical reversal of negativity and its sublation into the positivity of a being. It is, rather, in a kind of pre-dialectical burst, the deepening and intensification of negativity up to the point of affirmation. Freedom = the self-deepening nothingness.

In this way, there may be a beginning, arising, and breaking open of an opening. Not only is there nothing *before*, but there is nothing *at the moment* of freedom. There is nothing on which it depends, nothing that conditions it or renders it possible—or necessary. But neither is there "freedom itself." Freedom is even free *from* freedom: thus it is free *for* freedom (through its conditional—compare note 1—Hegel's text in some sense presents the freedom that comes before freedom, or the very birth of freedom). With freedom, the dialectical linkages are interrupted or have not yet taken place—even if their possibility has already been offered in its entirety. No identity preserves itself in negation in order to reappear affirmed (understandably, since the nothingness is here none other than the nothingness of being as such in its initial abstraction). This is so because freedom is not itself negated during the course of its own trial (as would be the case on the further register of a dialectic of slavery): freedom is itself nothingness, which does not *negate itself* properly speaking, but which, in a pre- or paradialectical figure of the negation of negation, affirms itself by making itself *intense*. The intensification of the nothingness does not negate its noth-ing-*ness* [*néantité*]: it concentrates it, accumulates the tension of the nothingness as nothingness (hollowing out the abyss, we could say, if we were to keep the image of the abyss), and carries it to the point of incandescence where it takes on the burst of an affirmation. With the burst—lightning and bursting, the burst of lightning—it is the strike of one *time*, the existing irruption of existence. In this black fulguration, freedom *is* not and does not *know itself* to be free *from* anything; nor is it or does it know itself to be free *for* anything determined. It is only free from all freedom (determined in this or that relation, for example, the relation with a necessity), and it is only free for every freedom. In this way, freedom is neither in independence nor in necessity, neither spontaneous nor com-manded. It does not apprehend itself [*s'apprend*], but takes itself [*se prend*], and this means that it always surprises itself [*se surprend*]. Freedom = the nothingness surprised by its fulguration. Despite its having been foreseen, the free act surprises itself, beyond fore-seeability. Foreseeability could only concern its contents, not its modality. This is also why the will foresees—in fact it does only this—but it does not foresee itself (it is by confusing the two that we make the will into its own subject). Freedom defies intention, as well as representation. It does not answer to any concept of itself any more than it presents itself in an intuition (and it doubtless there-fore belongs neither under the term "freedom" nor in any image or sentiment that could be associated with freedom), because it is the beginning of itself at the same time that it is itself the beginning—which is to say, the maximum intensity of the nothingness and no origin. "*No notion of beginnings*," writes a poet.[2]

Heidegger interpreted freedom's nothingness (even if he was not formally interpreting Hegel's text) in the following way:

Freedom is the foundation of foundation. . . . The breaking-forth of the abyss in founding transcendence is the primordial movement which freedom makes with us.[3]

The transcendence that makes freedom is the transcendence of finitude, since the essence of finitude is to not contain in itself its own essence, and consequently to be, "in its essence" or in its in-essence, the existing of existence. It is a *finite freedom* which is the "foundation of foundation." This absolutely does not mean that this freedom would be a limited freedom having no space of play except between certain borders or frontiers (which is how freedom is almost always understood in every ethical, political, and even aesthetic conception of freedom). *Finite* freedom, on the contrary, designates freedom *itself*, or the *absolute* freedom of being whose essence essentially withdraws: from existence. Thus, freedom here comes to characterize *the foundation which by itself does not secure itself as foundation* (cause, reason, principle, origin, or authority), but which refers through its essence (or through its withdrawal of essence) to a foundation of itself. This latter foundation would be the securing of every foundation—but it cannot be precisely this on the model of any other foundation, since no other foundation *fundamentally* secures itself as such. The foundation of foundation consequently founds in a mode which is also that of a nonsecuring, but which this time refers clearly to the withdrawal of its own essence and to what we could call the definitive in-dependence of its own independence. The foundation of foundation therefore founds, in Heideggerian terms, in the mode of "the abyss": *Abgrund*, which is the *Grund* of every other *Grund*, and which is of course its own *Gründlichkeit* as *Abgründlichkeit*.

The abyss is "no-thingness" (*né-ant, Un-wesen*), which it is perhaps not illegitimate (but up to what point and in what sense must we *legitimate* here? Up to what point, without insolence or arrogance, are we not given over to the freedom of recommencing the thinking of freedom, of *repeating*, which means asking again, a certain *fundamental* il-legitimacy which is nothing other than the object of these pages?) to think of in its turn as the Hegelian "intensification" of the nothingness. The word "abyss" says too much or too little for this intensification: too much *figure*, in spite of everything (the contours of the abyss), and too little *intensity*. But the truth of the abyss and of intensification, as the truth of the *no-thingness*, can be named as *experience*. (This does not mean that we would be naming it properly. We will play the game of impropriety with every other term. But we will attempt to experiment here with precisely this impropriety as the very foundation of freedom, and to experiment with what it tests in thought and language: the finitude of their infinite freedom, the infinitude of their finite freedom.)

The foundation of foundation that is freedom is the very experience of founding, and the experience of founding is nothing other than the essence of experience in general. The act of founding is indeed the act par excellence of *experiri*, of the attempt to reach the limit, to keep to the limit. Is not the model of all foundation the founding of the ancient city—the marking of the outline of the city limits? (By the same token, this is also the model of political foundation, even if, as we have seen, the outline of the model of political foundation should be understood as a network of paths and directions rather than as a circumference already in place.) It is not a foundation in the architectonic sense of the excavation and preparation of a ground that will support a building. In order to construct an architectonic foundation, one must first have founded in the sense of having topographically surveyed (or having founded the survey itself. . .), which means having delimited the space of the foundation. This delimitation, in itself, is not anything; it is the nothingness of productive construction. In this sense, it *makes* nothing (and is not *poiesis*), and *there is* nothing, nothing given or preestablished (not even the idea of a plan of the city or building). There is nothing but the indeterminable *chōra* (not an undetermined place, but the possibility of places, or rather pure matter-for-places) *where* the foundation takes place. This foundation is more or less the *nothing* itself, this ungraspable *chōra*, carried to the incandescent intensity of a decision. Here, now, where there is nothing, here and now which are anywhere and anytime, existence is decided for—for example, the existence of a city. This is not the production of the city, but that without which there would be neither plan nor operation to produce it. The decision outlines a limit by bringing itself to the limit that owes its existence only to this founding gesture.

If it is therefore, despite everything, a *poiesis*, this time in the sense of what "brings into being," it is a *poiesis* that brings neither to the being of essence (the plan, one could say), nor to the being of substance (stone, mortar), but only to the being of existence. One must think here of a *poiesis* which is in itself a *praxis*. What is founded exists insofar as it has emerged, by a free decision, from the in-itself, from the abstract night and depth of immanence, but it has not emerged therefrom in the sense of something having been extracted: it has not yet emerged except in the sense of a free decision, which at the same time makes the inaugural incision into the surface of the in-itself—and the in-itself withdraws. This is experience itself, because it neither gathers nor produces anything: it decides a limit, and thus at the same time—at one *time*—it decides its law and its transgression, having in sum already transgressed the law before setting it, making it exist without essence, transcendent without a transcended immanence.

(We have related, through concepts and languages, "experience" to "piracy." But foundation always has something of piracy in it, it pirates the im-propriety and formlessness of a *chorā*—and piracy always has something of foundation, unrightfully disposing rights and tracking unlocatable limits on the *chorā* of the sea. In order to think the experience of freedom, one would have to be able ceaselessly to contaminate each notion by the other, and let each free the other, pirating foundation and founding piracy. This game would have nothing to do with amusement; its possibility, or rather its necessity, is given with thought itself and by thought's freedom.)

The experience of founding takes place on the limit. What is founded *exists* (it is not only projected, but is first thrown, as founded, into existence) and it exists according to the limit's mode of existence, that is, according to the mode of the *self-surpassing* (overcoming and emancipation, gestures of liberation), which is the very structure of the limit. Foundation is the experience of finite transcendence: finitude, as such and without escaping its non-essence, decides or decides itself on existence—and this decision is already its existence, at the same time that it is the foundation of its existence. What makes experience here is the carrying to this extremity where there is nothing except through the decision of foundation, and *as* this decision. It is decision that produces, one could say, the founder (freedom) as much as the thing founded (existence). But the founding gesture, the experience of the limit, does not belong to a founding subject, nor does it support a founded object. And the founding gesture *carries* itself—*at once* anterior and posterior to the tracing of the limit it traces—to the contour, path, and outward aspect of a singularity whose freedom and existence it makes arise simultaneously, the freedom of existence and the existence of freedom: *the experience* of having nothing given, nothing founded, the experience of owning no capital of experience, the inaugural experience of experience itself.

The "foundation of foundation" supports itself alone, having nothing to support it, not even "itself," since "itself" comes to light, or to the world, in a founding gesture, sustaining itself only on its existence, which is sustained only by its own freedom. And this freedom is only sustained by the free decision of being-free, which is in turn only sustained by an infinite withdrawal of *being* and a non-being intensification of the nothingness, pushed all the way to an affirmation of existence as existence, that is, as its own essence—or in-essence. Here (and now), existence tries itself (*experiri*) before and beyond itself, it traces and crosses the limit of its being-thrown-into-the-world, it tests its every chance of existence: it founds itself and pirates itself at the same time, which amounts, furthermore, to saying that *existence makes itself its own chance to which, at the same time, it lets itself be given over.* This is why the "foundation of foundation" is experience itself: experience does not experience anything, but it experiences the *nothing* as the real that it tests *and* as the stroke of luck it offers. There is no freedom and there cannot be the slightest act of freedom without this experience, despite whatever calculations we could or would want to make of the possibilities of choice, of the powers of the will, and of the physical and social laws that constrain or emancipate.

The experience of freedom is therefore the experience that freedom *is* experience. It is the experience of experience. But the experience of experience is nothing other than experience itself: trying the self at the self's border, the immediate testing of the limit which consists equally in the tearing apart of immediacy by the limit, the passage of the limit, which passes nothing and which does not surpass itself, but which *happens* [*se passe*], in the sense that "*it happens*" [*ça arrive*] and in the sense that "*man infinitely surpasses man.*" Experience is the experience of experience's difference in itself. Or rather: *experience is experience's difference,* it is the *peril* of the crossed limit that is nothing other than the limit of essence (and therefore existence), the singular outline of shared being. Experience is thus also its own différance: experience does not belong to itself, nor does it constitute an appropriation of "experiences" (in the sense of knowledge obtained through experimentation), but it is returned to what it is not—and this widening of the gap of difference is its very movement. This gap into which being withdraws is a gap or withdrawal of a self-presence, a gap or withdrawal of a self-knowledge.

Freedom is not "inconceivable": freedom is not conceived, and this is why it is freedom. Its self-evidence beyond all evidence, its factuality more undeniable than that of any fact, depends on this non-knowledge of self, more buried and exposed than any consciousness or unconscious. For Descartes, all that can be said of freedom is "that each individual should encounter it and experiment with it for himself."[4] Like the *ego sum* and the *unum quid* of the union of the soul and body—and no doubt in direct connection, which should be demonstrated, with these two instances—freedom proves itself by testing itself. This does not refer to any introspection, nor to any intimate sentiment, for freedom is anterior to every empirical certitude, without being, properly speaking, on the order of the transcendental. Or rather—and this is what constitutes the difficulty, but also the urgency and the liberating force of this *thought* for philosophical discourse—freedom is *a transcendental experience* or *the transcendental of experience,* the transcendental that *is* experience. What "I experiment with for myself" is in no way a power I could withhold, or a capacity I could get in touch with in myself. Instead, I experiment *that I am* in the experience of myself—this intensity of (un)founded no-thingness—I experiment that the withdrawal of essence *is* an affirmation of my existence and that it is only on the "foundation" of this affirmation that I can know myself to be the subject of my representations, and give flesh to my singular being in the world.

All there is to think of freedom is this affirmation of its experience. But affirmation in general cannot be thought of simply as the negation of negation. Affirmation can only be *thought* through the intensity of affirmation. A thought affirmative of this affirmation, a thought that would be neither the product of a dialectic nor the arbitrary prophecy of a subjectivity is what a logic of the experience of freedom must propose.

In a sense, Hegel's "science of the experience of consciousness" proposes nothing else: it guides the concept of experience to the necessity for experience to be its own subject. At every instant of this trial, the constitution-into-subject, given over to its own experience, is carried to its limit. But the Heideggerian *Dasein*'s "thrownness" also says nothing else: it guides this necessity for experience to be its own subject to the necessity for the subject to be, in its (un)foundation, abandoned to experience, which means abandoned to the freedom to exist. This freedom to exist is not a choice that could be made by a subject, but is that existence decides itself as existence, that is, as being which is shared outside of itself and which has in this sharing *not its renewed essence* (dialectical logic), *but precisely its existence as its own (in)essence*.

Heidegger did not keep the word "experience" here. Yet he did judge that Hegel had "retreated" from what was fundamentally implied by the use of this word in the title of the *Phenomenology*. Indeed, Heidegger had already indicated the nature of this implication or "resonance": more profoundly than "the appearing in its own present being to itself,"[5] which for him translates "experience of consciousness," experience should open onto the exact reverse (not the opposite—and hence more "profound," without depth, the foundation of foundation . . .) of this self-presentation, which means onto the other side of this same limit on which the "self" is located: "Undergoing an experience in the sense of letting the mat-

ter itself demonstrate *itself* and so be verified as it is in truth."[6]
Experience: letting the thing be and the thing's letting-be, and the
thing-in-itself, as we have said, is existence (the existence of *Dasein*
and the existence of beings in general in their common reciprocal
openness). The experience we have is existence—rather than the
experience *of* existence. Experience of the *thing itself* and experience as the thing itself, sameness of the thing and thingness of the
same. Letting the thing of existence give itself over into truth, to its
truth—which is above all the freedom with which, each *time*, it
exists. We have this experience which makes [*fait*] the *fact* of freedom, yet we do not "have" or "make" it (in the sense of *poiesis*).
Neither would we say that it "makes us." Let us say, rather: experience's self-without-subjectivity—which experience singularizes—
is attained in full force by *its* freedom.

This is not empiricism's experience, though it is not an experience
that a subject could teach. It is not the experience of classical empiricism, nor even that of an "empiricism without positivity" as
Lévinas's is reputed to be.[7] It is not these because it is the experience
of experience, in the sense that has been mentioned, and because it
is therefore always the experience of thinking. But if, by this very fact,
it is also a question of a thought of experience, it is nevertheless in
no way a question of an "experience in thought," which would
designate nothing but an imaginary experience. It is a question of
thought as experience: this is as much empirical as transcendental.
Moreover, the transcendental is here the empirical. It is this empiricity of thought itself that is attached to "conditions of production," for example, history, society, institutions, but also language,
the body, and always chance, risk, the "strike" of a "thought." *In the
investigation that brings to light its own condition of possibility as freedom, thinking cannot "think"* (whether in the sense of the construction of the concept, or in the sense of self-reflexivity) *without at
the same time materially touching on this very condition of possibility.*
This materiality is not that of a simple physical exteriority (it is
not a pineal gland . . .), and yet it is no less the body or flesh of
thought—thought not "incarnated" by some aftereffect, but more
initially delivered to itself in the fold and refolding of what Descartes

had to resort to calling a "substantial union."[8] If freedom gives thought to thought—even more than it simply gives it something to think about—this happens in the materially transcendental experience of a *mouth* at whose opening—neither substance nor figure, a nonplace at the limit of which thought passes into thought—thought tempts chance and takes the risk (*experiri*) of thinking, with the inaugural intensity of a cry.

~

One will perhaps argue that this logic does not strive to escape from self-presence except in order continually to return to it and confirm it. Ultimately, in spite of everything, freedom has experience of "itself," and one could even go so far as to affirm that it has experience of the purest ipseity: the "foundation of foundation" is nothing other than the foundation that is rigorously no longer founded on anything but itself. With good reason, one will recall that in the certitude of the *cogito*, in Descartes's own terms, necessity and freedom are each as powerful as the other, or rather are converted into one another. One might then be tempted to conclude that freedom does nothing but recognize its own proper necessity, and necessity is then recognized as the freedom of what is absolutely proper and self-present.

Nothing of the above is incorrect, and all of it can be summarized by the following pronouncement: freedom frees itself. Philosophy has certainly never said anything else. But this still does not mean that freedom, in freeing itself, *appears to itself* [*s'apparaître*]. That which, in making itself, does not appear to itself (that which, consequently, does not "make" itself according to the mode of producing its *eidos*), does not have the property of subjectivity. Nevertheless, it should not be understood that "self-appearing" would be a particular attribute which, in the subject, would come to be added to "making oneself," whereas it would be absent in the case of freedom. The two things are indissociable, and it follows that *freedom actually has the exact structure of the subject*: in a sense, it appears to itself by making itself, and it makes itself by appearing to itself, present-to-itself in the absolute unity of its autooriginarity. But what appears to it (itself . . .) is that it does not make itself, and what it makes (itself . . .) is its not appearing to itself. In other words, *freedom grasps itself in a mode of releasing*. It is not a pirouette—and not a dialectic. Freedom grasps itself released; it is a releasing of the grasp at the heart of the very gesture of grasping. It is the no-thingness of the mastering of its own mastering. For there would be no free thing or person if what was free commanded itself from a position of certitude and presence that would not be put at stake by free action.

Thus freedom is not the negative of the subject. It is, on the contrary, the affirmation of self-presence pushed to the very end— or rather *initially carried to the intensity of incandescence*—to this extremity at which, simultaneously, the self disappears into a pure presence without any relation-to-self (but, at the same time, with an infinite relation to others) and presence vanishes into a self purely given over to itself (to the sharing of singularity). None of these "pure" essences is presentable as such, because none subsists as such in any region where the unpresentable in being would be concealed. But their absolute mixture, as well as their infinite distension, produce the "strike," syncope, and pulsing in which freedom is decided, and was always decided, before any free subject appears to itself, which means, finally, before any "freedom" presents itself as such. *Freedom renders the self to the self outside of all presence.*

Freedom operates here as the ancient condition of free human beings, at least in the way that we think we understand this condition or in the way that philosophy needed to represent it to itself (and with it, all the originarity of the political). Being free "by birth" signifies being free since before birth, before there was the being of being free. This means that the possible place, in a particular lineage or particular city, for a new future individual is the place for a free human being—a free place for a free human being—who receives the condition of freedom when he comes to be conceived, just as infallibly as a slave's son receives his condition. (In the same way, moreover, the contingency of a war or of a decision for emancipation can suddenly deliver each individual to his inverse condition, and this possibility is also part of the scheme.) There is no other task of thought, on the subject of freedom, than that which consists in transforming its sense of a property held by a subject into the sense of a condition or space in which alone something like a "subject" can eventually come to be born, and thus to be born (or to die) *to* freedom (was this not already in some sense the effort of Spinoza's thought on freedom?). What makes this task so difficult and perhaps even impossible to accomplish as a task of philosophical discourse is that the ontological condition required here is not a *status*, as was that of the free human beings of Antiquity (who were in this sense from the start the owners of their freedom), but consists in a releasing of being. We *are born free* not in the sense that a law of nature or of the city guarantees for us in advance the enjoyment of freedom, but in the sense that every birth is a releasing of being, abandoned to a singularity or to a trajectory of singularities. Now, being does not have freedom as a property it could distribute, by releasing from itself, to every existent—nor is being the necessity whose discovery across the movement of existence would produce itself as freedom. Rather, freedom is the foundation that is discovered in the fact that being *is* essentially abandoned—or that it *exists*.

Freedom is the withdrawal of being, whose existence founds itself. This "foundation" is nothing other than an exposure. Freedom exposes existence, or rather, freedom is the *fact* that existence is exposed.

> Ek-sistence, rooted in truth as freedom, is exposure to the disclosedness of beings as such.[9]

Exposure proceeds from "truth as freedom" because truth, before being the adequation of a verifiable utterance, resides in the very possibility of such an adequation (or in the foundation of this foundation). This adequation supposes that there is a *coming*, a coming-into-presence-of. . . . Coming-into-presence is not simple and pure presence: it is not the given, but the gift of the given. The gift, the coming-into-presence, or, one could say, the presentation, tears presence itself from the depth of the presence immersed in itself (immersed to the point of being able to be converted only into absence, as is regularly done by the supreme presence of every negative ontology, theology, or eleutherology). *At this point, where dialectical thought sets into operation the power of the negative in order to reveal the presence at the heart of its absence* (which presupposes subjectivity, insofar as subjectivity is itself what hollows out negation *and* what confers on it, not an intensity of the nothingness, but a potential for conversion: the subject has always already supported the absence of presence, it has always already founded its freedom in this necessity), at this point *the thinking of the withdrawal of being requires thinking that there is not an operation, but a liberation.*

This means that before every process of a spirit appearing to itself as the becoming of being in its phenomenon and in the (self-) knowledge of the phenomenon, being as being makes itself available for every subsequent process, of this kind or of another, and being *is* this "making itself available." But "making itself available" *does not appear to itself:* it does not represent, objectify, engender, or present itself to itself.[10] (And if we can somehow think and say this, it is not because we make use of the concept of such an "a-presentation"; on the contrary, it is because thinking and saying are themselves given and made available by this setting into availability: they are and have experience of it.) Similarly, "making itself available" does not imply any conversion of essence that would mediate itself. That which makes itself available remains unchanged in what it is. But what it is, it frees for. . . . For example, for a subjectivity—not, however, in the sense that a liberation would be ordered for this subjectivity as it would be for its foundation (in consciousness, intentionality, will, in the freedom conceived of as the freedom of aim or use of being), but in the sense that the advent of such a subjectivity remains itself free, existing, and able to take place or not to take place (and, as we will say later, exposed to good as well as to evil).

Being frees itself for existence and in existence in such a way that the existence of the existent does not comprehend *itself* in its origin and finally never comprehends *itself,* but *is at the outset grasped and paralyzed* by this freeing which "founds" it (or "pirates" it). Moreover, existence is to being not as a predicate is to a subject (Kant was the first to know this) but as the improbable is to necessity: given that there is being, what is the chance of its withdrawal freeing an existence? . . . The existence of being is improbable for the existent—and is what frees thought in it: "*Why is there something rather than nothing?*" In this way there is a coming-into-presence: in the *coming* to presence of that whose presence in itself has no reason or foundation for coming to presence. (This is exactly what the entire ontotheological tradition has relentlessly sought to present, even resolve, as the problem of freedom or of the necessity of a "creator" and its "creation.")

To use the terms that haunt all of Kant's thought, there is no reason that there should not be chaos and no reason that anything should appear. If something appears, it is therefore not through "reason," but through its freely coming. And if existence, somewhere, appears to itself as subjectivity, which also means as "reason," this is also through its freely coming.

The "disclosedness of beings as such" (= "there is something") does not refer to a deep-seated constitution of being in being-disclosed (here no doubt is where the possibilities for a general phenomenology end), but refers to the improbable, to the unexpected, to the surprise of a disclosure. Without this surprise, there would be no disclosure as such (and there would be no experience), there would be "revelation" in the ontotheological sense of the term, whose formula comes from Hegel: "What is revealed is precisely that God is the revealable." With respect to disclosure, one would have to say instead: "What is disclosed is precisely that the disclosed is not in itself disclosable—it is being—and that its disclosure exceeds and surprises it instead of coming back to it: it is being 'founded' in freedom, it is existence." For this reason, disclosure also offers itself—this is the logic of *alētheiā* in Heidegger—as the renewed concealment of the very being that discloses itself, and of the being of disclosure itself: in other words, as the concealment of the being of being, and of the being of freedom, of the freedom of being, and of being as freedom. Freedom: what is concealed in disclosure, if we can understand this not as a remainder that stays concealed in disclosure, but as the very movement of disclosure, or as its aspect or tone (its intensity): what is "veiled" in a voice, for example.

In this way existence is exposed: *Dasein* is exposed to the surprise of the disclosure of beings, because this surprise happens in the *da* of *Sein* and as this *da*—as "being's being-the-there"—whereas the being-there of *Dasein* does not belong to it as its own before this surprise. The *there* of existence is definitively not a position, neither spatial nor temporal, though it involves space and time, but it is a surprise. *It is its being-there* that makes its surprise, its being-there in the world of beings disclosed as beings.

To be exposed means to be surprised by the freedom of existing. This also means to be given over to the risk of existing, to the risk of never appropriating for oneself this surprise, of never *re*appropriating for oneself one's foundation. I will never appear to myself as my own surprise, as my own birth, as my own death, as my own freedom. This *never* contains at once all the finitude and infinitude of finite transcendence. It contains my pure presence in its own difference of being, exposed to its unlikely coming.

Once again we touch on the question of relation (actually, we never left it). Being-*in*-common is what presents to me this *never*: my birth and my death are present to me and are my own only through the births and deaths of others, for whom in turn their births and deaths are neither present nor their own. We share what divides us: the freedom of an incalculable and improbable *coming* to presence of being, which only brings us into presence as the *ones* of the *others*. This is the coming to presence of *our* freedom, the common experience of the exposure in which the community is founded, but founded only through and for an infinite resistance to every appropriation of the essence, collective or individual, of its sharing, or of its foundation.

§9 Freedom as Thing, Force, and Gaze

One will ask whether we are still free when we are free to the point that Being is what is free in us, before us, and ultimately for us. This very question could not help posing itself to Heidegger, who finally answered—during the period in which he still thematized freedom, although this was a decisive step toward the abandonment of the theme—that freedom considered as the "root" of being in no way agreed with freedom represented as the property of man:

> But if ek-sistent *Da-sein*, which lets beings be, sets man free for his "freedom" by first offering to his choice something possible (a being) and by imposing on him something necessary (a being), human caprice does not then have freedom at its disposal. Man does not "possess" freedom as a property. At best the converse holds: freedom, ek-sistent, disclosive *Da-sein*, possesses man. . . . [1]

In what sense, however, is man "possessed" by freedom? Sartre interpreted this thought in his celebrated formulation: "We are condemned to freedom."[2] Now this is certainly not the sense in which freedom should be understood, unless we confuse a thinking of the existence of being with an "existentialism." For Sartre, this "condemnation" means that my freedom, "which is the foundation," intervenes in order to found—which means, according to Sartre, to engage in a "project" of existence—in a situation of "determinism" by virtue of which I am not free:

Thus my freedom is condemnation because I am not free to be or not to be ill and illness comes from without: it is not from myself, it has nothing to do with me and is not my fault. But since I am free, I am constrained by my freedom to make it mine, to make it *my* horizon, *my* view, my morality, etc. I am perpetually condemned to will what I have not willed, no longer to will what I have willed, to construct myself in the unity of a life in the presence of destructions externally inflicted on me. . . . I am obliged to assume this determinism in order to place the ends of my freedom beyond it, to make of this determinism one more *engagement.*

Thus the condemnation to freedom is itself the consequence of a condemnation to necessity. Because I cannot avoid illness, I also cannot, in order to be a human being, whose essence lies not in an object but in a project, exempt myself from the necessity of making this accident the means, opportunity, and stepping-stone of a new overstepping of my accidental and accident-prone being in the project of "the unity of a life." I must "assume" my nonfreedom; more exactly, I must assume one of the "aspects of the situation," namely, the "passivity" surrounded by "the totality of the world," by means of the other aspect, which is the freedom to make a life project out of every condition.

This analysis fundamentally refers to a lack as well as to an excess in the apprehension of existence. It refers to a lack insofar as the freedom that is posited here as the taking charge of what it cannot choose or decide is itself definitively considered a power (or perhaps only an obligation . . .) commanded by its own deficiency, which corresponds to a deficiency in the essence of human beings: freedom "is the foundation" in human beings who "*lack* . . . being their own foundation." Freedom here is not "the foundation of foundation," as we have analyzed it, but is the foundation *in default* of foundation. It is also not experience as the experience of the limit at which experience itself does not belong to itself or return to itself—which is what gives it its freedom—but it is the proof that there is something other than freedom, a default of the autonomy and autarchy of a freedom that remains in itself a full power of self-determination. It is no longer a question of the foreignness of freedom to itself, but of a hindrance or constraint that limits it from the exterior, through "determinism." Thus freedom finds itself again endowed with an essence (the project) and with an aseity (the decision to assume itself) which operates, within its own limits, as a foundation whose foundation (which is apparently to be found in subjectivity) we would not question. And we doubtless understand the distracted desire that compelled Sartre to restore a consistency to a traditional power of *homo metaphysicus,* who had been made so anemic by the modern awareness of the world's implacable "investment." But this simply amounts to an attempt to provide a compromise solution for the most classical freedom of subjectivity in a space henceforth conceived and lived as foreign and hostile to this subjectivity (whereas this space is precisely the deployment of this subjectivity, as could be shown, for example, by a detailed analysis of the idea of "illness" that governs the text's example). In this sense, the Sartrian freedom that "assumes" objectivity without any of the means of objectivity is desperately in need of itself.

As for excess, the case is of course symmetrical. What is at stake for me, as I act on my "condemnation" to freedom by assuming the situation and overstepping it, is that "the world must appear to me as issuing in its being from a freedom which is my freedom." The goal and obligation is nothing less than to find a way of relating an absolute subjectivity to the very order of the world whose reality denies the absoluteness of subjectivity. (Furthermore, it is perhaps only a question of acting as if "the world must *appear to me as* . . . "; at the limit, the self-deception of freedom is clearly what is being claimed). If this goal has any meaning (and for Sartre it is "meaning" itself), it would have to be based, as in Hegel, on the presupposition of an infinite Spirit—which, however, could not be admitted here. If the subject is finite, the goal has no meaning. Sartre will of course be able to say: "Each person must realize the goal, and it must still remain to be realized afterwards. The *finite* pursuit of each person in the infinite pursuit of humanity." The *finite* and the *infinite* are juxtaposed here in such a way that no ontological community could be found for them, except in a mode of foreclosure: Sartre's "finite" is *a pure and simple hindrance* to being infinite (compensating for this anguish by vaguely projecting an infinite humanity—which is only a bad infinity. . .), and his "infinite" is *a pure and simple avoidance* of the condition of the finite.

One could not accomplish with greater consciousness, with a tenacity made more striking by its insistence, the unhappiness of consciousness that Hegel recognized in order to sublate it into the self-knowledge of actualization. Deprived of this sublation (or only proposing it in the mode of a deliberate "as if"), Sartrian freedom—in some ways the last "philosophical freedom," already prepared to cede its ground to the juridical defense of freedoms—is the final name of this unhappiness of consciousness: condemned to being, in the infinite form of the project (which would ultimately be the will's unhappiness), the infinite consciousness of the finite and the finite consciousness of the infinite.

Sartre's man is not "possessed" by freedom: he is forced by it into the "free" knowledge of his infinite deprivation of freedom. But here again, definitively, freedom has been measured against the necessity of causality: the freedom of the Sartrian "project" is the will to be the cause of that for which causes are lacking or contrary in given reality. The project is a wishful causality launched in defiance of experienced causality: the heroism of despair. (This has marked up until now, we should not forget, a large collection of discourses, not always directly existentialist, on freedom conceived of as the assumption, the overstepping, or in some sense the redemption, of harsh necessity.)

As long as the concept of freedom remains caught in the space of causality—and of will as causality through representation—it does not permit us to think of anything other than a spontaneous causality whose reality will always remain at least doubtful (measured by the measuring instruments of causality as such, which means according to the anthropology of the "human sciences") and whose secret will be kept, in every case, in the principle of causality itself. Now, the principle of causality, in Kantian terms,[3] is that of the permanence of substance, to which the concepts of necessary force and action lead back in order for the problem of change in phenomena to be considered. This principle is formulated in the fol-

lowing way: "*all change. (succession) of appearances is merely alteration.* Coming into being and passing away of substance are not al-
terations of it, since the concept of alteration presupposes one and
the same subject as existing with two opposite determinations and
therefore as abiding."[4] Thus the only possible logic of freedom as
causality would require that I be the cause of my birth and death. I
can certainly be this cause, if not entirely explicitly for Kant, then at
least according to a coherent explicitation of his thinking, to the extent that I can be, as an intelligible being and outside of the succession of time, the subject of a specific causality that is itself of
the order of the intelligible, that is, "free." But this new causality
must be able to be considered as reunited with sensible or natural
causality. To think the permanence of the substance of the world
united with the spontaneity of a subject of action is to think the unconditioned causality of the totality (as it is represented in the Idea
by the subject of the imperative in view of the realization of a moral
nature). However, the idea of the unconditioned causality of totality is nothing other than the idea of being itself. Thus "the possibility of a unification of two quite different kinds of causality. . .
lies in the supersensible substrate of nature, of which we can determine nothing positively, except that it is the being (*das Wesen*) in
itself of which we merely know the phenomenon."[5] But to attribute
to being (or to essence, which is here precisely the same thing),
considered as cause, the character of the unconditioned and spontaneous is to withdraw this being as such from beings in their totality,
for whom alone the category of causality has validity. Furthermore,
it is to withdraw causality from itself or into itself. (This is why
Kant's logic could lead one to claim that freedom *is* and is only
causality itself, or that freedom is its fundamental *efficacity* whose
means remain hidden in the law of phenomenal succession. This
could also lead one to wonder whether it is schematism—and
specifically the first schema, the "I generate time"—that opens successivity, whose "hidden art" would finally harbor the secret of freedom. . . . But could this secret be reduced to anything that is not also
secret? . . . Unless the thinking of freedom must be that of something
like *the manifest fact of a secret.* . . .)

The idea of a "unification of two heterogeneous causalities" can only signify a *heterogenesis* of causality: a *cause* without causality, or a substance without permanence. But the *cause* without causality, that is to say exempted as much from determination *by* another cause as from the determination *to* produce an effect, is the *thing* itself, the thing *in itself.* The thing [*chose*] of the phenomenon is not its cause [*cause*] (even if, as everyone knows, it is the same word): it is its existence. *Existence is the withdrawal of being as cause and as permanent substrate,* or, further, it is *the withdrawal of the cause in the thing.* The fact of the existence of the thing (its *Setzung*) makes all the successive changes of its essence exist at the same time, but this fact, in conformity with the Kantian principle, has nothing to do with its changes as such. The idea of "causality by freedom" represents nothing other than this *Setzung,* or the *birth* (and death) of the thing, *except that its enunciation forgets* that the cause in question—freedom—*is precisely the thing without causality.* In this sense, one would be justified in saying that metaphysics is exactly the forgetting of freedom (resulting in Sartre), and that this forgetting is produced at the precise moment that it *carries over the determination of the essence of causality onto the pure determination of the existence of freedom,* whereas existence exists only as the withdrawal of essence and consequently the *thing* exists only as the withdrawal of *cause.*

It is therefore not "being free" in the metaphysical sense of this concept as much as it is being free where the thing, at the moment it is valued as the very "cause," withdraws from all causality, and consequently, so it seems, from every force and action necessary for the production of the effectivity expected of a free act. This is not actually "being free" in the sense of being able to *cause* "freely," but it is existence's being-free. In this sense, the existent is "possessed" by freedom: it is "possessed" by it not in the privative mode of the necessity of mitigating (more or less imaginarily) its inability to posit itself and think itself as unconditioned causality, but in the affirmative mode in which freedom measures itself precisely against the fact that its Idea (unconditioned causality) is finally the Idea (which is precisely no longer an Idea, but a fact) of the thing without causality. This is the Idea of existence, in which and as which the "Idea" is immediately given as *fact* and this fact is given as *experience.*[6]

Yet what is given in this way as fact and experience is thereby also given, without changing ontological registers, as force and as action. Being free is not given as a "property" that it would be possible to make use of *on condition* of disposing elsewhere of the forces necessary for this usage, which also supposes that when all forces are lacking for action (and usually almost all are lacking in this regard . . .) freedom withdraws into the interiority from which it never ceases to shine, superb and powerless, until a last fatal force comes to extinguish its mocking flame.

On the contrary, even though it is effectively powerless, freedom is given as force and as action. The reality of the freedom of him who finds himself deprived of the power to act is not a "pure interior disposition," it is not a simple protestation of the spirit against the chaining up of the body. It is, it should be said, *the very existence of this body.* The existence of a body is a free force which does not disappear even when the body is destroyed and which does not disappear as such except when the relation of this existence to an other and destructive existence is itself destroyed as a relation of existences, becoming a relation of essences in a causality: such is the difference of relation between the murderer and his victim, and the difference of nonrelation between the exterminator and his mass grave. This force is neither of the "spirit" nor of the "body"; it is existence itself, impossible to confuse with a subjectivity (since it can be deprived of consciousness and will) or with an objectivity (since it can be deprived of power).

Freedom as the *force of the thing* as such, or as the force of the act of existing, does not designate a force opposed to or combined with other forces of nature.[7] Rather, it designates that from which there can rise relations of force as such, between human beings and nature and between human beings among themselves. It is the force of force in general, or the very resistance of the thing's existence— its resistance to being absorbed into immanent being or into the succession of changes. Accordingly, it is a transcendental force, but one that is a material actuality. Because *existence* as such has its being (or its thing) in the act, or if we like, in the praxis of existing, it is impossible not to grant it the actual character of a force, the thought of which implies the thought of a transcendental materiality, or if we prefer, an ontological materiality: the withdrawal of being as a material *Setzung* of singularity, and the difference of singularities as a difference of forces. Prior to every determination of matter, this materiality of existence, which sets down the fact of freedom, is no less endowed with the material properties of exteriority and resistance.[8]

Being free as being "possessed" by freedom is being free with the actuality of a materiality irreducible to any "pure spirituality" of freedom (and yet, "spirit" *is* this material difference in which the existent comes to expose itself as such). Though we cannot represent this materiality without making it drift into the order of forces both represented and linked in causality, and though, because of this fact, we cannot avoid falling back into an (optimistic or pessimistic) appreciation of the possibilities of action available to freedom, which, because of this fact, is reduced to a causal property of "spirit" (but who would dare simply to appreciate in this way the free force of the cadaver before its murderer?), this does not testify against the ontological status of the force of freedom. This indicates, *in the very resistance to the concept, the impenetrability without which freedom would not be freedom.* (One should not forget that what resists in this way is found constantly lodged at the heart of causality itself, as the efficacity of its successivity. It is not in the "spirit" alone that the force of freedom resides and resists, but it is in the existence of every *thing* as such. One could say: "*we*" are the freedom of every thing.)

Here thinking appears to be most clearly removed from both comprehension and incomprehension:[9] thinking does not comprehend freedom's force, but also does not regard it as incomprehensible—actually, it is colliding, as thinking, with the hard matter of freedom itself, this foreign *body which is its own* and by virtue of which alone it can be what it is: thinking. *It is first in itself, and as its own/alien material intensity, that thinking touches the impenetrable resistance of freedom* (and it touches it, more precisely, as the resistance of *language*, as the resistance of the *singularity* of thinkers and thoughts, but also as this other resistance, again singular, of the *body* that thinks, with muscles tensed, strong flashes in the mind, and the silent density of a flesh that delivers and withdraws at will what we call "thoughts" . . .).

So then, freedom is far from being able to be only "a thought" and it is also not a freedom "in thinking." It corresponds instead to the following: the fact that the existent thinks does not constitute one property among others in the existent, but sets up rather the very structure of its existence, because in thought—or as thought—it is removed from the immanence of being. This absolutely does not mean that the existent exists only in the dimension of "pure thought": there is precisely no "pure thought" if thinking is existence according to the transcendence that delivers it to the world and to the finitude of shared being. Rather, this means that the *life* of the existent is identically its *thought* (and for this reason, moreover, a philosophy of "life" does not suit it any more than does a philosophy of "spirit"). Before or beyond every determinate thought, in particular every deduction of its "freedom" or "nonfreedom," as well as every intuition of one or the other of these, thinking is the act for which its essence of act (its force, and therefore the "substance" that should be endowed with this force) is no more present in immanence than it is conceived in representation. *Thinking is the act of an in-actuality*: this is why it cannot appear to itself in order to master itself, in the mode of a subjectivity, but is for itself—as that which it thinks and as that which thinks it, always other than itself and always initial—the experience of the impenetrable force of its freedom.

This force can be considerable or minute in its calculable effects depending on the linking of causes (assuming we can calculate the effects of thinking and of freedom), but is in itself, as *thing* and not as cause, always the same. It always has the same intensity, which is not a relative but an absolute intensity. This is the absolute intensity that through and through *ex-tends* the play of differences by which we exist in the relation of singularities. Freedom is the absolute tension of the relation, this ontologically material tension whose impenetrability is the absolute price of existence ("dignity," in the Kantian lexicon, which means what is no longer a "value"). This tension is visible as soon as two gazes cross (it is not even certain that this has to be limited to human gazes, or that it must exclude what in our gaze looks at itself or is observed by the "inert" objects of the world): it is materially visible, or more than visible, "tangible," as the very invisibility of that which, in the gaze, gazes—and which is not *a* thought, nor a *face*, but the singular inactuality of this very act of the gaze, of this intense opening of an existence-in-the-world (well prior to any perspective-taking by a subject). This withdrawal of presence which lets and lets itself come to presence, this incandescence of nothingness in which every cause withdraws into the thing (here: there is something), this can only be freedom [*la liberté*], or perhaps it would be better to say: this can only be freedom [*liberté*]. This freedom "possesses" us in the same way that the gaze possesses: by delivering to presence. But it has no relation of any kind to a causality. Being as cause arises from several possible kinds of theoretical vision. Being as thing is offered by the force of freedom's gaze. It is always freedom that gazes, perhaps from the endless depth of the "starry sky," but also in a look exchanged by chance, or from the depths of a prison, or even into the eyes of someone who has just died. And if it is always freedom that gazes, it is undoubtedly also always the same gaze.

§ 10 Absolute Freedom

If freedom were not this being-free, this freedom of being (its own) and the freedom of existence in relation to being (which is the same freedom, the generosity of the withdrawal), we would not be free at all. We would be returned to the antinomy of caprice and fate, which could easily form the basis, and instantly the impasse, of Kant's third Antinomy—revealing that transcendental illusion is properly found neither in the thesis nor in the antithesis, but in the very antinomy purporting to give them their dialectical status (which thus exposes the general dialectic, in every sense of the word, of freedom for metaphysics). All philosophy prior to Kant knew, as he did, that caprice can depend on fate, just as fate can be understood as a caprice (perhaps this is where the philosophical interpretation of tragedy begins, or ends, unmindful of a "tragic freedom" which we will have to discuss further). By imagining the difference in nature of two causalities, Kant made possible both the exposition of the antinomy and its transcendental solution. But once this difference in nature is shown to be fallacious, since on both sides it is still finally a question of causality, we find ourselves relegated to the perpetual and derisory displacement at the interior of the antinomy, a displacement that condemns to inanity every interrogation of freedom, including finally even the concept of freedom, which engages one or another of the following possibilities: the subjective assumption of necessity, the relative freedom at the heart of a determined group, spiritual and nonmaterial freedom, ethico-political freedoms incapable of understanding themselves, and so on.

Freedom is not if it is not absolute, and it can only be absolute by being a possibility of causality, or even only by being finally (as everything in Kant would lead us to read it) the very intelligibility of causality—for it is the thing, not the cause, that can be absolute; it is presence, not essence; it is existence, not being. The thought of this absoluteness is the categorical imperative of every thought of freedom, and perhaps of all thought in general, even and exactly if this task of thought can never present itself as the program of a deduction or demonstration, even an infinite one, and if on the contrary it always offers itself as thought's testing of its own limit (but also of its own *matter*).

If the categorical imperative only has meaning insofar as it is addressed to a freedom, its meaning is that freedom, for its part, only has meaning in receiving such an imperative (whether this is literally the Kantian imperative, or whether it is an entirely different pronouncement: for example, "always think freedom!". . .). In other words, freedom is *essentially*, not accidentally, the speaker of the injunction,[1] and is perhaps therefore essentially only the allocutor of a categorical injunction on the subject of freedom, and the allocutor, consequently, of its own injunction: be free! Or: free yourself! (Or, more elaborately: be what you are, that is, freedom, and for this, free yourself from an essence and/or concept of freedom!) Perhaps there has never been anything else at the extremity or inauguration of every thought of freedom, whether the necessary free condition of the philosopher for Plato, the Cartesian free decision to be oneself, Spinoza's exclusive freedom of God, or even the Hegelian State as the total and singular actualization of freedom.

Auto-nomy, which has always represented the very regime of freedom, must be understood on this basis: as a legislation by the *self* in which the *self* does not preexist, since its very existence is what is prescribed by the law, and this law itself is not based on any *right*, since it founds with its own *juris-diction* the possibility of a "right" in general. Freedom is not a right, it is the right of what is "by rights" without right: with this radicality it must be understood as *fact*, as initial and revolutionary. The *law* here is law itself, in its pure essence (what it prescribes is subordinated to nothing prior, *not even to some non-freedom from which it would have to free itself*: freedom cannot but precede itself in its own command), and is, by the same fact, the law that never ceases brushing the limit of law, the law that does not cease freeing itself from law. Freedom: singularity of the law and law of singularity. It prescribes a single law, but this single law prescribes that there be only cases, that there be only singular instances, singularly impenetrable and unapproachable by this prescription. At the same time, freedom is preeminently approachable and penetrable: it is the law without which there would be neither hint nor expectation of the slightest law.

"Be free!" (perhaps, by way of an improbable verbal use of the substantive or adjective, one would have to be able simply to write "*free!*" [*libre!*]—unless this sounds, yet why not, like a training command . . .). "Be free!" therefore commands the impossible: there is no freedom that is available or designatable *before* this injunction or *outside of* it—and the same command commands impossibly, since there is no subject of authority here. Once again we touch the limit of comprehension. But we do so in order to find ourselves once again before the necessary anteriority of freedom,[2] which is no longer illuminated here only in regard to thinking but also in regard to freedom itself (if we are still permitted to make this distinction). Freedom must *precede itself* in its auto-nomy in order to be freedom. It cannot be ordered, its advent can be prescribed only if it has *already* freed the space in which this prescription can take place without being an absurdity, or rather without being anterior to the slightest possibility of *meaning* in general (and yet, is it not *also* a question of this? . . .). We cannot say "be free!" except to someone who knows what this phrase means, and we cannot know what it means without having already been free, without having already been *set free*. In the imperative in which freedom differs in itself, it must also *have preceded itself*. "Be free!" must occur unexpectedly as one of freedom's orders. Freedom must have already freed itself, not only so that the imperative can be pronounced, but so that its pronouncement can be an act endowed with the force of freedom.[3]

(In this sense, if it is correct to claim that the imperative, in general, is powerless over the execution of what it orders—it is not the cause—it would not be correct to claim that it is without force. This force is what makes *intonation* (a form of intensity) a remarkable element in linguistic descriptions of the imperative mode.[4] This force forces nothing and no one. In a certain way, it is a force without function, or is only the intensity of a singularity of existence, insofar as it *exists*.)

In this way, autonomy as the auto-nomy of freedom is absolute. This does not mean, as it could be understood on the most obvious register of Hegelian logic, that the Absolute is free. This means—the exact reverse of Hegel—that freedom is absolute, which is to say that freedom is the *absolutization of the absolute itself*. To be absolute is to be detached from everything. The absolute of the absolute, the absolute essence of the absolute, is to be detached from every relation and every presence, including from itself. The absolute is being that is no longer located somewhere, away from or beyond beings, with whom it would again have this relation of "beyond" (which Hegel knew well), and it is not an entity-being, but is being withdrawn into itself short of itself, in the ab-solution of its own essence and taking place only as this ab-solution. The absolute is the being of beings, which is in no way their essence but only the withdrawal of essence, its ab-solution, its dis-solution, and even, absolutely, its *solution*, in the *fact* of existence, in its *singularity*, in the *material* intensity of its coming and in the *tone* of the autonomous Law whose autonomy, autofoundation, and authority depend only on the experience of being the law extended to the edge of the law like the throw of an existence.

If such is indeed being's absolute extremity, to which we must absolutely grant existence, the very thing of thinking, then *"freedom" is the philosophical name of this absoluteness*, or is nothing. Freedom is the detachment—and unleashing—of being insofar as being is not retained in being and is absolved of its being in the sharing of existence.

§ 11 Freedom and Destiny:
Surprise, Tragedy, Generosity

Because of this absoluteness, freedom must be thought of in a way that distinguishes it from every concept of freedom opposed—and therefore relative—to something like fatality.

The idea of fatality, whether it takes on the resonance of a Destiny controlled from beyond the world, or of a necessity of the immanent development of a History, presupposes an ontological consistency proper to the course of events as such, either in its origin or in its linking process. This course of events must *be* (and it must be as a *course*) in accordance with succession and direction. On account of this, there can only be freedom in relation to this course of events; that is, there can only be freedom from the point of view of a non-finite transcendence that permits it to occupy a position outside of time. In this position, freedom can be identified with fatality, whether on the model of an ecstasy in God (or in the Subject of History) or on the model of the "resolve to the inevitable as essential self-deception."

The consistency proper to the course of events is the being of time: not being as time, but time as being; time as substance and as subjectivity. The question of, or obsession with, fatality is constantly present in the Occident (and without it, the thought of freedom falters, or else thought and freedom become dialecticized), to the extent that temporality is there substantivized. But to the inverse and symmetrical extent—which in fact also works through the entire tradition—that temporality is recognized as presenting an obstacle to substantivization in general, and in particular to its own substantivization,[1] the perspective shifts. The *course* of events should not be denied, but rather brought to light as the course of *events* and as the eventfulness of the very "course" as such. We will not address the Heideggerian analyses of temporality here, nor the persistent if unobtrusive thread of tradition that was to lead to them (history) and that was simultaneously freed by them from its course (event). We will bring ourselves immediately to this extremity at which the very concept of *time*, and almost even its name, is found suspended:[2] to this point at which the temporality of time proves to be nothing temporal (or where the temporality of time is temporal to the extent that it gives the time of time, in some sense its rhythm rather than its course—if we can risk forgetting that this rhythm occurs only in the very course itself).

This means that *across* time itself, so to speak, rather than in the depth of a temporal essence of time, what can finally be discerned is what we could call the *origination* [*provenance*] of time, or more exactly, the coming-forth [*pro-venance*] of time's *present.* Indeed, time as such, however fluid and even fugitive its flowing, is held fast for all of philosophy in the dimension and grasp of presence (the having-been-present, the being-present, the being-present-to-come). Thus time as such was for Kant the only thing that does not flow *in* time: it is the permanence of the present that succeeds itself. Just as beings, which are to the extent that they are beings-present, disclose themselves by concealing being in its withdrawal, likewise (this "likewise" actually responds to the intimate interlacing of both questions) time's present cannot present itself without signaling (concealing is also and above all signaling, without signifying) toward the coming-into-presence of this present (or, if one likes, toward presence's being-presented). The present cannot originate from another present; each present as such holds itself back from an *absolute* (past, present, or future) presence that, as such, is detached from all successivity. In Kant's terms for causality: each present of a presence is a *birth* (or a death) to existence, it is not a modification of a permanent substance (which as such would never have come to presence). Or further: the phenomenon in its phenomenality involves the couple of permanence/succession, which itself involves the couple of substance/accident, whereas the phenomenon considered as the *existence* of the thing involves, if we may say so, simply (but in fact it is simplicity itself, so close and so distant . . .) the "setting into position" of the thing, the *Setzung* of the existent into existence. This *Setzung* escapes permanence as well as succession and escapes substantiality as well as successivity. It is the origination, in time, of presence insofar as presence, as the present of its presence, depends on nothing that founds or produces it. This *Setzung* comes neither from time nor from anything in time, nor from anything outside of time. It is in some sense the coming-forth of time in time. In this, it proceeds from a "coming" that is itself not temporal, neither in the sense that it would come in time, nor in the sense that the duration of its procedure would there present itself (in this sense, it is not even a "coming"—it does not properly *come*, but it perhaps comes forth, comes up, comes back). It is a coming-forth that does not precede the present, but gives it as present, gives it its presence of present, or gives it to presence (and in this it way *gives time*—the origination [*provenance*] and obligingness [*prévenance*] of being for existence). Heidegger named this *Ereignis*. He says: "The giving of *presence* is the property of *Ereignen*. Being vanishes in *Ereignis*." Under the term *Ereignis*, whose current sense is "event," Heidegger therefore tries to think not temporal and present punctuality, which is what we normally understand by "event," but rather the advent of the event, the origination of a present and thus of the appropriation (*Eignung*) of being as being, of time as time, and of being and time in the opening of a presence (which also implies space).

Heidegger left the explication or exploration of *Ereignis* partially suspended. I will not attempt to take it up and prolong it: this would require an entirely different work. I will content myself with freely using what this motif seems necessarily to indicate in the direction of freedom, or in the direction of what we persist in calling here "freedom." It is thus a question of the coming-forth of time. If time is considered as originating from itself, it is considered to be the subjectivity of a necessity: an ineluctable course of events, with which freedom would have to reduce itself to practicing imaginary ruses. But what about the event or advent of the *course* as such? What about the advent of time itself, as the course of presents and as the present of the course? (What then, ultimately, about the first Kantian schema and the "*I*" who there produces or engenders time even before being able to be by definition a subject)? This entire question is doubtless that of a singular *I* who engenders in being born, who *is* only his birth and who is only birth: once again, a cry—of surprise?)

What about the coming as such, insofar as it, as we have said, does not come? What about the coming-forth of the coming, of the *e-venire* and *ad-venire* themselves? This coming-forth is not an origin in either time or being. It is only the origin of a possible origin—and perhaps it is, even more secretly and in accordance with a theme already evoked here, the origin of an improbable origin. It would be better to call it a *coming-up* [*sur-venue*].[3] Time, time as course and as event, time as the course of events and as the event of its own course, which means in all the modes of its coming-to-presence, time comes-up. This coming-up does not consist in the sudden character of the coming-to-presence, for its sudden character is still a mode of presence (if we understand this sudden character in connection with the "instant"—"suddenness," however, might be susceptible to a different analysis). But the coming-up is in the fact that "coming" does not *come*, that "happening" [*arriver*] does not *happen*. We must think here far from all that temporal thought supposes concerning coming, event, advent, and arrival, insofar as it is the thought of their presence. By keeping the word "event," but in trying to think it, with *Ereignis*, as the appropriation of a presence and not as the (sudden) presence of a property, we would say: in the event, time comes-up to time, time happens as time (as present), without happening in time or temporally. The birth of time that would also be the time of birth: time withdrawn from time, the time of a passage without present, the passage from nothing to nothing—but the delivery of existence.

What "happens" without happening, without coming from an origin, but in coming-forth or coming-up at the very origin (as a cry, perhaps, would come up at the originary orifice of the mouth, and not come from it), is surprise. Surprise as surprise does not come up in order to add itself to the course of events and to modify it. It offers another course, or, more decisively, it offers in the "course" itself the withdrawal of the course of time, the withdrawal of all its presence. In fact, we could say that surprise is already inscribed in the heart of all philosophical analyses of temporality and, in a singular manner, in the analyses of the present instant: on the limit between the already-having-been and the not-yet-being, the present has always also proved to be the limit of presence—the already-having-passed of what has-not-yet-come. This is the structure of the surprise (and it will form the exact reverse of the structure of the present): it takes place without having happened; it will therefore not have taken place, but will have opened time, through a schematism of the surprise whose "I" would surprise itself. Open time could be the time of astonishment and upheaval, or that of interrogation and explanation. For example, the time of the question: Why is there something?—or even of this (other?) question: Why pose the preceding question? We can always take the time to respond to the question, and we must, even if only to respond that there is no "reason" for this "why?" Yet this time that we will take will have been opened only by the surprise that did not take time, the surprise for which there was no longer time—or not yet time—to take one's time. The surprise will not even have taken the time to come, it will have come-up at every coming and will have been the event of a *free time*, of a free opening of time so that time could present itself.

The time of the response will be the time of necessity—as indeed the time of the question already was, since the "why?" presupposes the regime of necessity. But no necessity opens by surprise, which means that time as such will always be that of necessity. For time is always the course of the presentation of events, as well as the course of questions, doubts, responses, or silences—the time of "life" as the time of "philosophy" and as the time of the "philosophy of time." Yet the time of time, or this syncope of time that makes presence present itself by surprise (an empiricist's question: Will the sun rise tomorrow? In this sense, there is no response to empiricism, except in the *experience* of surprise, which does not respond, but which says only that tomorrow's sun, if there is one, will not be the same sun)—this can only be called "freedom."

When it is *no longer time* to live and philosophize, or when it is *not yet* time (birth and death outside of causality, birth and death of a singularity, of an "I" or of a sun, birth and death of "philosophy," or of a single "thought," a pulsing of existence), then it is surprise: it is "there" before ever having been there, and it is not "there" once it has arrived. An essence precedes itself and succeeds itself by a syncope: this is the logic of freedom as the logic of an essence whose access is not prescribed by this essence,[4] a "free" essence because it is nothing other than the surprise of a delivered existence. Freedom surprises— or rather, because freedom is not the subject of an action, freedom *surprises itself.* "Surprising itself" is the act of the subject at the limit of subjectivity: at the limit, which means where the self essentially differs and differs in itself (for example: *ego sum*). Freedom does not depend here on the will as the fore-seeing of the coming-forth of a representation's reality: it surprises with a *strike*, at every *moment* (not an instant, but a strike in an instant, an improbable cutting of the instant), the entire system of will:

And the gesture was made before she even realized it, so much had she thought about it.

Or:

She throws herself beneath the train without having made the decision to do so. Rather, it was the decision that took Anna. Which surprised and over-took [*a sur-prise*] her.[5]

Freedom always surprises when there is no longer or not yet time. That is, when there is no longer or not yet time *for time,* and for the opposition of a "freedom" and a "fatality." Not that freedom is resolved only to be "resignation to the inevitable" (which doubtless shapes the result of the metaphysical concept of freedom, but which at the same time has never formed the essential thought of any great philosophy; exemplary and even of primary importance in this respect, the Stoic's will to will the order of the world cannot be analyzed as resignation).[6] Yet neither does it lend itself (and this again is Stoic) to the illusion of a revolt that would in reality be subjected to the binding power of destiny. Freedom separates itself from resignation and revolt not in order to do nothing, but in order to open up this separate place, which is that of the free act in its proper and revolutionary force.[7] (Undoubtedly, neither the attitude of revolt nor that of resignation is excluded: but it is freedom that decides, freedom makes them free or not.)

When it is no longer or not yet time for the opposition of a will and a destiny, this is because it is no longer or not yet time for time. In freedom, it is not time for time. It is "time" for a cutting of time, for a coming-up that surprises time by presenting what has not come, withdrawing presence from what has been presented. The free act ignores the present of the past and does not ensure the present of the future; yet it also does not keep itself within its own present: it is not the event, but it happens to the event and appropriates (*ereignet*) it as the opening or closing of time, as a gift or refusal of coming-into-presence. In a sense, Kant is correct: if right now I get up from my chair, there is no other causality that comes to interfere without interfering in the mechanical causality of the world; but there is inevitably in this event a coming-up of what does not come there and of what does not appear there, of what delivers the time of this gesture to existence, which means to the (usually improbable) possibility of a syncope of time and presence *wherein that which does not present itself as present presents itself,* namely, the withdrawal of essence in which existence *exists.*

Freedom "presents itself" ahead of/behind itself, in excess of and in retreat from what could assign or institute it within a presence, whether the presence of a will or of a destiny. It is free for will and/or destiny, but it does not mingle with their subjectivity or substantiality: it is the possibility of having to make oneself the subject of a free will and/or the possibility of being taken by the force of a destiny, but it will be neither free will nor destiny; in them it will be existence exposed in an arbitrary and/or destinal mode, *but this exposure itself will be neither arbitrary nor destinal,* it will be what exposes itself without foundation, what is exposed by the releasing of its foundation to the chance of the will, to the risk of destiny. It will not be the event of a choice or of a transport, it will be what comes-up in such an event: an exposed existence.

In this way freedom is absolute: detached even from its own event, unassignable in any advent, it is the cut within time *and* the leap into the time of an existence. It enters time and in this sense we could say it "chooses" time, but it does not enter time except by way of the excess and withdrawal where time as such—which could be the presentation and the present of a freedom, of an act, and of a free subject—is surprised, since freedom there surprises itself, opening time on the surface of time, through the course of time, on time or at the wrong time. In this sense, we could not even say that freedom "chooses itself" or that it "chooses" time.[8] It is a question neither of choice nor of constraint. The issue is that existence as such is pure-ly offered to time—which means to its finitude—and that this of-fering, this presentation that comes before any presence, this com-ing-forth that only comes up unexpectedly, *is* existence in with-drawal from essence or from being. Its surprise does not let it "choose." Nevertheless, surprise does not determine existence: it exposes existence as an infinite generosity to time's finitude (as an in-finite, unexpected coming-up in finite presence).

Only thus can time become "filled" or "fulfilled," according to Benjamin's model:

> Historical time is infinite in every direction and at every moment not filled . . . the determining force of the historical form of time is never plainly discernible through any empirical event nor can it be reduced to any event. An event, as it would be fulfilled in a historical sense, is much more something entirely undetermined empirically, an idea.[9]

This fulfillment appears to me as analogous to what I have named the unexpected coming-up of and to the event. The "idea" suscep-tible to coming-up unexpectedly and grasping the "force of the historical form of time" (which means, in fact, the force of its very fulfillment) can only be freedom—in this case, the freedom of the tragic hero exposed to his "flaw," which, as Benjamin explains, is nothing other than the filling up of his "time proper." This freedom fills time, withdraws it from infinity as well as from its empty form, and *finishes* it because it *completes* it: a finished finitude, infinitely finished, we could say, and exposed as such in tragedy. This occurs in an instant (as Benjamin notes elsewhere, the unity of tragedy's time is a figure of the instant), which means not within an instant, in the present time of an instant, but by a cut in the middle of the instant: the cut of freedom that unexpectedly comes up in this time and fills it. Yet, "in tragedy, the hero dies because nobody is capable of living in filled time. He dies of immortality." We will transcribe this: his freedom withdraws his presence and essence in the very gesture by which it completes the existing finitude of time. It is also surprising. Death comes to surprise the tragic hero:

> For it is not rare that it is in moments of full repose—in, so to speak, the hero's sleep—that his time's decree is fulfilled; and likewise, in tragic destiny, the meaning of filled time comes to light in great moments of passivity: in the tragic decision, in the moment of delay, in catastrophe.

We see how this surprise of finite immortality—if it can be thus expressed—has little or nothing to do with this vision of the tragic, which is concluded by being made into the metaphysical paradigm of the conflict between a "freedom" and a "destiny." Tragic destiny is here nothing other than freedom's destiny, *or the free destiny of what brings time to the saturated intensity of a "time proper*," the finite/infinite burst of existence, which withdraws from being and time. The tragic, which knows nothing of sadness, as Benjamin has also noted, is the surprise of a time filled with freedom: unpresentable surprise, unsustainable and yet perfectly present, offered at the surface of the unimpeachable *fact* of its very surprise.

If one does not die from each act of freedom (but if there is no freedom that does not involve death, as Hegel knew), free existence nonetheless is never contained in the time filled with its freedom. It is never contained in a "free time," or in a fulfilled time, but in a necessary time from which freedom withdraws. Yet this withdrawal is precisely what renders existence to the absolute surprise of the experience of freedom's unexpected occurrence.

Finally, one does not die from each act of freedom, but one dies. Similarly, each time freedom exposes us to the possibility of death, death in turn exposes us to the surprise of freedom—as birth does also. Birth and death actually have the same structure, which does not simply join the two extremities of a lifetime, but which happens to the entire course of this life's events and which is none other than the unexpectedly occurring structure of *existence* as such: the one through which it is never present except in being freely offered to presence—to its own presence as well as to the presence of a world. Birth and death: what we can think of only as the appropriation of a presence (*Ereignis*) unexpectedly coming-up without origin to presence and to time's present. Birth and death are caught in time by a fatality—itself without origin or end—but are at the same time withdrawn from time, in a finite eternity that is itself only a free existing exposure. *For freedom, which is initial, is to the same extent final,* not, however, in the sense of a goal or result but in the sense that it, always fulfilled, does not cease exposing existence to the fulfillment that is its own: being its own essence, that is, withdrawing from every essence, presence, substance, causality, production, and work, or being nothing other than (to use Blanchot's term) the workless inoperation [*désoeuvrement*] of existing. "To be born free" and "to die freely" are not merely formulas coined for the determinations of right or for ethical exigencies. They say something about being as such, about the being of time and about the singular being of existence.[10] They say that we are not "free" to be born and to die—in the sense of a free choice we could make as subjects—but that we are born and we die *to nothing other than freedom,* where "dying to freedom" should be understood as "being born to freedom": we do not lose it, we accede to it infinitely, in an "immortality" of freedom which is not a supernatural life, but which frees in death itself the unprecedented offering of existence.

Perhaps Heidegger tried to think something similar by the term *destination.*[11] Destination would be the very movement of *Ereignis,* or of the appropriating coming-up: not destiny—the domination of the present—but the "donation of *presence.*" This presence is given, held out, offered from its withdrawal and in its withdrawal, and this means the liberation of presence and for presence in the with-drawal of present time: a presence which proves to *be* not *present*, but destination, sending, liberation of itself as the infinite sharing of existence. Yet "destination" and "liberation" still risk saying too lit-tle, as long as these words continue to mark conscious and willed ac-tion. In order to try to free in words another designation of freedom, let us say: *a surprising generosity of being.*

§ 12 Evil: Decision

What if thought found itself harshly summoned to modesty and reduced to powerlessness by evil? More serious still, what if it found itself confronted by evil with its own worthlessness?

Auschwitz demonstrated irrefutably that culture had failed. That this could happen in the midst of the traditions of philosophy, of art, and of the enlightening sciences says more than that these traditions and their split lacked the power to take hold of men and work a change in them. There is untruth in those fields themselves, in the autarchy [we would add: free thoughts, thoughts freed, always joined to an essential freedom of humanity's thought] that is emphatically claimed for them. All post-Auschwitz culture, including its urgent critique, is garbage. In restoring itself after the things that happened without resistance in its own countryside, culture has turned entirely into the ideology it had been potentially—had been ever since it presumed, in opposition to material existence, to inspire that existence with the light denied it by the separation of the mind from manual labor. Whoever pleads for the maintenance of this radically culpable and shabby culture becomes its accomplice, while the man who says no to culture is directly furthering the barbarism which our culture showed itself to be.[1]

As a consequence of his last proposition, Adorno adds:

Not even silence gets us out of the circle. In silence we simply use the state of objective truth to rationalize our subjective incapacity, once more degrading truth into a lie.

Therefore we cannot remain silent. We cannot remain silent before what has blocked the "freedom" that was our culture's main thought and before what has almost made us renounce all thought of freedom (Heidegger undoubtedly thought he was recognizing this, among other things, when he acknowledged "the greatest folly of my life";[2] however, he did keep silent,[3] and this silence, as we have claimed, was also a silence concerning "freedom"; in the meantime, he never ceased trying to think the "free space" of *Ereignis*: this too meant recognizing the worthlessness and futility of the "culture" of freedom, without, however, giving way to . . . freedom.) If every thought of freedom must be renounced in order to make room for the hastily acquired consensus of a moral and political liberalism, then thinking as such must be renounced. This would not be a serious matter if thinking were only "some thought"; on the contrary, it would be to renounce that which can be evil and do evil in thought: illusion, facility, irresponsibility, and intellectuality, which only considers itself free and easily affirms freedom as long as freedom does not put it to the test. However, thinking is not intellectuality, but the experience of its limits. This experience, as the experience of freedom, materially and in an unapproachable corporeality, is nothing other than birth and death. Indeed, to say of birth and death that "we can only think them" means that we can only think in them, and that freedom is at stake in them. Auschwitz signified the death of birth and death, their conversion into an infinite abstraction, the negation of existence: this is perhaps above all what "culture" made possible.

We cannot remain silent and we do not have to choose. The experience of freedom is not *ad libitum*. It constitutes existence and must therefore be grasped at this extremity of the negation of existence. Henceforth, there is an experience of evil that thought can no longer ignore. In fact, this is perhaps the major experience of all contemporary thought as the thought of freedom, which means precisely as the thought that no longer knows if and how "freedom" could be its "theme," since the negation of existence was systematically undertaken freely at the heart of the culture of freedom. Thought thinks nothing if it is not tested against declarations such as this one by Thomas Mann from 1939: "Yes, we know once again what good and evil are."[4] Yet the first requirement is not to understand by this the return to a "well-known" good and evil. It is on the contrary to take the measure of a new "knowledge of good and evil" and of a knowledge that cannot avoid the inscription of evil, in one way or another, *in* freedom.

Concerning evil, the lesson we must heed consists of three points:
1. the closure of all theodicy or logodicy, and the affirmation that evil is strictly unjustifiable;
2. the closure of every thought of evil as the defect or perversion of a particular being, and its inscription in the being of existence: evil is positive wickedness;
3. the actual incarnation of evil in the exterminating horror of the mass grave: evil is unbearable and unpardonable.[5]

Under this triple determination is constituted what we could call—not without a somber irony—the modern knowledge of evil, different in nature and intensity from every prior knowledge, though it still harbors certain of its traits (essentially, in sum, the evil that was "nothing" has become "something" that thought cannot reduce).

(In addition, this knowledge also includes the history of the modern *fascination* with evil, for which it will suffice to recall, all differences aside, the names of Sade, Baudelaire, Nietzsche, Lautréamont, Bloy, Proust, Bataille, Bernanos, Kafka, Céline, without forgetting the *roman noir*, in the various senses that two centuries have given this term, or the "horror" film, including private productions of films showing actual murders of prostitutes.)[6]

This knowledge is above all the knowledge that there is a proper "positivity" of evil, not in the sense that it would come to contribute in one way or another to some *conversio in bonum* (which always rests on its negativity and on the negation of this negativity), but in the sense that evil, *in its very negativity, without dialectical sublation, forms a positive possibility* of existence. This is the possibility of what has lately been called the diabolical or satanic and for which we no longer have even these designations, which are still culled from the sublimity of "an appalling black sun from which the night radiates."[7] For us the night can no longer radiate; on the contrary, it plunges into the dissolution of a fog that thickens it all the more: *Nacht und Nebel.*

This positivity of evil—as a kind of hard block that philosophy rejected or threw out before itself in the fulfillment of subjectivity, ignored or denied by a subject (God, Man, or History) who by rights could only rediscover and recover his "good"—represents precisely what Kant would not and could not think with regard to what he brought to light as the "radical evil" in human beings.[8]

> We are not, then, to call the depravity of human nature *wickedness* taking the word in its strict sense as a disposition (the subjective *principle* of the maxims to adopt evil as *evil* into our maxim as our incentives (for that is diabolical); we should rather term it the *perversity* of the heart, which, then, because of what follows from it, is also called an *evil heart.*

However, despite everything, it is in diabolical wickedness that Kant will recognize, several pages later, the biblical representation of an incomprehensible origin of evil in human beings. In other words, for there to be relative evil (which is called "radical" evil and for which there is always the hope of a "return to the good"), there must be in the origin the absolute evil of the determination toward evil. Yet all that we can picture of it is its incomprehensibility, which is the incomprehensibility of a "discord in our free will": our free will is "primitively disposed toward the good," and yet, if it is possible for our weakness to pervert our maxims, evil itself must first have been introduced as a motivation for maxims in general. This is what is figured by the devil, inasmuch as he is incomprehensible: "for whence comes the evil in this spirit?"—this spirit whose original destiny, Kant specifies, was "sublime." The wickedness of Lucifer/Satan figures an incomprehensible, absolute evil at the root of the root of human evil.

Accordingly, the incomprehensibility of evil is lodged—since Kant's time and almost without his knowing it, or at the limit of his thought—at the heart of the incomprehensibility of freedom. Yet in the final analysis nothing else is incomprehensible about freedom except the possibility of wickedness—and this to the extent that this "possibility" is a reality effectively present in freedom's factuality. Once again, our world presents us with this reality every day in various ways, ever since it entered into the age of exterminating fury. Nothing else is incomprehensible about freedom except this wickedness, once one recognizes the necessity of exempting the thinking of freedom from its dependence on the thinking of causality. The mystery of freedom is no longer that of a spontaneous cause, it is that of a spontaneity of wickedness. (But wasn't this issue at once prepared and concealed in Kant's thought, as well as prior to him, by the following: that authentic freedom was the freedom of the good, whereas evil was the fact of nonfreedom letting itself be dragged along by the mechanics of the sensible? Isn't this more clearly illuminated by the passage, in Kant, from theoretical freedom to practical freedom, as well as in the passage from Kant himself to Schelling and Hegel—a passage to the necessity of evil which Heidegger sought to repeat and to which we will return?)

The causing of evil does not pose a problem of causality but a problem of maxims. Freedom spontaneously admits, of itself, a maxim of wickedness. This does not exactly mean the design to "cause evil *for the sake of* evil," if we wish to object to this formula that implies that there always subsists a good that is subjectively represented as the finality of an act, or at least as the triumph of a force or as the pleasure of the subject. However, this "good" can no longer be represented as one in which an evil deed would be a moment or mediation. For this "good" is carried out or gratified by the perpetration of evil as evil. In evil, as evil, it is *good* that is ruined absolutely. That evil and good are relative to each other does not signify (rather, no longer signifies as soon as "the Good" can no longer be designated in a transcendent essence, to whose absolute only evil would be relative) that evil is the privation of a good, insofar as this privation leaves the essence or ideal of the good unscathed (we will neglect for the moment the fact that the good, at another level of philosophy, is perhaps thought of entirely differently once it is thought—including and since Plato—to be situated beyond essence itself, *epekeina tēs ousiās*; we will return to this). Nor is good relative to evil insofar as it would be the cessation of an evil (in this minimal version, cynical or pragmatist, evil is barely evil: it is the inconvenience and hardship of living). But evil is, if we can say it thus, "absolutely relative" to good in that it is the ruin of the good as such, not its privation, but its crushing in a night where nothing any longer gives one the slightest right to say that it would still be the gloomy evening preceding a dawn. Neither good nor evil precedes. Freedom alone precedes and succeeds and surprises itself in a decision that can be for the one or the other, but only insofar as the one and the other exist by the decision that is also, fully and positively, for evil as much as for good. Deciding for evil is not therefore deciding "not to do" good, it is deciding to ruin in the very decision the possibility of the good. Evil does not impair the good (it could not be impaired), nor does it disregard it (for evil knows and wills itself as evil and is therefore knowledge of the good), but it refuses its coming to life. Wickedness causes evil by withdrawing from the good its possibility *in statu nascendi*. It does not consist in an attack against the good (the polemological metaphysics of the combat between the powers of good and evil loses all relevance here;[9] besides, here there is no power of good *per se*, and it is with power as such that evil ultimately identifies). Wickedness consists in surprising the good where it has not even occurred: wickedness is stillborn good. Wickedness is the infinite tenacity that tears apart the mere promise of the good, again without signification or consistency.

In this way, wickedness is freedom unleashing itself in the destruction of its own promise—just as Lucifer was promised to a sublime destiny. Yet because there can be no pure "promise" of freedom, and because freedom is entirely there, given in its surprise, *it is freedom that unleashes itself against itself.* Freedom knows this as a "good" and it is this good that freedom devastates as it exercises itself as freedom. Freedom destroys itself in every freedom as if with an initial self-hatred. *Freedom's self-hatred* is perhaps the only formula (this gives a strange sense of vertigo and an oppressive threat) that can render what finally barely manages to be said in terms of "evil" and "good" and what nevertheless constitutes the absolute evil of resolute wickedness. The wicked being's tenacity does not wait for the victory of a freedom: it waits only for its own unleashing [*dechaînement*], to which it was previously and freely bound.[10] If this binding [*enchaînement*] is the fact of freedom, this is because freedom, insofar as it essentially *frees* or unleashes itself, *is* through itself the being-wicked as much as the being-good, or even, rather, because being-wicked is the first discernible positivity of freedom.

The thought of identity infinitely identical with and dissociated from "evil" and "good" (from this point on occasionally noted with quotation marks, as in Hegel) in freedom was imposed on philosophy after Kant by way of Schelling, Hegel, Nietzsche, and Heidegger. Heidegger writes:

> The essence of evil does not consist in the mere baseness of human action but rather in the malice of fury.

And:

> To healing Being first grants ascent into grace; to fury its compulsion to ruin.[11]

If fury is predisposed in being as the equal of grace, this equality is immediately shattered in the very principle (the principle shatters the principle of equality), because fury *ruins*: it ruins "healing," but healing does not repair ruin, it "does" nothing: its only possibility seems to be to "rise up" in the middle of ruins. Therefore we can say nothing about it unless we already know what fury is.

This fury can doubtless be understood in greater precision (Heidegger gives none; but perhaps the mere date of this text, 1946, need be contemplated) with the help of the one from which it derives: the "fury" that the Hegel of *The System of Ethical Life*[12] made the "first level" of evil or of the negative as "crime." This is the fury of barbaric "devastation" or of the "purposeless destruction" that answers to the "absolute urge" "at the extreme of absolute abstraction," of "the absolute concept in its complete indeterminacy, the restlessness of the absolute concept's infinity." And this annihilating restlessness of abstract infinity is also "pure freedom" which aims at nothing other than its own unmediated passage into objectivity, or into "the real being of absolute subjectivity," which in "pure objectivity" can only produce itself as annihilation of the determinate and as "formlessness." Thus fury annihilates itself, but it only annihilates *itself* by annihilating with it the freedom that it is.

In passing from Hegel to Heidegger and to the experience of our world, which presents itself to itself as universal barbarism, we should say the following: fury annihilates itself, but it does not thereby suppress itself as fury: it institutes total devastation. This is not the self-suppression of abstract subjectivity, but *it is a free devastation that leaves freedom devastated*: this constitutes a relation to the "self" only to the extent that the "self" of freedom is the absolute detachment from self. Fury, however, does not suppress this detachment: it is its unleashing and its tenacity. Fury, in Heidegger's terms, has its possibility in Being because Being "conceals" in it "the essential source of nihilation." Yet it conceals this origin in freedom, which is the freedom of its withdrawal. In the freedom of the withdrawal, freedom can be essentially withdrawn, that is to say devastated by the fury of the nihilation that it *is*. The fury of wickedness does not seek to preserve or mediate its freedom. It simply and directly executes—this is why it is furious—the infinite possibility of detachment that freedom *is*: the abyss of being in which singularity is equal to the withdrawal of all presence, in such a way that the ruining of all singularity of presence and all presence (coming-up) of singularity is the very liberation of freedom.

Wickedness does not hate this or that singularity: it hates singularity as such and the singular relation of singularities. It hates freedom, equality, and fraternity; it hates sharing. This hatred is freedom's own (it is therefore also the hatred that belongs to equality and fraternity; sharing hates itself and is devoted to ruin). It is not a hatred *of itself*, as if freedom were already there and could end up detesting itself, and yet it remains hatred of the singular "self" that is the existence of freedom, and the freedom of existence. *Evil is the hatred of existence as such.* It is a possibility of the existent only in the sense that in evil the existent withdraws existence into the abyss of being—pure immanence or pure transcendence[13]—instead of letting being withdraw into the existentiality of existence. *In this sense, however, evil is in the existent as its innermost possibility of refusing existence.*

Here are the unjustifiable and the intolerable: in freedom's point of annulment where its own unleashing devastates it, where its own incandescence devours it. The fascination of modern thought and art with evil originates here: it is a fascination with the furious exasperation of the *propre*[14] itself, which is never more properly what it is than in the ruin of existence, since existence, which is still its appropriation (*Ereignis*), comes-up in it, whereas ruin comes back to it, as the profit and pleasure of being appropriated up to the point of appropriation itself. Evil: reappropriated coming-up, existence taken up again in essence, identified singularity, the relation taken as a mass—and the mass in a mass grave. No one doubts that a justification need not be attempted, no one doubts (this is the greatest danger) that evil need not be imputed to the few in order to spare the others: evil belongs to the essence or structure of freedom such as it has been freed and surprised in our history, as our history. This justifies nothing, since it is on the contrary what exposes us to the unleashing of wickedness. But this does justify that a thought of freedom must keep its eyes fixed on the hatred that delivers itself at the heart of freedom.

In these conditions, what remains of a freedom for the good? Can we even pose the question? Does not the end of philosophical morality signify, in some thinking of *ethos*, for which we would like to find a determination more original than the ethical,[15] that the good can no longer be viewed, except, we are tempted to say, as the abstract negation of the evil always already unleashed, or—which evidently appears closer to the Heideggerian inspiration—as a sovereign indifference, "concealed" in Being, to the double possibility of its freedom? But this indifference, as we have just seen, cannot prevent the (in some ways essential) opening of the abyss of fury, which is at least determined by its infiniteness, whereas a nonindifferent determination of the "good" is infinitely set aside.

Heidegger's commentary on Schelling confirms this. If man is the being in whom the "ground" (the divine essence as the ground-without-ground of absolute indifference) is separated from the existence (of God as his proper possibility of existence revealed in humanity), and if it is man who, acceding in his autonomy to understanding and language, lays claim to existence itself as the ground, which means to the "tendency to return to oneself" or to "ego-centrism," then evil occurs when "the ground elevates itself to existence and puts itself in the place of existence" and when man wants to be "as separated selfhood the ground of the whole."[16] But the separation of "ground" and "existence" that is the proper possibility of humanity is also, thanks to it, the most proper possibility of divine existence itself (in terms we have used: the hatred of existence is also the most proper possibility of freedom). Thus the possibility of divine revelation as human existence, and thereby the possibility of the unity of beings—and thus the possibility of the good—here have their primary resource in the freeing of freedom as the freeing of evil.

> For evil *is* truly in man's essence as the most extreme opposition and revolt of the spirit against the Absolute (tearing oneself away from the universal will, being against it, the will replacing it in this "against"). Evil "*is*" as *freedom*, the most extreme freedom *against* the Absolute within the whole of beings. For freedom "is" the capacity for good and evil. The good "is" the evil and the evil "is" the good.
>
> But why is evil spoken of at all? Because it produces the innermost and broadest discord in beings. But why discord? Evil is thought because in this most extreme and real discord as dis-jointure (*Un-fug*) the *unity* of the jointure of beings as a whole must appear most decidedly at the same time.

Heidegger finally decided that Schelling failed in his thinking of the articulation or jointure of being, that is, the adjoining of "ground," of "existence," and of "their unity." Schelling's failure, he explains, is due to the traditionally metaphysical positing of this unity as absolute (which Heidegger wants to understand as the absolute return to self, rather than as the absolute detachment that we mobilized earlier). It must be understood, and this is doubtless the whole intention of the commentary, that only the thinking of being as the withdrawal of being in *Dasein* and as *Dasein*—the thought of *existence* (just missed, dare we say, by Schelling, which explains why this commentary is so *interested*, in the best sense of the word)—escapes the preliminary and insurmountable designation of the unity itself or of the absolute as a *being*. But the beingness [*étantité*] of the absolute, because it offers the absolute to the grasp of the "tendency to return to itself" or because it opens "ego-centrism" to the absolute, is what unleashes evil as the truth of freedom. Since good is considered to be the return to self of the unity of the being (a return to self that would no longer be that of a separated ipseity, but one of nonseparation), evil is in fact already, in principle, dialecticized as a negative moment or power of good (but this last consequence no longer belongs, for its part, in any way to what we could legitimately understand in Heidegger's laconic conclusions; and this is certainly not by chance, as we will see from what follows).

~

The deviations, drift, or tangent that Heidegger seeks to take in relation to Schelling would therefore be this: a nonbeing [*non-étant*] adjoining of being (its withdrawal). But up to what point would this withdrawal affect the structure of freedom "for good *and* for evil"? This is what is not mentioned. In fact, here Heidegger is not far from abandoning freedom, from devoting himself to being (and the "self-deception of resignation toward the inevitable" that he would denounce a few years later, again in relation to Schelling, implies a critique of indifference to good and evil). Yet in this movement, is not the sovereign (and quasi-dialectical) indifference of Schellingian good and evil preserved? Does this more or less imperceptible preservation respect the most profound exigencies of the thinking of being itself, or of the thinking of existence, as Heidegger seems to have recognized in the analysis of "freedom" pursued thus far?

In other words: is it possible to say that the thinking of being, at least as Heidegger was able to announce it, has escaped the profound logic and tonality of the idealism of freedom, according to which freedom "for good and for evil" is first established and can only be established through evil, and must therefore, whether it wants to or not, in one way or another justify evil, which means dialecticize it, as is the case when "discord" is at best what makes "unity appear"? At what point does the identity of good and evil cease once "fury" and "the criminal" have equally been disposed of in the "nihilation" of being? At what point does this identity, specifically presented as not being "one," cease dialecticizing itself and producing a superior identity, the result of which seems to be nothing other than a deaf return to a theodicy or logodicy, this time in the form of an ontodicy? And yet, why does being need a justification if it is not and does not cause—unless we must ask ourselves whether it isn't the unjustifiable that, in spite of everything, we want to justify? (This clearly means: to what extent, in spite of everything and everyone, did Heidegger silently justify Auschwitz? Yet this also means, above all for us: *to what extent is this silent justification not a weakness of the very thinking of being*, understood, as we are trying to do here, as the thinking of "freedom" or of the generosity of being?)[17]

(We could pose a similar question to Bataille, considering that "the unleashing of passions is the good, which has always been able to animate human beings"[18] and that this unleashing occurs, by definition, by way of the violation of the prohibition, which defines evil— here again there is a sort of fury. A "life without prohibitions" is impossible, and we cannot, once God is dead, "*humanly* lift prohibitions without venerating them in fear." Thus, "we rob freedom of its salt, if we do not acknowledge its price. Freedom demands a fear, a vertigo of freedom."[19] To what extent doesn't unleashing here dialecticize itself? To what extent isn't there here an "atheological" theodicy of sacred evil which is unleashed passion? To what extent didn't Bataille want, following a certain theological tradition of the economy of redemption, to justify sin [*etiam peccata . . .*], whereas sin, according to another less "economic" and more "spiritual" tradition, is never justifiable, though it can be pardoned? Finally, to what extent—in order to relate Bataille and Heidegger in a more obvious way—do we not yield to a fascination for the "vertigo" or "abyss" of freedom, which leads in turn to a fascination with the evil that engulfs and repulses [and at bottom, to a way of being tempted or of attempting to bear the unbearable, which does not mean tolerating or defending it, but which despite everything implies entering into a strange and somber relation with its positivity], while the *releasing* of being-free, and indeed its *syncope*, are so *groundless* that the horror and attraction of the abyss form only one of their possible figures—no doubt the one *figuring* them precisely with the most presence and thickness, conferring on them a profound and shadowy substance. Yet the positive presence of evil rightly announces that it comes from an abyss of the will to presence, from the "restlessness of the absolute concept's infinity." What is *groundless* is also to the same extent, perhaps more "profoundly," what comes-up from nothing, on nothing, what, instead of climbing out of the abyss, freely rises up, suspended in free air, the simple pulsating of a released existence. Let this be clearly understood: it is not a question of playing the idyll against the drama; the existence released from existence is delivered to every weightiness, on the edge of every abyss; evil has not only been confirmed as a positivity, it is perhaps confirmed as *the* positivity of freedom; yet it is a question of knowing whether freedom is constructed and reconstructed there, dialectically, subjectively, economically, or if it is torn apart there—purely and simply.)

In other words, we could ask, as we face the empirico-transcendental unleashing of freedom *and* fury, of a furious freedom: has the thinking of being avoided moving backward, if imperceptibly, toward an ontodicy in which is preserved the possibility of a "safeguard" or "shelter" of being (an *ethos* as an abode) in the midst of fury itself, and in proximity to "peril" and "safety"? Is this how we should think a thought that "lets Being be" and which is necessarily the thinking of being's being-free—as free in "fury" as it is in "grace"? Does being's being-free threaten to fall into the indifference of the absolute (which is nothing other than the freedom of its subjectivity, the basis from which it can and must appear to itself as the act of its own potential, as potential for good *and* evil),[20] or can and must the absolute of freedom engage it in a nonindifference?

Undoubtedly, the answer seems to be interwoven in the question and especially in the entire enunciation of the thinking of being: letting being be is to let it withdraw from what Hegel called "concentration in itself," which he designated as the first form of evil

in the *Phenomenology* (in sum, the phenomenology of the spirit of
fury: the absolute return to self of the consciousness that has not
gone out of itself). In a basically similar way, it is to let withdraw the
ego-centrism of Schelling's "ground." The entire tradition has understood evil as ego-ism, and egoism as the fury that in itself determines the undetermined absolute, finitizing the infinite and in-
finitizing the finite. (Likewise, in Bataille, the freedom of passion is
in no way egoistical: it is the very place of communication and it is
communication. For Bataille, egoistical freedom annuls itself. But at
the same time, in its transgressive unleashing, passion does nothing
but unleash *itself*). And yet, if the question of a secret, imperceptible
ontodicy is not entirely illegitimate, it is perhaps also not illegitimate
to suspect, despite everything, a secret egoity of being:

> What properly is, that is, what properly dwells in and deploys its
> essence in the Is, is uniquely Being. Being alone "is"; only in Being and
> as Being does what is called the "is" appear; what is, is Being on the ba-
> sis of its essence.[21]

The deployment of Being can certainly never be thought except
from the point of its withdrawal and its no-thingness. But cannot the
being-its-self [*être-propre*][22] of being preserving its property always
once again *withdraw from the withdrawal* of being, and reappropriate the *Ereignis* where it appropriates itself by "vanishing"? One
could find the question scandalous in view of the whole logic of this
thought, in which being *is only* the *singular* existence of *Dasein*. If we
must, despite everything, pose this question, this is first of all by reason of, if not the logic of this thought, then at least its *tonality*
(which also means its tension and intensity, if not its intentions).[23]
With the liberation of the thinking *of being as being* as sole exigency, as a kind of paradoxical but inevitable harmonic (at least
up to a certain point), this tonality makes possible a certain abandonment of the *being of beings*, given over to the fate of the deployment of the essence of being, and with it, in an indifferent
way, to a fury *properly* consubstantial with this essence. This tonality does not arise from a simple *critique*: rather, one should hear resonate, like an echo, the tension in the *concerned* response to the

material/transcendental irruption of devastating evil in this epoch of being. Nor is it a question of "relaxing" this tension: the unbearable and the unjustifiable have not ceased. But if we must ask ourselves to what extent this unjustifiable would risk being justified, this is because the thinking of being offers the demand and resource for this question, as we should have understood from the beginning. Another tonality is at stake, and we must try to understand it. There is yet another reason to pose the question, which the mere *logic* of the thinking of being (it is a logic, how could it be anything else?) will never be able to answer: the affirmation of *Dasein* as the existence of being will always be answered by the affirmation of being's being-free as the "concealment," no doubt dissymmetrical, but always dialecticizable, of good and evil. This is truly why Heidegger's abandonment of the theme of freedom will have been logical: as a power of subjectivity, freedom will in effect only have been the illusion in charge of covering over the profound acceptance of the course of things. And freedom's own factuality will always be dissolved into that of necessity. Freeing oneself from this freedom will have remained a wish suspended at the limit of this logic which itself traced the limit of philosophy.

⁓

Short of taking a step further—short of taking a step further, if we can say this, *into* the irreducible and singular factuality of freedom, and short of taking a step further into the very logic of the thinking of freedom, it is one step further to say *that the answer, here, is in the decision.*

Freedom is freedom for good *and* evil. Its decision, if it is in the decision that freedom occurs or happens to itself, is therefore the decision for good *and* evil. Yet, insofar as it decides, freedom is this decision, the decision for good *or* evil. Denying that freedom presents itself as an arbiter placed before values or norms transcendent to its own finite transcendence does not amount to denying that freedom, in deciding, decides for good *or* evil. Only freedom in action (there is no other), at the limit of thought—where thought is in turn finally the act that it is, and consequently, where it is also decision—decides as it liberates (itself) from good *or* evil. This means that it is necessarily, in its act, or even in the very *fact* in which it *freely surprises itself,* not the united and indifferent unleashing of good and evil, but in and through itself good *or* bad decision. Only unleashing unleashes itself, but this does not mean that it unleashes indifferently, for it would finally only unleash unleashing itself, "concentrated in itself," and consequently always wickedness. Undoubtedly, this does not mean that it unleashes a little of one and a little of the other, or the one as much as the other, without itself being implicated in this difference or opposition. In unleashing *itself*—and thereby releasing itself and knowing itself as the possibility of evil—it also releases itself and knows itself as fury *or* as liberation. We would at least like to try to show this much.

"Decision" does not have merely the irreducibly formal status given by its enunciation at the limit of its event (or *Ereignis?* Would *Ereignis* be decision?): we name the decision, but in so doing we do not enter it; we describe from without a gesture which can then be interpreted either as the simple passage into action of a considerable potential freedom for good *and* evil, or as the decision between a "good" and "evil" previously furnished by the most classical morality, or on the contrary as the arbitrariness, also most classical, of a free subjectivity deciding on *its* "good." Decision does not have merely this formal status because, as it is thought in all the rigor of the thinking of existence, the "concept" of decision itself refers *to a decision effectively taken in this thought.* The thinking of existence cannot think free decision without having *actually* decided *for its own existence,* and not for its ruin—not because of a choice and a moral preference anterior to the development of thought, but *in* the act of thinking posited at the existing limit of thought. (What then comes to light is not a novelty: there has been no philosophical thought worthy of its name that has not proceeded from this thinking decision of thought. But henceforth it has to think thought as such.)

In *Being and Time,* the analysis of *Gewissen* ends up at the thought of decision *and at a decision of thought* which still remains to be brought to light in this very thought.[24] *Gewissen* means "conscience" in the moral sense that French sometimes accords to the word *conscience* ["consciousness" or "conscience"—Trans.] but that is not "morality" in the sense of still having to do with any distinction of "good" and "evil." In *Gewissen* is attested *Dasein*'s "ownmost potentiality-for-Being" insofar as, because it is unfounded foundation, which means "existing as thrown," "it is *never* in possession of its ownmost being." In this "nullity," *Dasein* is discovered as essentially "*indebted*" (*schuldig*, which also means "guilty"). The existent, as existent, is indebted to and guilty for the being-itself which it is not and which it does not have: it is indebted to the withdrawal of being, we could say in reassembling the vocabularies of various periods in Heidegger, and this debt *must not be canceled in the mode of a restitution of being-one's-self, but precisely in the mode of existence and of the decision for existence.*[25]

Debt is revealed to the existent by the call that is addressed to it by the voice of its own/alien "foreignness," which characterizes its being as being-abandoned-to-the-world.[26] With originary debt or guilt (whose connection with Benjamin's tragedy could be pursued) "being-wicked" is also revealed. "Wickedness" here corresponds to being-indebted. For if, on the one hand, it cannot be a question, at this ontological level, of moral values, which have here only their "existential condition of possibility," and if, accordingly, the Kantian image of conscience as a "tribunal" cannot be taken up again, on the other hand "every experience of conscience begins by experiencing something as a 'debt,' " and this is what, in the "ordinary" experience of conscience, the primacy of "a bad conscience" responds to. In other words, what is ordinarily considered as "bad" is this being-guilty of not properly being one's being, or of not properly being being, but (which is not specified but which must become explicit in order to come to the decisive point of this entire thought) *of not being being in the mode of its being, which is the mode of existing.* Ordinary comprehension here has nothing of the "ordinary" [*vulgaire*] about it: it grasps evil as that which does not decide for the being-existing of existence. What is inexact about ordinary comprehension is the attribution of "bad conscience" to a "reprimand" that consciousness would address to itself for a wrong already committed. The existential interpretation grasps that "the attestation of being-wicked" is "more ancient" than every act committed and submitted to judgment (whose possibility, on the contrary, it founds). (However, it is equally possible to claim that *Dasein* has always already committed the wrongful act of not existing according to existence's ownmost possibility—always already, it has not properly and absolutely rendered itself to its world, and it has not freed itself—it has always already skirted the generosity of being—and not even vulgar consciousness would be so vulgar in this respect.)

The ontological undecidability of moral good and evil thus rests in fact on what should be called an ontological archi-decision of the existent, attested as wrong by the call sent to it by its own existentiality. If it is not wrong in the sense of a choice made between good and evil, it is wrong (and how would it not then have *already*, infinitely *already*, decided on a good and an evil? . . .) in that it is in debt and has to decide. The decision, *Entscheidung*, here is not the choice produced at the end of a deliberation[27] (the existent does not deliberate whether it exists or will exist; meanwhile, in another sense, we could say that its existence is in itself essentially *deliberated*, in the two valences of the word), but if it *cuts* [*trancher*], it does so between an undecided state and a state of decision. It decides for decision and for decidability. This could also come to mean that if the existent is not "wrong" in any determinable sense of guilt, it is, meanwhile, wrong (as Hegel knew) *in that it is not innocent* (literally, not to be in-nocent is to cause harm). It is not innocent, since, as an existent thrown-into-the-world, it is in the very element of its freedom, it is its *fact*, and freedom is the freedom to decide on good and evil. The non-innocence of freedom constitutes the existential condition of possibility of the decision, which makes the existent exist as "resolute." So:

> Resoluteness, by its ontological essence, is always the resoluteness of some factual Dasein at a particular time. The essence of Dasein as an entity is its existence. Resoluteness "exists" only as a decision [*Entschluss*] which understandingly projects itself. But on what basis does Dasein disclose itself in resoluteness? On what is it to decide? *Only* the decision itself can give the answer.[28]

That the answer is given only by the decision means that there is no sense in deciding, by way of the analysis of the ontological structure of existence, on what the singular existent *must* decide. This would be to remove it from its very decision, to fold up its freedom and suppress the possibility that it recognize itself as indebted to decision by the very fact of its existence—by this fact (of being its own essence) *that the decision presents above all*—and this would therefore be to have fundamentally missed the originary phenomenon of existence.

In proceeding as thinking does here, which means in letting be the being-free of existing being—*for* the factual and singular *decision*—hasn't thinking decided, in itself and for itself? *From the comprehension of the non-innocence of freedom, hasn't it decided for decision and for its singular factuality?* This also means: from the comprehension of the existent's being-itself as *decided existence*, hasn't thinking decided for the decision that decides in favor of existence, and not for the decision that decides *to stay indebted to existence and consequently to appropriate itself as the essence outside of existence?* Hasn't thinking decided, at the most intimate point of its decision for decision, in favor of the "grace" of existence, and not of the fury of essence? (And moreover, since it is henceforth time to ask the following: can we speak of "grace" and "fury," of "healing" and of "ruin," without having allowed a decision to be made by language, whereas what is at stake is allowing every decision as such, in its freedom, to decide for one or the other side of what is equally "concealed" in being? For if the existent can decide on ruin and on its own ruin, and if this possibility is inscribed in the very being of existence, such a decision is no less what also ruins the decision in its existential essence.)

This is not written as such in Heidegger's text. Here, the stakes are those of a decision of reading, less in the sense of a question of interpreting the discourse of a thinker more or less correctly and faithfully, than in the sense of a question of being addressed by a freedom to freely share his thought. The act of reading is here no doubt in retreat as much from scrupulous review as from interpretive violence. It reads by sharing the freedom through which thought as thought is always *offered*: held out, proposed, to be taken and decided, at the surface of the text. (Now it is in the same context that Heidegger writes: "It is the authentic Being-one's-Self of resoluteness that makes leap forth for the first time authentic Being-with-Others"; there is no sharing except of freedom, but there is also no freedom except in sharing; the freedom of deciding to be-one's-self outside of sharing is the freedom, lodged at the heart of freedom, to ruin freedom. We can only come back to this decidability.)

Thinking here decides for decision, or it decides, if we like, for the in-decision in which alone decision can occur as such. Decision is singular, it is "at every moment that of a factual *Dasein.*" It is not a decision *of* singularity (since singularity is not a preexisting subject, but is singular "in" the very subject and decides in deciding *itself*), but it is a decision *for* singularity, which means for freedom itself, if freedom is in the relation of singularities and of decisions. Singularity, as decided and deciding itself, is no longer in the non-innocence of the freedom to decide. Yet neither has it become innocent and "good." It has entered into the decided decidability, so to speak, of existence at each *moment* of its existence. Now decision, as singularly existing and as engaging relation and sharing, engages the withdrawal of being. If decision keeps itself as decision, it also keeps being in its withdrawal, as withdrawn. It "saves" it, as Heidegger says elsewhere, in the sense that "this means releasing, delivering, liberating, sparing, sheltering, taking into one's protection, guarding."[29] What is thus saved is the finitude of being. It is "the essential limitation, the finitude [that] is perhaps the condition of authentic existence."[30] Finitude is what, in singularity and as singularity, withdraws from the infinite grasp, from the molar expansion and furious devastation, of an ego-ity of being. Being withdraws into finitude; it withdraws *from* "concentration in itself": it is its very being, yet insofar as the very being of being is being-free, being cannot be this withdrawal *except by decision.* Only decided existence withdraws being from the essential "self" and properly holds back its possibility for devastating fury. Only existence, as the existence and singular factuality of freedom, offers, if not exactly an ethics, in any case this "shelter" of being *which is its ownmost ethos as the ethos or abode of the human being who dwells in the possibility of his free decision.*

There is therefore an authentic decision—though it has its authenticity in the very decision and without the prior distinction of an inauthentic or authentic content of decision. Or there is an authenticity of decision, that is to say, an authenticity of freedom. There is an authentic freedom, which decides freedom *for* existence and for the singular relation that it is, and which decides it from the heart of an infinite non-innocence where the in-finity of being (which does not have its own essence) can always unleash itself, and in a sense has always already been unleashed, as fury. There is a free decision that frees freedom for itself, for its finitude, for its sharing, for equality, for community, for fraternity, and for their justice—singularly, singularly shared/divided, singularly withdrawn from the hatred of existence.

§13 Decision, Desert,
Offering

Would authentic decision then be the good? There is no positivity of the "good" and the *epekeina tēs ousiās* of Plato's Good must again be understood here. Decision cannot appear to itself as "good" insofar as it will have truly decided. It cannot, quite simply, appear to itself,[1] and it is doubtless less free the more it wants to appear as such. Nothing therefore can assure it, and even less forewarn it, without suspending its essence of decision. It is delivered to its freedom as to that which comes-up to it and surprises it. Every decision surprises itself. Every decision is made, by definition, in the undecidable. In this way, essentially (and it is in this sense that I have said "authentic" here, a word taken from Heidegger, in spite of or in defiance of its moralizing connotation), decision cannot decide without letting being be in its finite singularity. *I* cannot decide without infinitely abandoning myself to the finitude of my singularity and thus I cannot, in the strike and cut of *my* decision, renounce appearing to myself as the "deciding" subject. This is also why my decision is identically, each time, a decision for relation and sharing—to the point that the *subject* of *my* decision can appear to itself as not being simply "me" (but also a "you" or an "us") without it being any less singularly my own, if it is authentic. Yet it must be repeated that the decision does not appear to *itself*: in this way it *decides* and is decided.

Nothing finishes with the decision, but everything begins. It is indeed only here that wickedness can begin to be wicked and it is here that non-innocence can become fury. For fury needs singularity: wickedness *wants to enjoy* [*jouir*] the spectacle of its ruin and thus fury must maintain its presence. Wickedness too lets existence be, in its own way, in order to ruin it. Otherwise what would it address?[2] Isn't decision also the choice of a line of life, vice or virtue, that it would fix upon the existent? Yet decision is the access to letting-be. Letting-be, which is always the contrary of a "laissez-faire" or "letting-happen," will ceaselessly have to decide, at every moment, its "ethical" relation to the existence it lets-be. It will be in the duty, or in the shirking of the duty, in virtue or in its exhaustion, in malignity or goodness, in the calculated appreciation of circumstances, or in the stoic *eukairia* that welcomes the right moment. Yet it cannot avoid acceding to the relation with existence, which means to the relation in existence with the being-singular that alone *exists* and that exists in the withdrawal of being. It can unleash the nothingness of this withdrawal in essential devastation, or expose itself as if to its very existence. But it cannot avoid—and this is wherein freedom is a fact—acceding to the singular dissemination of being, and dividing it. Nor, consequently, can it avoid *exposing* itself as the being-singular of its own decision, exposed to this coming-up of being in its withdrawal, which only places us into presence as the ones of the others: this is properly, in constitutive and irreducible alterity, to place freedom into the "presence" of itself.[3]

This does not arm us with a morality. This does not dictate to us what it will mean, and when and how, "to respect others," "to respect oneself," "to treat humanity as an end," or to want equality, fraternity, and justice for the human community. This does not even dictate when and how to respect, and not give, death (my own or that of others) as this singular possibility that "belongs" only to singularity.[4] This gains us neither determined duties nor rights. Undoubtedly, their determination can itself be nothing other than the product of infinitely renewed decisions that are rediscussed and renegotiated in the general space of the decision. But this frees us for duty and right, and for the perversion of the one and the other.

What makes us free, then, is the freedom that exposes us and that is only what it is in this exposure. Neither will nor destiny, but the gift of what Heidegger calls "disclosedness:"

> In the term "Situation" ("situation"—"to be in a situation") there is an overtone of a signification that is spatial. We shall not try to eliminate this from the existential conception. . . . But spatiality of the kind which belongs to *Dasein*, and on the basis of which existence always determines its "location," is grounded in the state of Being-in-the-world, for which disclosedness is primarily constitutive. Just as the spatiality of the "there" is grounded in disclosedness, the Situation has its foundations in resoluteness.[5]

Disclosedness [*ouverture*] and resoluteness are correlative, which means that decision as such is essentially "disclosive" or "spatializing" (a spatiality that does not return to time, but which is "at the same time" the spacing of the space and time of existence). Now, the disclosedness that characterizes the decision in its authenticity is the disclosedness to (or of) the "free." Once he had separated freedom as theme from the metaphysics of subjectivity, Heidegger will not have ceased to give more and more scope, if we can say this, to the motif of "the open" as a motif of "free space,"[6] itself considered either as a "prospatiality" of "the free space of time" (we could say: it is *here* that surprise is involved), or as a "spacing" that "carries the free, the disclosed, the spacious."

"Spacing is the setting free of places"

—and places that have been set free undoubtedly answer to what Bonnefoy calls "the true place":

> The true place is a fragment of duration consumed by the eternal, at the true place time is undone within us. . . . Perhaps it is infinitely close; it is also infinitely distant. Such are the ironic presence and being in our instant. The true place is given by chance, but at the true place chance will lose its enigmatic character. . . . There is beauty in this kind of place, but a beauty so extreme that I would no longer belong to myself, in being governed and assumed by its perfect command. In this place I would also be profoundly free, for nothing in it would be foreign to me.[7]

This spatiality, or spaciosity, is the space of freedom, inasmuch as freedom is, at every moment, the freedom of a free space. Which means that it constitutes the spatializing or spacing essence of freedom. Spacing is the general "form"—which precisely has no form, but gives *room* for forms and formations, and which is not general, but which gives *room* for singularities—of existence: the spacing, exposure, or retrenchment and cutting (decision) of singularity, the *areality* (which is, as we have indicated elsewhere, the character of *air*) of singularity in its difference which relates it to its limit, to others, and to itself: for example, a mouth opened in a cry.

This spatiality is not so much a given free space—different in this from Hannah Arendt's public space, which takes the form of an institution or of a preliminary foundation, unless it should be understood as the very foundation of this shared areality—as it is the gift of a spatio-temporality (if we may speak thus), which is engendered (gift of the first schema—schema of the gift itself = offering?) and which is followed by the very liberation of space—and as the exact reverse of its devastation. Its description could be borrowed from the description of nomadic space in another thinking, distanced from the thinking of being and whose distance itself here signifies the free space of thinking:

> The nomads are there, on the land, wherever there forms a smooth space that gnaws, and tends to grow, in all directions. The nomads inhabit these places; they remain in them, and they themselves make them grow, for it has been established that the nomads make the desert no less than they are made by it. They are vectors of deterritorialization. They add desert to desert, steppe to steppe, by a series of local operations whose orientation and direction endlessly vary. . . . there is no line separating earth and sky; there is no intermediate distance, no perspective or contour; visibility is limited; and yet there is an extraordinarily fine topology that relies not on points or objects but rather on haecceities, on sets of relations (winds, undulations of snow or sand or the creaking of ice, the tactile qualities of both).[8]

As this desert which is not an increase of devastation, but the growth of its own spacing as the nomad's dwelling place, freedom does not receive a space that would be given to it, but it gives itself space and gives space to itself as the incalculable spacing of singularities. In other words, freedom itself is not the essence of the free, but the "free" is the existing opening by which freedom takes place. It is not *pure* spacing, it is also "habitation"—habitation in the open—if the nomad does not represent errancy without at the same time representing a dwelling, and thus an *ethos.*

This is not exactly what one would understand as an "ethics of freedom." It is the *ethos* itself as the opening of space, the spacious shelter of being in existence, deciding to remain what it is in the distancing from self, in this distancing that delivers it to its retreat, to its existence, generously. It is a generosity of *ethos* more than an ethic of generosity. "Freedom" itself, in the spaciosity of being where freedom is opened rather than engulfed, proves to be generosity even *before* being freedom. It gives rise, in the exposure of being, to its own singularity always newly decidable, always newly surprised by its decision. This generosity does not dominate fury, which is born with it. Yet it gives, without counting—without counting anything but fury—it is the infinite gift of finite freedom, while fury is the finite appropriation of infinite freedom.

It gives freedom, or *offers* it. For the gift is never purely and simply given. It does not vanish in the receipt of the gift—or of the "present." The gift is precisely that whose "present" and presentation are not lost in a realized presence. The gift is what comes-up to the presence of its "present." It also keeps itself, in this coming-up and surprise of the gift, as gift, as the giving of the gift. In this it is an offering, or withdrawal, of the gift in the gift itself: the withdrawal of its being-present and the keeping of its surprise. It is not a question here of the economy of the gift, where the gift comes back to itself as the benefit and mastery of the giver. On the contrary, it is a question of what makes the gift as such: an offering that may not be returned to anyone, since it remains in itself the free offering that it is (this is why, for example, one never gives what one has received to a third party, lest one annul the gift as gift). One must keep the singular present in which the gift as such is kept, that is, offered: it is presented, made freely available, but is freely held back at the edge of the receiver's free acceptance. The offering is the inestimable price of the gift. The generosity of being offers nothing other than existence, and the offering, as such, is kept in freedom. All of this means: a space is offered whose spacing, each time, only happens by way of a decision. But there is not "a" decision. There is, each time, my own (*a* singular mine)—yours, theirs, ours.[9] This is the generosity of being.

There is, then, that which should become more and more urgent for our thinking, as its theme *and* as its decision: this generosity of being, its *liberality*, which dispenses *that there be something* and that we exist. This taking place of something offers itself in the opening that frees places and the free space of time. The opening does not open unless we let it open, and we only let it open if we let ourselves be exposed in existence. We are exposed to our freedom. There is therefore finally the generosity of being dispensed in the plural singularity of "us": the freedom of the decision, which is always "mine" in the sense that all property of my essence vanishes and that the entire community of existence is involved. Yet this gift is kept in the offering. It is kept there as what is unfounded in freedom, as the inessence of existence, as the desertlike and nomadic character of its dwelling, as the risk of its experience or the pirating of its foundations—and consequently also as the threat of a free hatred of freedom.

If there is a hope of thinking, without which we would not even think, it does not consist in the hope of a total liberation of freedom that was to occur as the total mastery of freedom. The history of a similar wait is over. Today the threat of a devastation of existence alone has any positivity. Yet the hope of thinking signifies that we would not even think if existence were not the surprise of being.

§14 Fragments

How might a discourse of freedom correspond to its object (supposing this made sense)? How might it "speak freely" (as one "speaks frankly" or as one "speaks up") in speaking of freedom and in order to speak of it, or to let it speak?

I give no particular credit to the form of the fragment, inasmuch as I employ it here (as occasionally elsewhere) and entitle this paragraph with this form, and with no theme or concept. As a form, the fragment is exposed to all the ambiguities of which its history since Romanticism, if not since the moralists' maxims, has made us perfectly aware. These are the ambiguities of a freedom represented simultaneously as disengagement, as a surpassing of all rules and of all literary genres, and as a concentration of self-constitution and self-sufficiency. Because they are essential to the brevity and discontinuity of the fragmentary form, these ambiguities cannot be removed. Nevertheless, as Blanchot indicates in one of his fragmentary texts, if the fragment is "something strict," this is "not because of its brevity (it can prolong itself to the point of agony) but because of a tightening and strangling to the point of rupture."[1] In principle the fragment can be, even should be, singular and continuous. It should be a single, continuous fragmentation—neither "just one" fragment nor detached fragments. I would even say: philosophical discourse today is fragmentation itself. Philosophy no longer stops being written at the limit of the rupture of its discourse—which means philosophy's "end," but likewise its "liberation." Why is it, then, that fact does not make itself the equal of right, and why decide to finish-unfinish here, in the form of the fragment, an essay aspiring to be philosophical?

Because of poverty, simply because of insufficiency. It is too clear to me, too harshly visible, that the sketch barely outlined in the preceding pages of a free thinking of freedom has at this point merely begun, that nothing has been said, and that this discourse comes too soon for something that undoubtedly precedes it from afar. It is too clear to me that every continuation of this discourse as it is (not mine, but ours, this discourse in which the word "freedom" can in no way approach the liberation of its own meaning, nor of the meaning of ownership in general, of what frees it and of what frees from it, etc.), every use of supplementary philosophical resources (which are not lacking), is from the start committed to the continual fragmentation that is in question here: the fragmentation of a thinking of freedom. Consequently, freedom cannot be signaled except as that which comes to thought only through the "agony" of this thought, with the "strangling" of this discourse.

To conclude—and to begin—it is freedom's own fragmentation that in fact escapes discourse. Philosophy rejoins neither its own "end" nor its own "liberation." It pettily crumbles, short of the "fragment" as well as of "discourse." In speaking of freedom, one has to accept being confronted by this insistent stripping away.

If I attempted to reach the end (as if there were one . . .) of this agony, to use discourse untiringly against this rock (thing, force, gaze) of freedom, until exhaustion, until syncope, until death, I would doubtless not be wrong, and yet I would be cheating. I would keep the surprise and experience of freedom for a beyond that I would pretend to attain in disappearing. But the experience is already taking place, as I have continually said, and all philosophy has said it without ever being able to say it (except by cheating . . .).

And I would be cheating no less with the community, which is the site of this experience but which cannot communicate this experience to itself as its common essence, because it is not an essence, but a sharing. Freedom shares and shares itself. Philosophical discourse

cannot think of representing it or of presenting it: in thinking freedom, philosophical discourse must think of itself as shared, as at the
same time "communicating" something (of the concept, and even
of the concept of the limit of the concept), and as *apart*: separated
in its praxis from other praxes where experience takes place, similar
and infinitely dissimilar.

Freedom places philosophy before its strangest, most disconcerting truth.

So then—fragments. They run the risk of appearing to bring
about an ambiguous reversion of "philosophical discourse" to a
"literary form" and of seeming to give in to another trick. But without this risk, despite everything, no matter what I did I would be be-
traying yet more certainly the experience of freedom. I would claim
to offer it as a concept (even if as a concept of the limit of the concept) or to draw it as a conclusion from an analysis, or to identify it
with the movements of a discourse, and even with its tightening, its
continual fragmentation. But the experience of freedom is already
taking place, and it is only a question of this, along with our for-
midable insufficiency to "know" it, "think" it, or "say" it. So then,
fragments, as vague, uncertain marks of this insufficiency.[2]

⌒

The risk of seeming to reappropriate through "literature" what
would be lost in "philosophy." At least since Nietzsche, and up until all of us today—all those who dare philosophize—there has been
no philosophical writing exempt from this risk, or from coming
to terms with it: Bergson as much as Heidegger, Deleuze as much as
Derrida. In certain respects, the history of contemporary philosophy
is the history of this risk, in all the diversity of its variations—
which means, in all the diverse ways in which freedom has come to
implicate itself as a writing of philosophy (style, genre, character, address, audience, company, proximity, translations, untranslatabilities,
words, metaphors, fictions, positions of enunciation, and so on
and on: all that renders the "philosophical genre" hardly recognizable and yet perfectly identifiable in the concept, analysis, demonstration, systematicity, self-grounding, and self-questioning that
were always its own).

⌒

Concerning the insufficiency I have mentioned, I would claim neither that it is necessary, nor that the constraint of freedom is to bend us securely to the necessity that freedom should be seized from us, nor that it has "appropriated" us in such a way that there is no longer any sense, "afterwards," in wanting to appropriate it to oneself. Undoubtedly, this is true. It is even truth itself. But "insufficiency," and its correlate in the "strangling" of discourse, *are precisely not yet at the level of what is in question here*. It is not a question of an impossible appropriation because it is "above our means" or because it happens in death and as death. It has to do with a question that an appropriation here cannot and must not pose in any terms. There is nothing to ask of this genre, or to look for, or to interrogate positively or negatively. And that it should be so is in no way a deprivation, but is freedom itself. —Still, I cannot avoid saying, this is freedom *proper*.

～

Yet another thing (or the same thing, differently) must be at stake in this chiaroscuro necessity of the fragment: something, clearly, that touches on the relation of philosophy and literature. It is not that the fragment would give a literary form to philosophical thought and its un-thought (one knows, from here on, how the thought of the form/ground couple must be deconstructed, and I might add that the entire question of freedom perhaps finds itself invested here, beginning with, for example, classical motifs of the "freedom" or "necessity" of the "form" in relation to the "ground"). Rather, what is at stake in the relation of philosophy and literature is what Derrida has named writing. (Perhaps we should say that he has *surnamed* it "*writing*," recapturing and rewriting words and concepts that the period brought forth on the basis of Nietzsche, Benjamin, Heidegger, Bataille, and Blanchot.) Writing is the movement of meaning in the suspension of signification, which withdraws meaning in giving it, in order to give it as its gift. (I would say: its offering.) (In a more recent vocabulary, accompanying Blanchot, Derrida chooses to say: the step, the past, the passage and pace of truth "which becomes irreversible in the truth of the *pas*,"[3] where this last truth should be understood as the last truth of meaning.) In writing, there is nothing philosophical or literary. Rather, writing traces an essential indecision of the two, between the two, and consequently, an indecision in each one. It may even become necessary to include the discourse of science here. This indecision reveals that the withdrawal/offering of meaning occurs *from* "philosophy" *to* "literature"—and to "science"—and reciprocally. It does not happen in the absolute and as a single gesture. Its absoluteness is precisely its transmission from system to system (each of these systems being itself plural), which renders the distinction between systems undecidable, but which at the same time demands this distinction. (It works in an analogous way in "art," between *the* arts.) It is undecidable, and yet *there is* "philosophy," "literature," "science." It is undecidable, and yet we know very well what this sharing is. This "knowledge" does not come from another discourse that would oversee the others; it is therefore caught in the sharing and exchange or change—but "we know very well." We know that we change systems in writing—occasionally within the same text, within the same sentence. Fragments represent this, no doubt poorly. Nothing says that we have to adhere to this fragmentation, or that there should not be "even more" literature, "even more" philosophy, or "even more" science. In any case (and this is what matters to me here), each time, with every change, when we are aware of changes without knowing exactly *what* changes, decision appears: each time, we decide on a writing, we decide on a writing of writing, and therefore we decide on writing and on the meaning in its offering and withdrawal. Sharing voices: never one single voice, the voice of meaning *is* the decision, each time, of a singular voice. Freedom.

But in writing there is still something else, namely, communication (actually it is not something else). Writing is for reading, issues from it, and is also for other writings—even and precisely if its gesture is the withdrawal of communication, writing "only for" itself. Writing is of the community or it is not writing. And reciprocally: the community is of writing (in every possible sense of such an expression). Which means, as this essay has already recalled, that the community does not found itself in a common essence, but that its being-in-common obeys the double logic of sharing, which is an extension of the logic of offering and withdrawal. We communicate—that is to say, above all we "are *in* common" or we "compear" [*com-paraître*] in the withdrawal of communicated sense and in the withdrawal of the sense of communication—*and* in the sharing of "genres" or systems of discourse. I cannot pretend to communicate a common sense (even though such a "pretension" must also be what decides to write). But if I decide to write, I am subject immediately to the sharing, and to the incommensurability of the *in-*common (compare above, Chapter 7).

If I say "so then, the fragment . . . ," I am allowing, or trying to allow, something of this sharing to play "in" "my own" discourse and in "addressing" "my" readers. Something, certainly very few things, but I cannot master the calculation of its effects (readings); I cannot refuse its game or risk, I cannot set aside its decision. It is a political and ethical minimum. Freedom is at stake here, without which the most open, communicative, and democratic writing, the writing that is most careful of common sense and also most rigorousiy philosophical, can cover up the worst lie and accompany the worst politics.   ∼

"We must not give ourselves illusions: freedom and reason, these two ethical as well as ethico-aesthetic concepts that the classical age of German cosmopolitanism bequeathed to us as distinctive signs of humanity, have not done very well since the middle of the nineteenth century. Gradually they became 'off-beat,' we no longer knew 'what to do with them,' and if we let them get corrupted, this is less a success of their enemies than of their friends. We must therefore not give ourselves illusions concerning the fact that we, or our successors, will certainly not return to these unchanged representations. Our task, and the sense of what will put our spirit to the test, will be much more—and this is the task of pain and hope, so rarely understood, that weighs on each generation—to effect the always necessary and longed-for transition to the new, with as few disasters as possible!" (Robert Musil, *On Stupidity*, 1937; must we specify that this lecture, as its title ought to show, unambiguously targeted Fascism?)   ∼

Freedom can experiment with itself up to the limits of its own experience—where nothing separates it any longer from "necessity."

～

I have been told: "You offer no semantics of the word 'freedom.'"
True. The senses of this word matter little to me (but its strategic position, much). It does not cease, in tradition as well as for us, to approach "necessity." And this is exactly the question: from such a
proximity of the two, something entirely other must inevitably free
itself: the truth of experience.

～

We can no longer even say: "Freedom, Diotima, if only we understood this sublime word! . . . " (Hölderlin, *Hyperion*).

～

Let us give without commentary the elements of an etymological
semantics: according to a first derivation, *libertas*, like *eleutheria*,
has a base *leudho/leudhi* signifying "public," attached to *leudh*:
the idea of growth, increase. Another etymology, less certain, makes
libertas come from *liber*, book: the *libellus*, little book or booklet of
free expression, would account for its moral meaning. As for the
Anglo-Saxon *free/frei*, its first signification is: beloved, cherished
(friend and *Freund* are from the same family), because in my house
there are those I love, and slaves. *Liberi*, children, first designates the
children of a free man. But in fact there are two categories: "*libero-
rum hominum alii ingenui sunt, alii libertini*" (Gaius, *Institutiones*,
I, 10). The *ingenus* is born from a free father (and means "distinguished, liberal, generous, sincere, refined"), the *libertinus* is born
from a father who was himself freed (enfranchised). (Of course,
these ingenuous or libertine children are not the rejects—*proles*—of
the proletariat.)

Necessarius, for its part, primarily designates a person with whom
one is close, but not consanguineous: hence a friend, someone from
whom one cannot separate.

～

What other semantic is there, which would not be the complete
program of the philosophy of freedom? Freedom to do, to act, or

freedom in view of . . . , freedom as an essence to be realized or as a given nature, responsible freedom and responsibility toward freedom, freedom as right or power, self-determination, free will, recognition of common law, individual or collective freedom, civil, economic, political, social, cultural freedoms, the assumption of necessity, anarchy, libertine or libertarian freedom, liberality, freedom of movements, freedom of spirit, the free end of a rope or chain— none of these should escape our attention, yet none of these exactly matches what is at stake here under the name of "freedom."

～

Such are the stakes of the limit that freedom *is*, or rather that it always surpasses: in touching the outside *of the inside*, one does not therefore pass the limit, for the exhaustion of this touching is unlimited. And this exhaustion is equally what effaces itself before, and in the coming to presence of, the thing itself—a coming to presence that no present will ever capture, that no presentation will ever secure or saturate. The coming to presence of the other of thought exhausts all thought of the other.

～

One could say that in freedom there is the ontological imperative, or being as intimation—but under the condition of adding that this is without commandment (no commandment/freedom dialectic) or that the commandment is lost in freedom's abandonment to itself, all the way to caprice and chance.

～

Under the name of freedom, it now seems to me that I have tried to discuss something that would have, in a sense, the structural position of Hegelian death (of metaphysical death, therefore—and is this not always the site and operation of deliverance?). Yet this would not be the negative and hence would not lend strength to a dialectic. (The negative is the negation of freedom, of which freedom itself is alone capable. It is the fury of evil. But evil likewise does not exist as a dialectical moment; it is an absolute possibility of freedom.) Something else then, in place of death: putting the existent into the world. Birth, which is doubtless birth to death—not, however, in the sense that birth would be "for" death (with this doubtful

value of "for," if it is used to translate Heidegger's "*zum Tode*"),
but in the altogether different sense in which death is that to which,
or in which, there is birth: once again, exposure to the limit. Not
"freedom or death!" (though I want to erase nothing of the power
or nobility of this cry in our history), but: freedom *in place of* death.

Thought, then, does not have the relation with freedom that
Hegelian spirit has with death. It does not have to "dwell in it fear-
lessly." In the first place, thought is not a dwelling, not a tomb or an
abode, but a nomad space (and yet it is also a place to *stay*, perhaps
even a house . . .). Next, thought cannot be exempt from fright
in the face of the freedom which precedes it, which always surprises it, and toward which it can never turn back (thought is therefore
not a fear "in the face of," as there is no Hegelian "face-to-face"
with the abyss). It cannot but be anxious about freedom to the
point of making a mockery of all thought—or to the point of freeing a laugh whose joy is limitless. In freedom, thought encounters
not so much an "unthinkable" as the unthinking (and it does not
"encounter" it: there is no "encounter" here, not even the so-called
encountering of others' freedom, because this freedom is not exterior to me). The unthinking other weighs thought and gives it
weight or withdraws its weight. The transcendental materiality or factuality of freedom is the unthinking other, which does not even
think thought, but delivers it to itself.

~

I would have liked, and it would have been necessary, for this work
to have been able to go further—I do not mean only in analysis or
problematization, but actually to the point of withdrawing and
putting under erasure all its discourse into material freedom. I
could have been tempted to make you hear music now, or laughter,
or cannon shots taken here and there in the world, or moans of
famine, shrieks of revolt—or even to present you with a painting, as
we find in Hegel when the young girl presents the outstanding
products of ancient art and the divine places that the gods have
left.[4] Quite clearly, this would be temptation itself, the cunning
abdication of thought into the immediate, into the "lived," into
the ineffable, or into the praxis and art designated as the others of

thought. On the contrary, it is a question of returning praxis to thinking. Something from Marx inevitably resonates here with something from Heidegger. A material thinking of the action of thought?

But it remains equally certain—and this is an indestructible remainder—that on the limit of thought, thought is exposed to the indecision between discourse and gesture, both of which are *of* thought, but threaten at every moment to break out of it. That is, they threaten to be only discourse or only gesture. Here again, there is sharing, between "the weapons of criticism" and the "critique of weapons," between the "action of thinking" and the "thinking of action." This sharing must be thought *or* practiced by deciding each time the undecidable.

One could also say: thinking in action is always suspended (and "in potential," so to speak) between these two ultimate possibilities: "the words to say it *are lacking*" and "the words are lacking *not to say it*, but to do it." Only in and through this primary indecision is there any decision of thinking (since thinking always engages itself where "words are missing": this is its freedom, for which precisely nothing is missing, except words).

∼

Note 2 to Chapter 7 (p. 192) says: "there would be the freedom of *Dasein* and the freedom of beings in general, one in the other and one through the other." This is one of the most difficult points, but doubtless, finally, one of the most necessary. Heidegger, in the period of *Being and Time*, means to distinguish the factuality of *Dasein* from the factuality of, for example, the "stone" (see §27 of *Being and Time*). It seems to me that this cannot be so simple. There cannot be, at least on what we could call a first level (but is it only the first? What would this distinction of levels mean?), several factualities. *There is* the factuality of the world. Again, what I insist on calling *factuality* and what, under this name, gives the most reliable (and most problematic) guiding thread of freedom from Kant to the freedom *we* have to think (this thread passes through Hegel, Marx, Nietzsche, and Heidegger), *is* the "there is" with all its force of "real presence" (without forgetting any of the problems related to such a "presence"—first and above all, that presence is in its coming, not in its being-present). Factuality as factuality is also (I would almost say "and first of all," were it not preferable not to introduce any order here) the factuality of the stone, the mineral, as well as that of the vegetal, animal, cosmic, and rational. Presence, impenetrability, *there* without "ek-stasy," *also* form the material-transcendental condition of a *Dasein* (and *with this name* one must rename "man" in the sense that this man is a singular material presence: a man, and not a stone, but the one and the other there, the one beside the other; in this regard, moreover, we see that we should no longer be able to say in such a context "man" in the generic sense, but only "man" or "woman").

Will I then say that in this unique (which does not mean "identical in all its modalities") factuality a unique (and nonidentical) freedom must offer itself? Will I say that all things are free? Yes, if I knew how to understand this. But at least I know that it would have to be understood (even while I know that such an "understanding" would have to be disentangled from the "understanding" of philosophers). We cannot content ourselves with sharing the world between *Dasein* and beings that are *Vorhanden and Zuhanden*—not only because these categories do not permit, or permit poorly, making space and allowance for the animal and vegetal, other modes that are also undeniably modes of "ex-istence," though in a way that remains obscure to our understanding. But also, *and above all,* because one must be able to affirm, for every *thing,* the withdrawal of the *cause* in it (analyzed above; see Chapter 9). In the thing without causality (neither caused nor causing) there is beingness [*étantité*] as the positing (*Setzung,* not *Stellung*) of the thing, existence as what makes the being-thrown, not only *in* the world (of *Dasein*), but *of* the world. The world is not given, substantial and immobile, *in order* for us to come *there.* The *there* of the "there is" is not a receptacle or a place arranged in order for a coming to produce itself *there.* The *there* is itself the spacing (of space-time) of the coming, because there is *all* (and totality is not the fastening, the completion without remainder; it is the "having there" [*y avoir*], the taking place [*avoir lieu*], the unlimited "coming there" [*y venir*] of the delimited thing;

which also means that totality is all, except totalitarian, and it is obviously a question here of freedom).

Nor is the world (this is clear in Heidegger) the correlate of an intentionality. (Perhaps it should be said, from the very interior of a Husserlian logic, that the "transcendence of the world" cannot work without the factual-material effectivity of a world that no longer arises from any "naive thesis"; one must perform a "reduction" here that would no longer be "eidetic," but, if we dare say it, "hyletic.") In no sense is the world "for me": *it is the essential co-belonging of ex-istence with the existing of all things.* Without that existence would be only ideal, or mystical. . . . But existence takes place on the surface of things. If we thoroughly investigated this essential co-belonging (of the essence-less), we would find that no thing can be simply "necessary" and that the world is not "necessary." We could not isolate on one side the causality of phenomena, and on the other noumenal freedom (this is what, ever since Hegel, we have not stopped debating with Kant). What would we find then? Let us try, provisionally, to say: something like a *clinamen,* which would not be chance (another necessity), but the free opening of the "there is" in general—which is never precisely general, but always on the order of "each time."

Clinamen, or declension, inclination of the "there is," of the "*es gibt,*" of the offering. For it to be, it must bend, it must slant—from nothing toward nothing. Or again, the blink [*clin*], the blinking of appearance, of the coming of all things, as secret as the "wink of an eye" (as the instant), but just as motivated and just as insistent as it is. Only in this way can there be an opening, a reciprocal clearing of *Dasein* and of beings in totality, without their becoming indistinguishable, but without their being submitted to the exclusive apparatus of subjectivity and representation. (The thought of representation inevitably condemns freedom, since the presence "beyond" representation is there given as "necessity," and freedom is content to play with representations, in order finally to dissolve into representation.)

In this sense, the stone is free. Which means that there is in the stone—or rather, *as* it—this freedom of being that being *is,* in

which freedom as a "fact of reason" is what is put at stake according
to co-belonging. (I do not deny, it should be emphasized, that in all
of this I am opening an enormous question in which one cannot but
find provocation, especially since I posit no result.)

I have tried to say that "we are the freedom of all things" and
perhaps this expression should not be kept. At least its intention is
in no way subjectivist. It does not mean that we represent the entire
world in our freedom, but rather that the freedom of being puts itself at stake as the free existence of the world and as our ex-istence
to this freedom—which also means that we are responsible for the
freedom of the world. And this could not be without consequences
for the question of technology (and on the at once open and aporet-
ic position of this question in Heidegger). Not that we have to pro-
tect nature *against* technical exploitation (when something of this sort
has to be done, it is always once again a matter of technology); but
in technology we liberate, and we liberate ourselves to the freedom
of the world. It is no surprise that this can cause anguish and profound ambivalence. But we do not have free access to what happens
here, as long as we think only of freely exploiting the unfree remainder of beings. This is also what makes us accommodate ourselves to entering into this class of beings . . . as workers. The
thought of a proletariat, like the thought of ex-istence in which a reciprocal liberation of "nature" and "history" would be played out,
could find something here to reconsider—mediated, it is true, by
many kinds of displacements and transformations.

I have absolutely no intention of extrapolating in a confused
way the idea of freedom. How could I do this without making use
of such an "idea"? Whatever the extreme difficulty and strangeness
of the problem, if the being of beings is the being *of beings*, and not
a kind of hidden *daimōn* telling its secrets to *Dasein*, we cannot
avoid detouring through the freedom of the world in order to come
to our own freedom. This is a necessity of thinking, a political and
ethical exigency.

~

"Authentic decision" (Chapter 12): a difficult thought, a limit-
thought, at least for the powers of this essay. How can we affirm that

there is an "authentic" decision, which amounts to affirming and announcing an ethical foundation without being able to present the
foundation or nature of this "authenticity"? (Keeping this word
"authenticity" is already more than ambiguous, since it means that
one is installed in an axiology . . .). Furthermore: how can we do it,
as long as we rest assured that freedom constrains us to undo or
frustrate the logics of "foundation"?

And yet, "we know what evil is" (compare Chapter 13). We know
it all the more since its overwhelming self-evidence has been made
even more widespread by our recent and present history. But what
we also know is that moral foundations have not only collapsed
under this evil, but have lent it a hand. And it is not for nothing that
the sentence "Freedom, how many crimes are committed in your
name!," whose author I have forgotten, has become a disabused
adage of modern times.

The undecidability in which there is decision is not the equivalence of all decisions. It is the impossibility that the "decider" of the
decision (at once its criterion and agent) precede the decision itself,
which is a very different kind of undecidability. But the decision that
decides itself decides for the authentic or not. Doubtless, in
Heidegger, this decision remains in at least one sense too "heroic"
and linked—why not say it thus?—to a "system of values" that up
to a certain point commands and secretly decides the very analysis
of the decision. This also amounts to saying that "authenticity,"
despite Heidegger's intentions, can only be cut from "inauthenticity," of which authenticity must be "only a modified grasp."[5]

Let us leave the examination of this point in Heidegger for later.
It seems to me that we can also seek to understand that there is a decision for freedom which is not the decision for the freedom to
suspend freedom, even though in both cases it would be the same
freedom that decides itself. Freedom is precisely what is free for
and against itself. It cannot be what it is except by remaining, at every
moment, freedom of "grace" *and* of "fury." This chasm is its "foundation," its absence-of-ground. But this is also the chasm through
which the freedom that chooses *itself* and the freedom that destroys
itself are the same and not the same. And perhaps freedom "is"

nothing other than this absolute difference in absolute identity. How can one grant that it is an "authentic decision?"

The decision that frees freedom against itself is the decision to suppress decision—and consequently to suppress the undecidable that renders decision possible and necessary. Or rather, it is the suppression of the existentiality of existence itself (a suppression that takes a thousand forms, besides murder). The decision for evil—which remains the possibility essentially conjoined and therefore absolutely proper to the decision for good—is a decision for what leaves nothing more to be decided. Authentic decision is on the contrary a decision for a *holding* of decision as such, which is its reappropriation and reconquest in the indecision that is itself maintained as an opening of the possibility of deciding. And this is why authentic decision *does not know itself* as such, or as decision for the good. It cannot present itself to itself as "good." It remains in itself different from itself. The decision for evil is what can appear to itself as "good," as a decision "taken" or "resolved," but not "held" in the sense indicated above.

One has to determine [*trancher*], that is, one has to determine that we will be able and will always have to determine again, even if it is only to make this "same" decision every time: because as *deciding*, and not as already decided, decision is at every moment new. Yet neither does this mean that authentic decision, reopening at every moment in itself the difference of in-decision, never decides except to . . . let everything happen [*tout laisser faire*]. Letting everything happen is also a way of annulling decision, as much in the liberal or anarchist sense that can be given this expression as in the sense of letting everything be done in the extreme, which completes the whole by exterminating it. The authentic decision *is* precisely against the possibility of doing "everything," or letting it be done. But as decision, it chooses not to do "everything." Prescription, obligation, and responsibility remain fastened to it.

One will say: now it is without content or ethical norms. No doubt. But did it ever have any of these? Decision is the empty moment of every ethics, regardless of its contents and foundations. Decision, or freedom, is the *ethos* at the groundless ground of every ethics. We have to decide on contents and norms. We have to decide on laws, exceptions, cases, negotiations; but there is neither law nor exception for decision. Its "authenticity" is not on the register of the law. Or rather, it is this law withdrawn from every form of law: the existentiality of decision, freedom, which is also the decision of existence and for existence, received well before every imperative and every law.

We therefore do not have to think in terms of new laws (even though we *also* have to make them), and we do not have to invent a "morality" (with hardly any irony, we can say: don't we have all we need in matter?). But above all, what is incumbent on us is an *absolute* determination, an absolutely originary, archi-originary determination of ethics and praxis—not a law or an ultimate value, but that by which there can be a relation to law or to value: decision, freedom.

If existence is without essence, this is because existence is entirely in its decision. It is entirely in the free decision to receive and hold itself as decision (a deciding decision, but in the mode of a receiving-itself, a letting-itself-be-taken by the decision . . .) *and/or* to decide on itself as such or such essence. Such is the *ethos* to which we must come, or which we must allow to come to us. This *ethos* would not correspond to a "progress of moral conscience," but would bring to light the archi-originary ethicity without which there would be neither Plato's Good, nor Kant's good will, nor Spinozistic joy, nor Marxian revolution, nor Aristotle's *zōon politikon.*

~

Why speak of "revolution" (for example, in Chapter 7)? In order capriciously to oppose the current discredit of this word? Why not? Ideology can always benefit from being shaken. But also: don't we have the responsibility of thinking the decision that opens onto the very possibility of deciding? Now which word has carried this thought, in a privileged way, through two centuries? And which word could replace it after two centuries? Enough has been said about how much "revolution" was a turn toward nothing, or even another turn of the screw. This is true—but this is also a mockery of history. Revolution brings to light common freedom, freedom's being-*in*-common, and the fact that this being, as such, is given over to decision. We cannot, despite everything, think this word differently. For a long time, the case of reform has been heard, and the more reform there is, the less anything changes. Revolt is a prisoner of the despair that produces it. Revolution does not at all exclusively signify the taking of power by a political faction. It signifies, or at least it signified: the opening of decision, the community exposed to itself.

I know that Fascism and Nazism were also revolutions, as were Leninism and Stalinism. It is therefore a question of revolutionizing revolutions. I understand all too well that this "pirouette" might not be appreciated. But what should we say and do if it becomes no less true that we must *again*, despite everything, decide to break with the course of things entirely decided? What should be said and done if the intolerable is always present, and if freedom has to make itself more and more skittish, more and more unbridled?

How can we think "revolution" without assault divisions or commissars of the people, and even without a revolutionary *model* (but on the contrary, as a reopening of the question of the model itself)? After all, the word matters little—but we still have not thoroughly thought through all that "revolution" gives to be thought. Above all, people continue to die of hunger, wars, drugs, boredom. A middle class continues to be generalized with its scruples relating to "technology," masking from us what is in the process [*technique*] of becoming class warfare.[6]

~

People die of hunger, drugs, wars, boredom, work, hatred, revolts, revolutions. They die or become mutilated in life, soul, and body. All liberations (national, social, moral, sexual, aesthetic) are ambiguous, and also arise from manipulations—and yet each has its truth. Freedom Manipulated (by powers, by capital): this could be the title of our half-century. Thinking freedom should mean: freeing freedom from manipulations, including, first of all, those of thinking. This requires something on the order of revolution, and also a revolution in thinking.

~

Democracy is less and less exposed to external criticisms or aggressions, but more and more preyed upon by its internal criticisms and disenchantments. Or rather: forces with incalculable effects (nuclear, physical, chemical, genetic) have been put into operation or unleashed, as we would say. All this leads back to the question of what "thinking freedom" means today. It means *at least* very clearly that received ideas about freedom, in all of their systematic frameworks (opposition to necessity, or assumption of necessity, assignation to the free subject, reciprocal delimitation and respect, repartition of the juridical, of the moral and political, of public and private, of the individual and collective, and so on), are themselves either "operative" in the least liberating practices of this frightening and disenchanted world, or constantly rendered "obsolete" by it. "Freedoms" are *also* pieces of "technology." This is why it is derisory to content oneself with reaffirming, in a Kantian mode, a "regulative idea" of freedom, or, in the mode of a "philosophy of values" (which we know was also able, more than others, to support Nazism), an "absolute value" of freedom. . . .

We always return to this: thinking freedom requires thinking not an idea but a singular fact, just as it requires carrying thought to the limit of a factuality that precedes it.

∼

In this essay, I was forced to repeat several times that freedom could not be "a question." This means that its thinking must be in search of a nonquestioning mode of thinking (but can we say "search" here? Would it not be too close to "question"?). Here is a profound and powerful trait of today's thinking: the demand for an affirmativity (we find it modulated differently from Nietzsche and Benjamin to Deleuze and Derrida).[7]

Yet perhaps neither affirmation nor negation may be substituted for the question. It could be a question of another disposition, one that has no logical name.

∼

What I wrote here concerning Heidegger and Nazism is necessarily insufficient after a year of commentaries occasioned by the renewed bringing to light of the "affair." Yet I have no intention of adding to these commentaries. A few words will suffice: that Heidegger never stopped thinking, in his most intimate and decided thoughts, something of "freedom"—by means of the abandonment of its theme or metaphysical question—and that *this itself* could command his political gestures, is what gives us something to think about. On the one hand, Heidegger was the first to take the measure of the radical insufficiency of our "freedoms" to think and open existence as freedom. But on the other hand, he still thought of "the free," up to a certain point at least, in the terms and in the tones of "destiny" and "sovereignty." In the name of this he was undoubtedly seduced by Hitler and later remained silent on the subject of the camps.

Destiny and sovereignty—whatever the names or figures they are given—are the sites where freedom obstinately renounces itself, even if freedom is what is destinal and sovereign. In this regard, Heidegger could not remain the thinker of existence humbly exposed to the world, which also means, but without fuss: free.

∼

"Being" just begins to clarify itself when we consider that "freedom" gives it, or that being *is* in freedom. We are then no longer thinking precisely according to a "thinking of Being," since we are in the process of rescuing this thinking from being "a thinking *of* something" (even if being *is* not). A thinking freed from being a thinking *of.*

∼

This essay proposes a thesis on being, in direct line from the one that Heidegger deciphers in Kant and from this other thesis, posited and withdrawn by Heidegger, on being "founded" in freedom. And what is more, it involves a thesis on theses, a positing and affirmation on the positing and affirmation of being, as posited and affirmed by freedom, as freedom.

To this extent, I run the risk of simply and naively reconstituting a metaphysics, in the sense in which this word designates "the forgetting of being" and the forgetting of this forgetting. Which means: the forgetting of the difference between being and beings is from the start lost from sight by metaphysics—this difference permits no *positing* of beings to be imposed on being, and no sovereignty over beings to be attributed to being.

But this difference *is not*—not even *the* "ontico-ontological difference." It is itself the very effacing of this difference—an effacing that has nothing to do with forgetting. If this difference is not, it in effect retreats into its own difference. This retreat is the *identity of being and beings*: existence. Or more precisely: freedom.

Freedom: *the withdrawal of every positing of being, including its being posited as differing from beings.* There is therefore no thesis here on being except insofar as there is no longer any possible thesis on being. Its freedom is in it and more ancient than it. This is its last thesis—or its first *doing [faire] (facere, factum* have the same root as *tithemi, thesis,* and even *tun* and *to do,* in German and English). "Doing" can no doubt be interpreted in many ways; I use it here only to show a difference within the thesis itself.

Philosophers have made theses on being; now the question has to do with the fact of its freedom.

~

Where thinking butts up against what renders it possible, against what *makes* it *think [faire penser].*

~

The "authentic decision" is made in "the beyond of the decision."[8] It does not arise from decisionism. It is much more and much less than what any theory of decision can represent (I am thinking of Carl Schmitt in particular, for whom the decision on the exception becomes the essence of the political, which is not foreign to Heidegger's politics.) Why? Because the decision does not tear itself away from the "inauthentic" in order to break with it; it happens within it and at its surface. Heidegger comes close to saying this—and does not. This is where, in Heidegger, one must break through "the thin wall by which the 'they' is separated, as it were, from the uncanniness of its Being."[9] The authentic decision is therefore also "short of [*en deçà*] the decision." But this "short of" is in no way the stupid and dismal acceptance of the quotidian and of all that is produced there. The "inauthentic" remains an *a priori*

warped category, marked by a loss even if Heidegger refuses to
make a "forfeiture" of it. But this "loss" is the loss of being, of its immanence and coming to the world, to presence, freedom. The place
of being-thrown—its place or its very "throw"—is not first of all the
"They," but freedom.

∽

The motto "liberty, equality, fraternity" seems to us somewhat
ridiculous and difficult to introduce into philosophical discourse, because in France it remains official (a lie of the State) and because it
is said to summarize an obsolete "Rousseauism." But for Heidegger,
does not "being-there also with others" (§26, *Being and Time*) determine itself according to "an equality [*Gleichheit*] of being as being-in-the-world?" Such an equality is unbreachable: it belongs
precisely to freedom.

As for fraternity, which gives one even more to smile about:
should it be suspected of coming from a relation to murdering the
Father, and therefore of remaining a prisoner as much of the sharing of hatred as of a communion with an identical substance/essence
(in the totemic meal)? This interpretation of the community as
"fraternal" must indeed be carefully dismantled. But it is possible,
even with Freud, to interpret it otherwise: as a sharing of a mater-
nal thing which precisely would not be substance, but sharing—to
infinity.[10] In this respect, Chapter 7 above has only gone halfway.
Perhaps the "mother" must also be abandoned, if we cannot avoid
her being "phallic" (but is this certain?). We must also think of the
fraternity in abandonment, of abandonment.

∽

"*Fraternity: we love them, we cannot do anything for them, except
help them to reach the threshold.*" Blanchot's fragment ascribes to
fraternity a love without effect, without affect, without communion. A strange restraint of love, yet still named "love." (Regarding
fraternity, Hannah Arendt could be invoked in the same sense.)
What, in these conditions, does "help" mean: not a support, not a
consolation, but the communal exposure of freedom.

∽

Pushed to the end of its experience, freedom would only result in
death. It could not meet up with itself except in the unleashing of

an absolute, unapproachable principle, where "grace" would be "fury" itself. The Terror, sacrifice, savagery, suicide. By reasoning in this way, we have already lost sight of the fact of freedom. As if in death this fact became presence, property, self-identity. But the experience of freedom remains the experience where these determinations collapse. Freedom is the inappropriable of death. In deciding on death, we think we are deciding on freedom, either to give it (suicide, or the Inquisition), or to kill it (murder). But what resists, resistance itself—which is properly the community's—is the freedom that *the* dead *person* (not abstract "death") never ceases to present, and that breaks loose more than ever from his being-dead. His death, whatever its cause, gave him back to an inappropriable freedom.

Thus inappropriable death delivers this freedom which gives birth to me. It is in this way that being-in-common takes place: through this free space where we come into mutual presence, where we com-pear. The opening of this space—spacing of time, exposure, event, surprise—is all there is of being, inasmuch as it "is" free. Death does not belong to this space, for it effaces itself in pure time as a figure of effacement and as an effacement of all figures. Yet common space, while it is at every moment new, also bears the mark, at this moment ineffaceable, of this effacement. We live with all the dead: this is what murder denies in vain. The community is entirely exposed to itself—including the community of the co-belonging of the world.

(Let us not be suspected here of an exalted, mystical vision of universal life. . . . It is certainly a question of life, but finite, humble, banal, and insignificant, in the sense that life exists, in effect, at the limit of sense: where the experience of freedom begins and ends.)

~

There is no "experience of freedom": freedom itself is experience.

~

Fighting "for" freedom, equality, fraternity, and justice does not consist merely of making other conditions of existence occur, since it is not simply on the order of a project, but also consists of immediately affirming, *hic et nunc*, free, equal, fraternal, and just existence. We ought to be able to say as much for writing and thinking "about" freedom.

~

"To die freely: an illusion (which is impossible to denounce). For even if we renounce the illusion of believing ourselves to be free with respect to dying, we return to confusing, in words constantly belated, what we call the gratuitousness, the frivolity—its light will-o'-the-wisp flame—the inexorable lightness of dying, with the insubordination of what every seizure lacks. Whence the thought: to die freely, not according to our freedom, but from passivity and abandonment (an extremely passive attention), according to the freedom to die."[11]

~

"Here is an appendix which develops, a spirit without canals or compartments, a freedom perhaps ready to be seized, perhaps also to annihilate other freedoms, either to kill them or better to embrace them."[12]

~

"Freedom is an *ethical* principle of *demonic* essence."[13]

~

There is this surprising freedom in which freedom leaves us, relative to it, free to let it offer itself, while it has nothing to make itself recognizable. This is all there is.

~

This freedom which asks us, proposes to us, requires us to be free to the point that we remain free with respect to it, to the point that we free ourselves from freedom . . .

~

Given the direction that certain commentaries are presently taking, what I will have tried to say here about a freedom which lays claim to republican and democratic mottoes, but which disengages itself from "democratic freedoms," will be charged with Jacobinism, even terrorism, if not outright Fascism (or, in another version, nihilism). (Recently, this type of accusation has been eagerly flung at every effort of thought that a reference to Heidegger in particular is reputed to expose.) Yet,

1. it should be known that in the move from a thinking, let us say of being, of essence, or of principles—it matters little here—to a politics and an ethics, the consequence is never good (why do we systematically forget the massive and enduring adherence of so many theorists of the "philosophy of values" to the Nazi regime?);

2. this consequence is not good because in drawing it we pass without passage from the regime of the interrogation of the "principle" as such, of its nature and "principiality" even, to the regime in which we fix these principles. Thus we remove freedom from the one and the other, for what is in play from the one to the other is precisely the indetermination, the undeducibility of putting freedom at stake and into operation. Or further: the "principle" of freedom—let's say, as foundation or as the sharing of being—precisely "founds" the exercise of an incalculable freedom.

That Heidegger should have been a Nazi was an error and a mistake. That he could have been one is what belongs to the archiethical principle of freedom. (Finally, in being a Nazi, in the very particular way we are beginning to be able to distinguish, that he could also have willed himself "to conspire with the liberation of the possible," according to Granel's expression,[14] is what requires an evaluation, undoubtedly infinitely delicate, which belongs to our tasks of thinking.)

∼

To depend on nothing—to give oneself one's own law—to be the opening of a beginning: in our discourse we cannot escape this triple determination of freedom, in which everything is held (and holds for both a *we* and an *I*). It is thus solely a question of making the following transcription: having no foundation—accordingly, having "one's own" law always this side of or beyond "oneself"—being as removed from oneself as an opening is, and grasping no more of oneself than can a beginning. Everything comes back to this, and the transcription appears simple enough. In reality, however, because transcription is impossible in our discourse, it remains equally impossible in the very description I have recorded here! Transcription has its freedom this side of or beyond itself (and cannot be verbal transcription only, or a changing of names or syntaxes, or even a "pure and simple" "act" outside of discourse). It is what is most difficult for thinking: at its limit, putting its limit at stake. Transcription is no doubt unachievable.

～

However, this does not mean that freedom would be, in Hegelian fashion, the infinite as the absolute in its negativity. Because freedom is the infiniteness *of the finite as finite*, and is thus itself finite, which means at the same time singular and without essence in itself, it consists in neither having nor being an essence. Freedom consists in not consisting, without any contradiction. This "without contradiction" makes the *fact* and secures the *presence* of freedom—this presence which is the presence of a *coming* into presence. Never infinite, never dialectical negativity, more buried than affirmation and negation, freedom is never this "freedom of the void" which Hegel designates as belonging to "fanaticism" and to "the fury of destruction."[15] Neither "full" nor "empty," freedom comes, it is what of presence comes to presence. In this way it *is*, or is the *being of being*.[16]

～

Thinking, undoubtedly, is for us what is most free. But freedom is this fact which less than any other can be reduced to thinking.

Reference Matter

Notes

Foreword

1. See p. 96 of this book.
2. John Stuart Mill, *On Liberty*, Elizabeth Rapaport, ed. and intro. (Indianapolis: Hackett, 1978), p. 1.
3. See John Locke, *An Essay Concerning Human Understanding*, Peter H. Nidditch, ed. and intro. (Oxford: Clarendon Press, 1975), p. 244: "The proper question is not, whether the Will be free, but whether a Man be free. . . . We can scarce tell how to imagine any *Being* freer, than to be able to do what he *wills*. So that in respect of Actions, with the reach of such a power in him, a Man seems as free, as 'tis possible for Freedom to make him."
4. See Thomas Hobbes, *Leviathan*, C. B. Macpherson, ed. (Harmondsworth, Eng.: Penguin, 1968), p. 127.
5. See Immanuel Kant, *Critique of Pure Reason*, Norman Kemp Smith, trans. (New York: St. Martin's, 1965), pp. 409–11.
6. See René Descartes, *Meditations on First Philosophy*, Donald A. Cress, trans. (Indianapolis: Hackett, 1979), p. 17. On this momentous statement, see the meticulous presentation of Jean-Luc Nancy, *Ego Sum* (Paris: Flammarion, 1979).
7. See David Hume, *A Treatise of Human Nature*, L. A. Selby-Bigge, ed., P. H. Nidditch, rev. ed. (Oxford: Clarendon Press, 1978), pp. 155–72; Book I, §14.
8. This also captures the analysis of modality that Kant undertakes in the section of the *Critique of Pure Reason* entitled "The Principles of Empirical Thought," but insofar as the *Critique* itself sets out to expose

the "conditions of possibility" of the unity of experience, it also allows for—if it does not already present—an experience of possibility, and it is this allowance that, according to Nancy, marks the decisive character of Kant's "revolution in the mode of thinking": "The becoming-world of world means that 'world' is no longer an object, nor an idea, but the place existence is given to and exposed to. This first happened in philosophy, and to philosophy, with the Kantian revolution and the 'condition of possible experience': world as possibly of (or for) an existent being, possibility as world for such a being. Or: Being no longer to be thought of as an essence, but to be given, offered to a world as its own possibility" (Nancy, Introduction, *Who Comes After the Subject*, Eduardo Cadava, Peter Conner, Jean-Luc Nancy, eds. [Routledge: London, 1991], p. 1).

9. David Hume, *An Enquiry Concerning Human Understanding*, Eric Steinberg, ed. (Indianapolis: Hackett, 1977), p. 64; cf. *A Treatise of Human Nature*, pp. 399–418. Hume's attempt to show the compatability of liberty—or, more precisely, the "liberty of spontaneity"—with thoroughgoing determinacy has set the terms in which numerous analyses of freedom have been cast; see the excellent discussion of this issue in Barry Stroud, *Hume* (London: Routledge & Kegan Paul, 1977), pp. 141–54.

10. Civil liberties were not, for Hume, an overriding concern, and he certainly did not conceive of their defense on the basis of "reason" as a legitimate philosophical exercise; in fact, his historical studies set out to demonstrate the need for the continuity of authority and to extol the power of precedent. On the sense of Hume's "conservativism," which, unlike modern conservativism, does *not* result from rejection of the French Revolution (although perhaps it took impetus from a revulsion for Rousseau), see the remarks of Donald W. Livingston, *Hume's Philosophy of Common Life* (Chicago: University of Chicago Press), pp. 306–42.

11. Hume, *A Treatise of Human Nature*, p. 7.

12. Ibid., p. 10.

13. Ibid.

14. See, in particular, Hume's renunciation of his earlier "solution" to the problem of personal identity in the appendix to *A Treatise of Human Nature*: "In short there are two principles, which I cannot render consistent; nor is it in my power to renounce either of them, viz. *that all our distinct perceptions are distinct existences,* and *that the mind*

never perceives any real connexion among distinct existences. Did our perceptions either inhere in something simple and individual, or did the mind perceive some real connexion among them, there wou'd be no difficulty in the case. For my part, I must plead the privilege of a sceptic, and confess, that this difficulty is too hard for my understanding" (*A Treatise of Human Nature*, p. 636). On this inconsistency and its relation to the problem of personal identity, see the well-known discussion by Norman Kemp Smith, *The Philosophy of David Hume* (London: Macmillan, 1941), pp. 556–58.

15. The most celebrated account of the alternative between "negative" and "positive" freedom can be found in Isaiah Berlin's "Two Concepts of Liberty," *Four Essays on Liberty* (Oxford: Oxford University Press, 1969), pp. 118–72. A more nuanced version of this alternative is pursued with surprisingly similar results by Richard E. Flathman, *The Philosophy and Politics of Freedom* (Chicago: University of Chicago Press, 1987).

16. Hume, *A Treatise of Human Nature*, p. 264.

17. Ibid., p. 265. In an earlier chapter, Hume had tried to distinguish imagination from memory and had further distinguished two senses of imagination (see pp. 117–18*n*), but each of these turn out to be "founded" on an originary if nevertheless heterogeneous imagination from which the others derive. The most extensive survey of Hume on the imagination is that of Jan Wilbanks, *Hume's Theory of Imagination* (The Hague: Nijhoff, 1968); the relation of Hume's faculty of imagination to Descartes's corporeal imagination and the medical theories it spawned is discussed by John P. Wright, *The Sceptical Realism of David Hume* (Minneapolis: University of Minnesota Press, 1983), pp. 187–246. The discourse of the imagination in eighteenth-century Britain was extraordinarily widespread. Along with Hume, the discussion was pursued by Alexander Gerard, Abraham Tucker, Adam Smith, Edmund Burke, Adam Ferguson, and Dugald Stewart, to name only a few (and to leave out the doctors entirely). It has been a traditional topos—or perhaps ideology—of scholarship to see in the discourse of the imagination the "foreshadowing" of English Romanticism, especially since Coleridge's presentation of the imagination has been so often viewed as its credo.

18. See p. 20. Cf. the explication of the word "experience" in Philippe Lacoue-Labarthe, *La Poésie comme expérience* (Paris: Bourgois, 1986), pp. 30–31. The German word *Erfahren* ("to experience") derives, of course, from *Fahren* ("to travel") and is related to *Gefahr* ("danger").

19. Hume, *A Treatise of Human Nature*, p. 264.

20. The most important of Nancy's writings in this context is *The Inoperative Community*, Peter Connor, ed. P. Connor, L. Garbus, M. Holland, and S. Sawhney, trans. (Minneapolis: University of Minnesota Press, 1991). A complete bibliography of Nancy's writings can be found in a volume of *Paragraph* devoted to Nancy's thought and edited by Peggy Kamuf; see *Paragraph* (June 1993).

21. Those whom Hume awoke include, at least on the "continent," not only Kant but at least two other no less significant sleepers: Johann Georg Hamann and Edmund Husserl. When Hamann went to England in 1757, he encountered "the Attic philosopher," David Hume, who, as he explained to Kant in a lengthy letter, has fastened onto "belief" or "faith" (*Glauben*) and is, to this extent, "a Saul among prophets"; see Hamann's letter of July 27, 1759, in Kant, *Philosophical Correspondence*, Arnulf Zweig, trans. (Chicago: University of Chicago Press, 1967), pp. 41–42. Hamann did not, of course, find "faith" in Hume, but he also experienced more than simply "frustration humienne" (Nancy's term, *L'Oubli de la philosophie* [Paris: Galilée, 1986], p. 47); as the reference to Saul indicates, he discovered in Hume an unlikely speaker, one in whom the classical forms of argumentation gave way to overjoyed nitpicking and argumentative exuberance. For Hamann's friend and student F. H. Jacobi, Hume's discourse on belief marks a gulf that neither traditional metaphysics nor its Kantian transformation could ever hope to overcome; only a "leap of faith" does so. See F. H. Jacobi, *David Hume über den Glauben, oder Idealismus und Realismus, ein Gespräch* (Breslau: Löwe, 1785). Although in a completely different sense, Edmund Husserl also conceived of a Hume who surpassed Kant in the depth and direction of his questioning. Hume was, according to Husserl, a decisive if nevertheless misguided predecessor in phenomenological research; see, in particular, the late reflections on the alienation from the "life-world" contained in Husserl, *The Crisis of European Sciences*, David Carr, trans. and intro. (Evanston, Ill.: Northwestern University Press, 1970), especially pp. 88–97: "the world-enigma in the deepest and most ultimate sense [not the sense Kant understood], the enigma of a world whose being is being through subjective accomplishment [*Leistung*], and this with the self-evidence that another world cannot be at all conceivable—that, and nothing else, is *Hume's problem*" (pp. 96–97).

22. Precisely what substance Hume understood a community to

share in, or to partake of, is the key question for any inquiry into his political philosophy, his conception of historical continuity, and his politics. To the extent that he thought it was nature and not reason, he opposed attempts to establish community on radically new, "rational" foundations. No doubt his bizarre encounter with Rousseau, who accused him of leading a worldwide conspiracy, also contributed to his conception of the political community. For an interpretation of this encounter, see Jerome Christensen, *Practicing Enlightenment* (Madison: University of Wisconsin Press, 1987), pp. 243-73.

23. See p. 87. Nancy does not in this context refer to Walter Benjamin's philosophical writings, but they often impose themselves on his analyses. In an early text that shows the confluence of Hermann Cohen and Edmund Husserl, entitled "On the Program for the Coming Philosophy," Benjamin, like Nancy, frees experience from everything "lived," from every subjectivism as well as every objectivism. The experience in whose presence philosophy will come is purely transcendental; it is "an experience of experience," and this experience could very well turn out to be that of pure language. See Walter Benjamin, "Über das Programm der kommenden Philosophie," *Gesammelte Schriften*, Rolf Tiedemann and Hermann Schweppenhäuser, eds. (Frankfurt am Main: Suhrkamp, 1980), II.1, pp. 157-71; "Program for the Coming Philosophy," Mark Ritter, trans., *The Philosophical Review* 15 (Fall–Winter, 1983-84): pp. 41-51. Benjamin turns from this program for philosophy to come, which is anything but a proposal for the renewal of philosophy, toward an exposition of the characteristically modern "shock-experience" in which experience (*Erfahrung*) breaks up into "lived experiences" (*Erlebnisse*); see, in particular, the third and fourth sections of "On Some Motifs in Baudelaire" in *Illuminations*, ed. and intro. Hannah Arendt, Harry Zohn, trans. (New York: Schocken, 1968), pp. 160-65. Baudelaire's *Les Fleurs du mal* registers "an emancipation from experience (*Erfahrung*)" (p. 162), and this emancipation gives rise to a poetry of *Erlebnisse*, which, precisely because it has destroyed what passes for the unity of *Erfahrung*, may constitute the "experience of experience" of which "The Program for the Coming Philosophy" speaks.

24. Martin Heidegger, *Sein und Zeit* (Tübingen: Niemeyer, 1979), p. 42; *Being and Time*, John Macquarrie and Edward Robinson, trans. (New York: Harper & Row, 1962), p. 67. See p. 9 of this book.

25. A spectacular example of the explication of essence as *potentia*—

and one that no doubt marks the beginning of speculative meta-physics—can be found in Leibniz's response to Spinoza: "The power of God is his essence itself, because it follows from his essence that he is the cause of himself and of the other things" (Leibniz, *Philosophical Papers and Letters*, Leroy E. Loemker, ed. and trans. [Boston: Reidel, 1969], p. 204).

26. One of Nancy's more programmatic writings, *L'Oubli de la philosophie*, is devoted to the exposition of the "sense" that is "us." See especially the chapter entitled "Le sens, c'est nous" (*L'Oubli de la philosophie* [Paris: Galilée, 1986], pp. 85–99). But this *sens* cannot be confused with the *Sinn* toward which phenomenology is oriented; the latter is, in Nancy's terms, "signification" and arises from a desire (or exercise of the will, or act of labor, or intention) to cancel the distance from ourselves that "sense" imposes on us. Nancy's *sens* should not, then, be understood as the equivalent of Husserl's *Sinn*, but it never-theless remains a question whether the term *sens* invites such equivoca-tions.

27. See Martin Heidegger, *Kant and the Problem of Metaphysics*, Richard Taft, trans. (Bloomington: Indiana University Press, 1990). In "La voix libre de l'homme" Nancy proposes a reading of freedom in Heidegger's Kant-book and in his subsequent disputation with Ernst Cassirer over the legacy of Neo-Kantianism; see *L'Impératif catégorique* (Paris: Flammarion, 1983), pp. 115–37. Nancy has written of the tran-scendental imagination and its "art" of schematism in many other con-texts. See, in particular, *Le Discours de la syncope* (Paris: Aubie-Flammarion, 1976), pp. 106–9; "La vérité impérative" in *L'Impératif catégorique*, especially pp. 106–8; "L'Offrande sublime" in *Du Sublime*, Jean-François Courtine et al., eds. (Paris: Belin, 1988), pp. 43–46. Reading Kant's chapter on transcendental schematism is, for Nancy, thinking the crisis it inscribes: "In the crisis, and by it, philosophy is therefore judged; it leads it to discern itself. (In this sense, there is a repetition of something of Kantian *critique*: schematism does not ask to be elucidated; it asks to be brought to light as the limit of the thought of signification, which it represents)" (Nancy, *L'Oubli de la philosophie*, p. 79).

28. See Nancy, *Le Partage des voix* (Paris: Galilée, 1982); "Sharing Voices," Gayle L. Ormiston, trans., *Transforming the Hermeneutic Context*, G. L. Ormiston and A. D. Schrift, eds. (Albany: State University of New York Press, 1990), pp. 211–59.

29. The prolegomenon for the discussion of the "fact of reason" in *The Experience of Freedom*, which describes itself as "prolegomena" for future thought of freedom (see p. 206), is Nancy's *L'Impératif catégorique*; see, in particular, pp. 20–22. Nancy's exposition of "the fact of reason" bears striking *contrast* to that of Theodor Adorno, who, during an analysis of the Marquis de Sade's moral theories, presents it as "a mere natural psychological fact" (Max Horkheimer and Theodor Adorno, *Dialectic of Enlightenment*, John Cumming, trans. [New York: Continuum, 1972], p. 94; cf. Adorno's more extensive analysis in "Freedom: On the Metacritique of Practical Reason," *Negative Dialectics*, E. B. Ashton, trans. [New York: Seabury Press, 1973], pp. 211–99). A discussion of the relation of Nancy to Adorno, which is undoubtedly warranted in this context, would have to consider Jacques Lacan's "Kant avec Sade" (*Ecrits* [Paris: Editions du Seuil, 1966], pp. 765–90) along with Nancy and Lacoue-Labarthe's early text on Lacan, *Le Titre de la lettre* (Paris: Galilée, 1972).

30. See Kant's admission of uncertainty and of the "veritative tone" in which this admission takes place in "On a Newly Arisen Superior Tone in Philosophy"; see *Raising the Tone of Philosophy: Late Essays by Kant, Transformative Critique by Derrida*, P. Fenves, ed. (Baltimore: Johns Hopkins University Press, 1993), especially pp. 71, 93.

31. See Kant, *Foundations of the Metaphysics of Morals*, Lewis White Beck, trans. and intro. (Indianapolis: Bobbs-Merrill, 1959), pp. 43–44.

32. For a particularly significant deployment of this often-found phrase in Kant's writings, see Immanuel Kant, *The Doctrine of Virtue*, Mary J. Gregor, trans. (Philadelphia: University of Pennsylvania Press, 1964), p. 37*n*.

33. See Nancy, *L'Impératif catégorique*, pp. 10–12.

34. See, for example, Kant's remarks on the execution of Louis XVI in *Metaphysical Elements of Justice*, John Ladd, trans. and intro. (Indianapolis: Bobbs-Merrill, 1965), pp. 87–88*n*; cf. Peter Fenves, *A Peculiar Fate* (Ithaca, N.Y.: Cornell University Press, 1991), pp. 272–75.

35. See p. 134.

36. See p. 89. Nancy in this passage refers to a phrase Jacques Derrida deploys in the conclusion of his analysis of the writings of Emanuel Lévinas: "Concerning death which is indeed its [the other's] irreducible resource, Lévinas speaks of an 'empiricism which is in no way a positivism'" (Derrida, *Writing and Difference*, Alan Bass, trans. [Chicago: University of Chicago Press, 1978], p. 152; Lévinas, *Difficult*

Freedom, Seán Hand, trans. [Baltimore: Johns Hopkins University Press, 1990], p. 188). This citation, like so many others found in *The Experience of Freedom*, implies a multiplicity of connections. At stake in Nancy's exposition of freedom is the issue of "violence and metaphysics," and this issue is greatly sharpened by the series of questions Derrida poses after he cites Lévinas's remarks on Rosenzweig: "But can one speak of an *experience* of the other or of difference? Has not the concept of experience always been determined by the metaphysics of presence? Is not experience always an encountering of an irreducible presence, the perception of a phenomenality?" (p. 126). *The Experience of Freedom*, which could also perhaps be called "the experience of the other" or "the experience of difference," takes up these questions not precisely to answer them as to show how "experience" has already done so. And this is not only what Derrida proceeds to do—"nothing can so profoundly *solicit* the Greek logos" (p. 126)—but also, as Derrida notes, what Schelling had set out to do in his *Exposition of Philosophical Empiricism*, and finally what characterizes the most important texts of Emanuel Lévinas as well as those of Franz Rosenzweig.

37. Nancy does not use the word "classical" lightly or loosely; its shifting meanings are explored in Jean-Luc Nancy and Philippe Lacoue-Labarthe, *The Literary Absolute*, P. Barnard and C. Lester, trans. (Albany: State University of New York Press, 1988).

38. See p. 154.

Chapter 1

1. *Encyclopedia*, §482, in *Hegel's Philosophy of Mind*, A. V. Miller, trans. (Oxford: Clarendon Press, 1971), p. 239. From Hegel to us, the vanity, ambiguity, and inconsistency of an idea of freedom incapable of obtaining foundation and rigor for itself, have been, in discourses that are just as moralizing as emancipatory, as reactionary as progressive, *topoi* as abundant as the *topos* of irrepressible freedom itself. Bataille has expressed this in another way: "The term freedom, which supposes a puerile or oratorical enthusiasm, is from the outset fallacious, and there would be even less of a misunderstanding in speaking of all that provokes fear." Georges Bataille, *Oeuvres complètes*, vol. 2 (Paris: Le Seuil, 1970), p. 131.

2. Karl Marx, *On the Jewish Question*, in *Early Writings*, T. B. Bottomore, trans. (New York: McGraw-Hill, 1964).

3. Theodor Adorno, *Negative Dialectics*, E. B. Ashton, trans. (New York: Continuum, 1987), pp. 214–15.

4. René Descartes, Fourth *Meditation*; Hegel, *Encyclopedia* §§478, 481 [translated in *Hegel's Philosophy of Mind*), pp. 237–39]. We add the following qualification: nothing of this scheme is fundamentally put in question when the subject of representation is situated in God and when, for man, freedom becomes more problematic (as is the case, in different ways, for Leibniz or Spinoza). It is no less true that the thought of freedom as the necessity of substance or of essence (from Spinoza to Nietzsche by way of German Idealism) combines the subject's "self-appearing" with a mode of bringing the subject, at the limit, to an exposure in which it no longer appears to itself. This is what Heidegger will have tried to grasp in Schelling (we will return to this).

5. Does this mean thinking? "In fact one cannot think for someone else, any more than one can eat or drink for him. . . . " G. W. F. Hegel, *Encyclopedia*, §23 [translated in *The Encyclopedia Logic*, T. F. Geraets et al., trans. (Indianapolis: Hackett, 1991), p. 55].

6. G. W. F. Hegel, *Lectures on the History of Philosophy*, E. S. Haldane and Frances S. Simson, trans. (New Jersey: Humanities Press, 1983), vol. 1, p. 150 [trans. modified].

7. Cf. Jacques Derrida, *Edmund Husserl's Origin of Geometry*, John P. Leavey, Jr., trans. (Lincoln: University of Nebraska Press, 1989), esp. pp. 145–46.

8. G. W. F. Hegel, *Encyclopedia*, §17 [translated in *The Encyclopedia Logic*, p. 41].

Chapter 2

1. We are not saying "political" here. Either what is understood by "political freedoms" more or less covers the series of epithets we have used, or we would have to consider in the political as such the specific putting at stake of the transcendence of existence. It is uncertain whether one could do this today. We must still rethink the political as such, or think differently what Hegel assigns to the political as the existent effectivity "of *all* the determinations of freedom" (*Encyclopedia*, §486, in *Hegel's Philosophy of Mind*, A. V. Miller, trans. [Oxford: Clarendon Press, 1971]). Later, we will consider the model of a free political space, without being able to keep it as constituting by itself the proper space of freedom. At the very least, we will be able to find a political "analogon" of what Alain Badiou seeks in the following interrogation on the subject of freedom: "What is a radical politics, one which goes to the root, which challenges the administration of the necessary, which reflects on ends, which

maintains and practices justice and equality, and which all the while assumes the climate of peace, and is not like the empty anticipation of a cat-
aclysm? What is a radicalism which is at the same time an infinite task?"
Alain Badiou, *Peut-on penser la politique?* (Paris: Le Seuil, 1985), p. 106. To
which we would add: what is a common freedom which presents itself as
such without absorbing into its presence the free event? Cf. Jean-Luc
Nancy, "*La Juridiction du monarque hégélien*," in *Rejouer le politique*
(Paris: Galilée, 1981).

2. "The concept of freedom, insofar as its reality is proved by an apodictic law of practical reason, is the *keystone* of the whole architecture of
the system of pure reason," Immanuel Kant, *Critique of Practical Reason*,
Lewis White Beck, trans. (New York: Macmillan, 1985), p. 3. Wasn't this
proposition an axiom for all of philosophy up until Marx and including
Nietzsche? If it lost this position, this was not due to a loss of a taste for
freedom, but rather to the closure of an epoch of history and of thought,
a closure for which the Kantian "keystone" provides a model (even though
the Kantian thought of the *fact* of freedom also constitutes the opening of
what we have to think concerning this topic).

3. In *Traditionis traditio* (Paris: Gallimard, 1972), p. 175.

4. "In the concentration camps, it was no longer the individual who
died, but a specimen." Theodor Adorno, *Negative Dialectics*, E. B. Ashton,
trans. (New York: Continuum, 1987), p. 362 [trans. modified]. That is, the
specimen of a *type* (in this context, "racial"), of an Idea, of a figure of an
essence (in this context, the Jew or the gypsy as the essence of a non-
essence or of a human sub-essence). Cf. on this subject the analyses of
Philippe Lacoue-Labarthe in the "Heidegger" section of his *L'Imitation des
modernes* (Paris: Galilée, 1986). On the question of evil, cf. Chap. 12.

5. "I generate time itself in the apprehension of the intuition" (*Critique
of Pure Reason*, N. K. Smith, trans. [New York: St. Martin's Press, 1965],
Transcendental Schematism, p. 184), and this apprehension is the "synthesis of the manifold"—i.e., the constitution of phenomena—"which sensibility provides in its originary receptivity" by "joining with spontaneity"
(Transcendental Deduction). This originary synthesis is nothing other
than the principial structure of finite transcendence (cf. Martin Heidegger,
Kant and the Problem of Metaphysics, Richard Taft, trans. [Bloomington:
Indiana University Press, 1990], §16). But, in these conditions, the
schematism should be elucidated no longer according to the guidelines of
a production of *Bild*—as Heidegger does, at least up to a certain point—
but on the contrary (even though this is not a contrary . . .) as the *freedom*

itself of *the withdrawal* from every figure (cf. ibid., §14). This would be the object of another work.

6. Martin Heidegger, *Gesamtausgabe* (Frankfurt-am-Main: Klostermann, 1982), vol. 31, p. 134.

Chapter 3

1. The inverted structure of the Deduction of the Second *Critique* in relation to that of the First *Critique* is indicated by Kant. *Critique of Practical Reason*, Lewis White Beck, trans. (New York: Macmillan, 1985), Book I, chap. 1, I, p. 17.

2. "The Canon of Pure Reason," I and II. Immanuel Kant, *Critique of Pure Reason*, Norman Kemp Smith, trans. (New York: St. Martin's Press, 1965), p. 637.

3. Immanuel Kant, *Critique of Judgment*, J. H. Bernard, trans. (New York: Hafner Press, 1951), §91, p. 320.

4. Martin Heidegger, *Gesamtausgabe*, vol. 31, p. 300. (We take E. Martineau's side in translating *Vorhandensein* as *être-sous-la-main*, and this is also an occasion to recall that Martineau initiated, on the basis of Heidegger, the opening of a problematic of freedom that is echoed here. Cf. his preface to R. Boehm, *La Métaphysique d'Aristote*. Not that this in any way diminishes our great esteem for the translations of Jean-François Courtine.) We will proceed by following the analyses of §§27 and 28 in *Being and Time*.

5. This could not be a moral conscience (we will discuss *Gewissen* later according to its analysis in *Being and Time*) whose ontological, non-anthropological character Heidegger emphasizes (*Gesamtausgabe*, vol. 31, p. 291). Nevertheless, respect could add a further twist to this determination of the fact of practical reason, but it will not appear here.

6. Nor does this mean that it would be a fact of the "interiority" of reason, accessible to some kind of introspection. The psychological is empirical, but not on the order of the transcendental experience which is the experience of freedom. On another level, this also does not mean that reality here would only be that of possibility, as it is, for example, in Fichte: "Freedom really and truly exists, and is the root of Existence; however, it is not immediately real, for its reality goes only as far as possibility." J. G. Fichte, *The Way Towards the Blessed Life*, William Smith, trans. (Washington, D. C.: University Publications, 1977). Fichte's formula undoubtedly restores philosophy's most constant thought, at least (if for the moment we leave aside Spinoza, whose proximity to what we are

trying to say should be studied, to the extent that for him freedom is identified with the effectivity of beatitude; but Spinoza does not think existence as such)—at least up to Hegel and to the conversion of freedom into effectivity (yet not simply into necessity, for Fichtean "possibility" is itself a necessity of the "independence of the absolute with respect to its own intimate being"). Freedom has been thought as the necessary existence of the subject's infinite possibility of relating to itself, but not as the existentiality of existence.

7. §76, Third *Critique* (New York: Hafner Press, 1951), p. 250. We choose "setting into position" for *Setzung*, in contradistinction to the simple *Position* (in the German text)·of representation. Our use of this motif liberally distances itself—because of this distinction of concepts in Kant— from Heidegger's use of it in *Kant's Thesis on Being*, where precisely this distinction is ignored.

8. *Setzung* therefore responds point for point to the dynamic of *différance* by which Derrida designates the infinite motion of finite being as such. *Différance* thus implies freedom, or is implied by it. Freedom frees *différance*, while *différance* defers freedom, which does not mean that *différance* keeps freedom waiting: it is always already there, but by surprise, as we will see.

9. Aristotle, Book I, *Nicomachean Ethics*, W. D. Ross, trans. (Oxford: Oxford University Press, 1975).

10. Translator's note—Nancy plays on the homonymic coupling in French of "*à faire*," "to be done," and "*affaire*," "affair, matter, concern, transaction, business, lawsuit," and their relation to "*faire*," "doing, making, producing," and "*fait*," "fact."

11. *Kant and the Problem of Metaphysics*, Richard Taft, trans. (Bloomington: Indiana University Press, 1990), p. 178.

Chapter 4

1. Sartre will have merely displaced and misinterpreted (on this point, as on others) Heidegger's thinking, as we will show later. Adorno, for his part, left behind in *Negative Dialectics* a thinking in which freedom is confined to its own movements rather than interrogated in its essence. It should also be recalled that Bergson too represents, in an entirely different way, a kind of stopping point of the thinking of freedom. Theodor Adorno, *Negative Dialectics*, E. B. Ashton, trans. (New York: Continuum, 1987).

2. *Gesamtausgabe*, vol. 31, p. 300.

3. Reuben Guilead's book, *Etre et liberté—une étude sur le dernier*

Heidegger (Louvain and Paris, 1965), unfortunately does not live up to the promises of its title. The fragmentary analysis of freedom in Henri Biraud, *Heidegger et l'expérience de la pensée* (Paris: Gallimard, 1978), with which we feel ourselves to be in agreement in several respects, does not consider the suspension of the theme in Heidegger. Fred R. Dallmayr, while he too does not consider this point, presents a very suggestive synthesis of Heidegger's thought on freedom in *Polis and Praxis* (Cambridge, Mass.: MIT Press, 1984), chap. 4, "Heidegger's Ontology of Freedom." Our work would have to engage in a complex discussion with Reiner Schürmann's book, *Heidegger on Being and Acting: From Principles to Anarchy*, Christine-Marie Gros, trans. (Bloomington: Indiana University Press, 1987). Schürmann does not really analyze the freedom which he supposes or implies throughout and which would have to be articulated with his theme of "coming to presence" (which is also an important motif for us, and to which we have devoted other analyses; cf. "Le Rire, la présence" in *Critique* 488–89, Jan.–Feb. 1988). We are less comfortable with his concept of "economy." If there is a certain community between us and these works (including those of Martineau, cf. note 4 to Chap. 3, and also Lévinas's "difficult freedom"), it consists less in a determinate "thought" (and still less in a "concept") than in the recognition of a necessary "liberation" of the thinking that tries to be the thinking "of" freedom. In other words, this is first a liberation with respect to the concepts and systems of freedom (among which we still will not include Spinoza without reservations; but that is another program of work), and secondly a less determinable liberation of thinking itself in its own praxis.

4. The call of care in *Being and Time* provokes and convokes *Dasein* to its freedom; cf. §§57 and 58, Martin Heidegger, *Being and Time*, John Macquarrie and Edward Robinson, trans. (New York: Harper & Row, 1962). We will speak again of the call.

5. G. W. F. Hegel, *Phenomenology of Spirit*, A. V. Miller, trans. (Oxford: Oxford University Press, 1977), p. 492; Friedrich Nietzsche, *Human All Too Human*, R. J. Hollingdale, trans. (Cambridge, Eng.: Cambridge University Press, 1987), I, §11, p. 217; Paul Celan, *Der Meridian*, in *Gesammelte Werke*, vol. 3, Beda Alleman and Stephan Reichert, eds. (Frankfurt: Suhrkamp, 1983), p. 200.

6. Martin Heidegger, *The Essence of Reasons*, Terrence Malick, trans. (Evanston, Ill.: Northwestern University Press, 1969), pp. 127–28.

7. According to the gesture whose model is given by *Kant and the Problem of Metaphysics*, Richard Taft, trans. (Bloomington: Indiana

University Press, 1990). Let us add here, as one document among others, these sentences from the *Introduction to Metaphysics* (1935; New Haven: Yale University Press, 1987), p. 170: "Being-human, as the need [*Not*] of apprehension and collection, is a being-driven [*Nötigung*] into the freedom of undertaking *techne*, the sapient embodiment. This is the character of history." In the pages of our text immediately following, citations refer to the English translation of Heidegger's *Schelling's Treatise on the Essence of Human Freedom*, Joan Stambaugh, trans. (Athens: Ohio University Press, 1985).

   8. Martin Heidegger, *Schelling's Treatise on the Essence of Human Freedom*, p. 192. Let us be clear about this: 1936–43, these dates speak volumes on their own, and one will not have failed to note, in the tone of the "resolve" to "destiny," an echo of the *Rektoratsrede* of 1933. The question of politics in Heidegger is obviously intertwined with the question of his debate on the subject of freedom and *with* the idea of freedom. One would have to consider this question with Philippe Lacoue-Labarthe, "Transcendence Ends in Politics," in *Typography* (Cambridge, Mass.: Harvard University Press, 1989), pp. 267–300; and with Gérard Granel, "Pourquoi nous avons publié cela," in *De L'Université* (Mauzevin: T.E.R., 1985).

   9. G. W. F. Hegel, *Hegel's Philosophy of Right*, T. M. Knox, trans. (London: Oxford University Press, 1967), p. 32.

   10. Martin Heidegger, "On the Essence of Truth," in *Basic Writings*, David Farrell Krell, ed. (New York: Harper and Row, 1967), p. 128.

   11. Ibid., p. 127.

   12. This situating of the theme was prepared by a passage from *The Question Concerning Technology* (1953), of which we will speak further. Martin Heidegger, *The Principle of Reason*, Reginald Lilly, trans. (Bloomington: Indiana University Press, 1991).

   13. Martin Heidegger, "Letter on Humanism," in *Basic Writings*, p. 223.

Chapter 5

   1. This also dates to before Rousseau and Kant (although the Spinozistic relation to civil law diverges, for its part, from this model; cf. in particular Etienne Balibar, "Jus-Pactum-Lex," in *Studia spinozana*, vol. 1, 1985).

   2. G. W. F. Hegel, *Science of Logic*, A. V. Miller, trans. (Atlantic Highlands, N. J.: Humanities Press International, 1989), p. 843.

   3. Jean-Luc Nancy, *L'Impératif catégorique* (Paris: Flammarion, 1983), pp. 58, 134. The text I refer to here is bound up with a network of

thoughts woven around the point of "unleashing" [*déchaînement*]: the law in Blanchot, judgment in Lyotard, (in)decision in Derrida, responsibility in Lévinas. Only responsibility is thematically constructed as prior to freedom and as "dominating" it. See Emmanuel Lévinas, *Totality and Infinity*, Alphonso Lingis, trans. (Pittsburgh: Duquesne University Press, 1969), p. 87. An additional remark: for Lévinas freedom is mingled, through itself, with "the arbitrariness" of an "egoistical ego," and its "essence" lies in "the imperialism of the Same." Responsibility, by "investing freedom" with the "presence of the Other," "*frees it from the arbitrary*" (my emphasis). This formula alone testifies to the fact that freedom cannot fail to precede itself or to precede every attempt to grasp it or to free it from grasp, even its own grasp. Lévinas himself, whose concept of freedom—at least in this work, since the rest of his work uses the word "freedom" in a wider sense—is thus strictly limited to that of free will, nevertheless appeals to "the critique in which freedom is capable of being called into question and thus preceding itself" (ibid., p. 89).

4. Martin Heidegger, *Schelling's Treatise on the Essence of Human Freedom*, Joan Stambaugh, trans. (Athens: Ohio University Press), p. 162 [trans. slightly modified]. The context gives these lines a remarkably ambiguous profile: they designate at the same time a limit of Kantian thought and, in order to indicate that Schelling finally does not overstep this limit, a positive affirmation from Heidegger himself. So freedom, undecidably, finds itself declared incomprehensible and, through a tacit promise of overstepping metaphysics, comprehensible to the thinking of being. Fundamentally, this is the constant ambiguity of the course and of the entire "path" followed by Heidegger on the subject of freedom.

5. Translator's note—*À la limite* may be rendered in English by any of the following formulations, depending on the context: "at the limit," "ultimately," "at the furthest extreme," "in the most extreme case," or even "in/as a last resort." *Entendement* may be translated as either "hearing" or "understanding"; it differs from *compréhension* by evoking an aural component, figural or literal, of comprehension. Finally, *accomplissement* has been rendered as "realization" in order to preserve most generally the various senses of "accomplishing, achieving, completing, fulfilling."

6. §142 (my emphasis), G. W. F. Hegel, *Philosophy of Right*, T. M. Knox, trans. (New York: Oxford University Press, 1967), p. 105.

7. §257, ibid., p. 155.

8. The possibility is not excluded that there may be other resources in Marx that should be pursued.

9. Martin Heidegger, "What is Metaphysics?," R. F. C. Hull and Alan

Crick, trans., in *Existence and Being* (Washington, D. C.: Henry Regnery, 1949, repr. 1988), pp. 357–58 [trans. modified].

10. G. W. F. Hegel, *Lectures on the History of Philosophy*, E. S. Haldane and Frances Simson, trans. (Atlantic Highlands, N. J.: Humanities Press, 1983), Introduction.

11. Must this be emphasized? From the "comprehension" of *Dasein* in *Being and Time* to the "thinking" of *What is Called Thinking?*, we are only following Heidegger's "path of thought," accenting it differently, freely, seeking to liberate what it proposes. It is understood that we are practicing a repetition which itself comprises the repetition of other repetitions: we are speaking not only of those we most frequently cite, here and elsewhere, several of which have been worked through in the repetition of Heidegger, but of still others, which have sometimes in self-defense repeated something of the same Heidegger (Adorno above all). Citation is not the entirety of repetition. Actually, an entire epoch was invented through repetition, and invented its difference as repetition, that is, difference as a secondary consequence of the "end of philosophy," as the re-demand (*repetitio*) for what is at stake in philosophy. But it is Heidegger himself who inaugurated thinking as repetition (and not as critique or sublation) of what had already been thought. To repeat is to experience the fact that thinking was closed in "metaphysics"—*and* the fact that this closure frees the possibilities and exigencies of finite thought, that is, of thought that takes up and replays all of its experience as experience of finitude. Freedom to repeat, liberation in repetition. In the "preliminary remarks" to *Wegmarken* (1967), Heidegger indicated the "necessity of later being understood otherwise than one understood oneself"; but "this necessity has its ground in the possibility that historical tradition and transmission still preserve a free space of play for what necessity demands." Thinking and its tradition free from themselves the possibility of their free repetition—and this is why there is *thinking*.

12. "Singularity" should here be understood at once according to the value Deleuze gives to the "ideal event" or to "essentially pre-individual, non-personal, a-conceptual" punctuality, and according to the value that common language gives to the word when it makes it mean "strangeness, anomaly," as well as according to the value of "surprise" which we will later analyze in the relation of freedom and time. Gilles Deleuze, *The Logic of Sense*, Mark Lester, trans. (New York: Columbia University Press, 1990), p. 52. For us, existence is above all what is singular. It happens singularly and only singularly. As for the existent, its own existence is

above all singular, which means that its existence is not precisely its "own" and that its "existing" happens an indefinite number of times "in" its very individuality (which is for its part a singularity). Singularity is what distinguishes the existent from the *subject*, for the subject is essentially what appropriates itself, according to its own proximity and law. Yet the advent of a subjectivity is itself a singularity.

13. Even free will would have to be reevaluated, especially if it is to be understood in its original form, as Vuillemin proposes: "It is said that Democritus' system suffered from having been transmitted through Epicurus' system, which subordinated theory to practice and introduced the metaphysical concept of freedom into philosophy. Actually, it is this concept of the freedom of indifference, of balance, or of will, which inspired the admiration of a Marcus Aurelius and which is the keystone of Epicurus' philosophy. And this freedom is primarily that of refusing the solicitations of opinion, for example the representation of future evils, in order to accept only the present, i.e. sensation cut off from the active movement of error." Vuillemin, *Necessité ou contingence—l'aporie de Diodore et les systèmes philosophiques* (Paris: Minuit, 1984), p. 205. An acceptance of the present which would be precisely a resignation to destiny (this is what Epicurus wanted) will later characterize freedom for us (Chap. 11). It is not a question of proposing a new Epicureanism, or an Epicurean derivative. It is only a question of stating that at the heart of the philosophical tradition surrounding freedom there is what could be called a "materialism of the present"—understood as the singularity of existence and not as appropriated presence—engaged in an intimate debate with the idealism of temporality understood as the perpetual presence of causal linking (cf. Chap. 9).

Chapter 6

1. Martin Heidegger, *The Metaphysical Foundations of Logic*, Michael Heim, trans. (Bloomington: Indiana University Press, 1984), p. 18.

Chapter 7

1. This analysis has been undertaken in Jean-Luc Nancy, *The Inoperative Community*, Peter Connor, ed. (Minneapolis: University of Minnesota Press, 1991). The law of the relation of singular existence is formulated in the following way by Francis Wolff (who concludes an analysis of Epicurus and Lucretius in Heideggerian terms, cf. note 13 to Chap 5): "A being which one could not relate to any other then does not ek-sist,

since it is the existence of one relation to another that determines the possibility of their ek-sistence." Francis Wolff, *Logique de l'élément—clinamen* (Paris: Minuit, 1981), p. 256.

2. In an analogous way, Merleau-Ponty tried to grasp the other [*autrui*] on the basis of freedom: "The other is no longer so much a freedom seen *from without* as destiny and fatality, a rival subject for a subject, but he is caught up in a circuit that connects him to the world, as we ourselves are, and consequently also in a circuit that connects him to us—And this world is *common* to us, is intermundane space—And there is transitivism by way of generality—And even freedom has its generality, is understood as generality: activity is no longer the *contrary* of passivity . . . the other is a relief as I am, not absolute vertical existence." Maurice Merleau-Ponty, *The Visible and the Invisible*, Claude Lefort, ed., Alphonso Lingis, trans. (Evanston, Ill.: Northwestern University Press, 1968), p. 269. Perhaps we should attempt to grasp not only *the other*—the other existent—but every other being—thing, animal, or instrument—from the starting point of freedom. The freedom that makes existence exist in the open also and at the same time produces the openness of the world and its free spacing. There would be the freedom of *Dasein* and the freedom of beings in general, one in the other and one through the other. But always, and in the final analysis, it is *existence* as such that puts at stake freedom and the openness in which beings present themselves. However, in this coming into presence, beings themselves in general also *exist* in a certain way, and singularly. We could say: because existence *is in the world*, the world as such itself also exists—it exists because of the proper existence of existence, which is outside of itself: *this* tree exists in its singularity and in the free space where it singularly grows and branches out. It is not a question of subjectivism, the tree does not appear to me thus, it is a question of the material reality of the being-in-the-world of the finite existent whose finitude comports the effective existence of the world as the singularity of existence itself.

3. Cf. Jean-Luc Nancy, "Shattered Love," Lisa Garbus and Simona Sawhney, trans., in *The Inoperative Community*, pp. 82–109.

4. This *one* [*on*] would refer to that of Blanchot, or to the parallel *they* [*ils*] which does not designate the anonymity of a banality, but corresponds to the event of what one cannot "grasp except by releasing oneself (from) the power of saying I." Maurice Blanchot, *L'Entretien infini* (Paris: Gallimard, 1969), p. 557. Cf. the consideration of this motif, as well as a collection of references to Blanchot on this point in Gilles Deleuze and

Félix Guattari, *A Thousand Plateaus*, Brian Massumi, trans. (Minneapolis: University of Minnesota Press, 1988).

5. Cf. "What is Freedom?" in Hannah Arendt, *Between Past and Future* (New York: Penguin, 1968), p. 148.

6. Philippe Lacoue-Labarthe, *L'Imitation des modernes* (Paris: Galilée, 1986), p. 188. (This sentence must be understood in relation to the following one: "Why, after all, would not the problem of identification be, in general, the very problem of the political?" p. 173.)

7. Jean-François Lyotard, *The Differend*, Georges Van Den Abbeele, trans. (Minneapolis: Minnesota University Press, 1988), p. 141.

8. Alain Badiou, *Peut-on penser la politique?* (Paris: Le Seuil, 1984), p. 113.

9. Immanuel Kant, *Religion Within the Limits of Reason Alone*, T. M. Greene and H. H. Hudson, trans. (New York: Harper), p. 176.

10. Martin Heidegger, *Gesamtausgabe* (Frankfurt-am-Main: Klostermann, 1981), vol. 51, p. 16 ("Grundbegriffe," course of 1941).

11. "Omnes et singulatim" in *Le débat*, no. 41, 1986, p. 7. In reality, we have the choice of defining politics between two poles: either the Aristotelian definition of the "political animal" in terms of the disposition of *logos* insofar as it involves justice, good and evil, etc., and in terms of the nonuseful finality of "living well" (*eu zein*); or, at the other pole, the technology of power. Perhaps the name "politics" should be reserved for one of the two; perhaps they should be thought together. Whatever the choice, it is remarkable that freedom is essential at both poles (and this is what demands that they be thought together). In the same text, Foucault could in fact write: "The distinctive trait of power can be found in the fact that some individuals can more or less entirely determine the conduct of other individuals—but never in an exhaustive or coercive way. A person who is chained up and beaten is subjected to the force exerted over him, not to power. Yet if he can be made to speak, when his last resort could have been to hold his tongue, preferring death, he has thus been forced to behave in a certain way. His freedom has been subjected to power and he has submitted to the government. If an individual can remain free, however limited his freedom may be, power can subject him to the government. There is no power without the potential for refusal or revolt" (p. 34).

12. Cf. Hannah Arendt, "What is Freedom?" in *Between Past and Future* (New York: Penguin, 1968). Is there then a mimesis of freedom, or does freedom on the contrary repudiate all mimesis? This question, briefly

skimmed several lines further on, cannot be treated here. We will simply indicate the principle: cf. note 9 in Chap. 13.

13. Cf. Chap. 2.

14. Saint-Just, *L'Esprit de la révolution* (Paris: 10/18, 1969), p. 79.

Chapter 8

1. G. W. F. Hegel, *The Encyclopedia Logic* (Indianapolis: Hackett, 1991), §87, p. 140. The conditional *would be* that replaces the indicative *is* of the first edition indicates, it is true, a slight retreat with respect to this determination of freedom. It is as if Hegel were saying, "Freedom would be this supreme form of nothingness, if nothingness were not itself already annihilated." Nonetheless, the dialectical conversion is not formally identified as such and is instead reabsorbed into "intensification."

2. Keith Waldrop, *The Garden of Effort* (Providence, R. I.: Burning Deck, 1975), p. 80.

3. Martin Heidegger, *The Essence of Reasons*, Terrence Malick, trans. (Evanston, Ill.: Northwestern University Press, 1969), p. 129.

4. René Descartes, "Author's Replies to the Fifth Set of Objections," in *The Philosophical Writings of Descartes*, vol. 2, John Cottingham, trans. (Cambridge, Eng.: Cambridge University Press, 1989), p. 241.

5. Martin Heidegger, *Hegel's Concept of Experience* (San Francisco: Harper & Row, 1970), p. 120.

6. Martin Heidegger, *Hegel's Phenomenology of Spirit*, Parvis Emad and Kenneth Maly, trans. (Bloomington: Indiana University Press, 1988), p. 20. And further: "To undergo an experience with something—be it a thing, a person, or a god—means that this something befalls us, strikes us, comes over us, overwhelms and transforms us." Heidegger, "The Nature of Language," in *On the Way to Language*, Peter D. Hertz, trans. (New York: Harper & Row, 1971), p. 57.

7. Cf. Derrida's analysis of Lévinas in "Violence and Metaphysics," in *Writing and Difference*, Alan Bass, trans. (Chicago: University of Chicago Press, 1978), pp. 79–153.

8. Cf. "*Unum quid*" in Jean-Luc Nancy, *Ego sum* (Paris: Flammarion, 1979).

9. Martin Heidegger, "On the Essence of Truth," in *Basic Writings*, David Farrell Krell, ed. (New York: Harper & Row, 1967), p. 128.

10. Thus, in Hegel, subjectivity first grasps that pure *being* is "only an empty word," which presupposes the mastering of signification and the relation to self given by representation. In this regard we might also adopt

Michel Henry's analysis in order to express the truth of subjectivity and its impossibility for freedom: "The moment of consciousness remains in fact the essential moment of self-consciousness, which remains an exterior consciousness, since exteriority is the medium in which consciousness is present to itself in self-consciousness. For consciousness, Hegel did not conceive a mode of presence-to-oneself other than the mode of the presence of the object, because the presence of the object as such is, in his view, none other than the very essence of consciousness. The essence of objectivity constitutes the unique foundation, it is the universal medium in which all that is manifested is realized." Michel Henry, *L'Essence de la manifestation*, vol. 2 (Paris: Presses Universitaires de France, 1963), p. 902.

Chapter 9

1. "On the Essence of Truth," in Martin Heidegger, *Basic Writings*, David Farrell Krell, ed. (New York: Harper & Row, 1977), p. 129.

2. The analysis that follows applies primarily to Sartre's efforts to elucidate and define the meaning of his formulation in the posthumously published *Cahiers pour une morale* (Paris: Gallimard, 1983), beginning at p. 447.

3. Cf. the first and second "Analogies of Experience" in the first *Critique*. The rest of our analysis addresses and expands certain elements of Heidegger's analysis in vol. 51 of the *Gesamtausgabe*. Our conclusions seem to be those that Heidegger reached but did not develop.

4. Immanuel Kant, *Critique of Pure Reason*, Norman Kemp Smith, trans. (New York: St. Martin's Press, 1965), p. 218.

5. Immanuel Kant, *Critique of Judgment*, J. H. Bernard, trans. (New York: Hafner Press, 1951), §81, p. 271.

6. The immediacy referred to here is not that of sensuous immediacy. Nor is it an absence of mediation in the intelligible. It is neither a sentiment nor an intellectual given of freedom. This might resemble what we could call the specific pregnancy of the "feeling of reason," which is for Kant the *respect* for the law of freedom, and as "what respect respects . . . , reason gives this to itself insofar as it is free." Martin Heidegger, *Kant and the Problem of Metaphysics*, Richard Taft, trans. (Bloomington: Indiana University Press, 1990). In some sense, the analysis made in this renowned paragraph 30 of *Kant and the Problem of Metaphysics* sets us in the direction we are attempting to follow here, to the extent that Heidegger, relating respect to transcendental imagination, makes it appear as "a transcendental and fundamental structure of the transcendence of the ethical self," where such a transcendence is nothing other than the structure of what we are des-

ignating as "experience." Still, Heidegger's extremely elliptical analysis does not seem truly to attain the unity it declares between the receptivity of imagination and the free imposition of law, because it is precisely in the unicity of an originary concept of experience that this unity should be found: in the experience of being-in-the-world as being-free; everything in Heidegger leads to this, without formally ending up at it; in *Kant and the Problem of Metaphysics*, this nonattainment, as well as the restricted place given to practical reason, seems commanded by a phenomenological (eidetic) hypothetic that burdens the directive analysis of the imagination and of schematism; but another work would need to be done in order to show this. Yet if there is a "self-evidence" of respect, it depends on the *factum rationis* and not on the sensibility that accompanies it without truly being at stake in that relation, since it is exempted from the "pathological," which, however, designates nothing other than the regime of the affectability of pure affection (cf. Michel Henry's analysis in *L'Essence de la manifestation* [Paris: Presses Universitaires de France, 1963], §58—from which we have strayed in our conclusions). We must therefore be able to think, if not a "pathology," at least a pure passion of pure reason, where reason is "practical" in all that it is (even when it is "theoretical"). But "purity" here will be nothing other than the material effectivity of being-in-the-world, and moral impurity (evil, which we will speak of later). This "passion" is the experience of freedom. The immediacy of this experience must therefore be understood as *the affective im-mediacy of freedom in existence insofar as freedom affects existence from an infinite distance*: from the point of an infinite withdrawal and in traversing existence with this distance-from-itself (its non-essentiality) which sets it outside of itself only in order to make it *exist* as the *thing* in itself. This im-mediacy of experience is the common originary structure of both sentiment and self-evidence, which it withdraws, the one as much as the other, from subjectivity.

7. It is therefore not a question of the man who is "immediately natural . . . bestowed with natural forces" of whom Marx speaks in his "1844 manuscripts" (*Collected Works*, vol. 3 [New York: International Publishers, 1975]) in order to distinguish him from the man "who exists through himself." But it is no less significant that Marx wanted to emphasize power in the same way that Hegel had emphasized consciousness. The experience of freedom is also the experience of a difference of forces at stake in being-in-the-world. We can recall, moreover, that in an entirely different but equally symptomatic way Bergson sought to present free action as the "detonation" of a material energy (cf. *L'Energie spirituelle*, I).

8. This ontological materiality seems to us to meet up with the analyses of Didier Franck in *Heidegger et le problème de l'espace* (Paris: Minuit, 1986).

9. Cf. Chap. 5.

Chapter 10

1. Cf. Jean-Luc Nancy, *L'Impératif catégorique* (Paris: Flammarion, 1983), and cf. Chap. 2.

2. Cf. Chap. 5.

3. The general and conjoined structure of order and event: "Come: how could this provoke the coming of what comes, the coming of the event, for example, if the '*come*' itself does not arrive, does not arrive at itself?" Jacques Derrida, *Parages* (Paris: Galilée, 1986), p. 62.

4. Cf. Emile Benveniste: ". . . the bare semanteme employed in its jussive form, with a specific intonation," which does not even constitute "an utterance." *Problems in General Linguistics*, Mary Elizabeth Meek, trans. (Miami: University of Miami Press, 1971).

Chapter 11

1. We must ignore here the articulation with space, which nevertheless belongs to this problematic. For this another work would be required. Further on we will find some indications in the direction of what would have to be thought not only as an originality proper to space (as does Didier Franck, cf. note 8 to Chap. 9, above), but as a "spaciosity" of time around the "event," which we will discuss here. Generally speaking, freedom offers itself as spacious and spacing: I will touch on this in the conclusion (Chap. 13).

2. Cf. Martin Heidegger, *On Time and Being*, Joan Stambaugh, trans. (New York: Harper & Row, 1972); and also Derrida's analysis of the "thoroughly metaphysical" character of the "concept of time" in "*Ousia* and *Gramme*: Note on a Note from *Being and Time*" in *Margins of Philosophy* (Chicago: University of Chicago Press, 1982).

3. Translator's note—"*Survenue*," "the unexpected occurrence," when emphasized by Nancy as *sur-venue*, has been translated as "coming-up" in order to preserve its sense of "coming" [*venue*].

4. Cf. Chap. 6. The entire thematic of the present paragraph should be compared to Lyotard's reading of *Begebenheit* in Kantian history, of the event's "fact of giving itself" as the "trace of freedom in reality." Although Lyotard, who does not propose an examination of freedom for itself, re-

tains the term "causality by freedom," the implicit concept of freedom that his text seems to suppose would perhaps find some analogies here. However, we would have some reservations with regard to the expression "trace of freedom," which implies both visibility (or sensibility; these are the stakes of Lyotard's "sentiment," which should lead us back to what is evoked in note 6 to Chap. 9) and intermittency; what is undeniable on the level of the "historical events" of which Lyotard speaks seems to me to refer, on the level of ontology, to what could be called the non-sensible constitution of the sensible and the non-intermittent constitution of evenemential intermittence. In a sense, there is constantly an event of freedom that opens existence as such. There is constantly a "coming-up" in time, and it is only from this point that one can accede to the possibility of thinking a "history" and its "signs." Cf. Jean-François Lyotard, *L'Enthousiasme* (Paris: Galilée, 1986), especially pp. 54–56, 100, 113.

5. Julien Green, *Minuit*, cited in Georges Poulet, *Mesure de l'instant* (Paris: Plon, 1968), p. 376; and Milan Kundera, *L'Art du Roman* (Paris: Gallimard, 1986), p. 80 (the author speaks of Anna Karenina—structurally speaking, would literature have to do with this surprise, many other literary examples of which could certainly be produced?). There is something of a syncope here—suspense and rhythm—of a beating at the heart of "reason," of a heartbeat. "A heart is already an event, an event is already a heart," wrote Dôzen. Freedom, in its event, is perhaps always of the order of the heart. But how does one think a heart of being? (We addressed the question in "Shattered Love," Lisa Garbus and Simona Sawhney, trans., in *The Imperative Community*, Peter Connor, ed. [Minneapolis: University of Minnesota Press, 1991].) What occurs in *Ereignis* is perhaps that occurring occurs to itself and appropriates itself as presence. But this can only occur in the mode of an unexpected coming-up. Occurring occurs to itself by coming up in the beating of the coming-up. It would be this—the heart of being—or its freedom (wouldn't the *heart* be for us a synonym or metaphor of freedom in all its states?). The opening of a world, as such and absolutely, is unthinkable outside of the freedom of the coming-up. Otherwise, it is not a *world*, but a *universe*. In a somewhat comparable way, Wittgenstein links wonder before the "miracle" of existence (which references Heidegger, in the German edition of the text, as Christopher Fynsk has shown us) with *ethics* as the proper order of expressions "whose very essence is to have no meaning," which we would interpret as: to have the "meaning" of the freedom of being (cf.

Wittgenstein, "Lecture on Ethics," in *The Philosophical Review* [Ithaca: Sage School of Philosophy, 1965], vol. 73, pp. 3–12).

6. Among many analyses, we can cite that of Vuillemin (who, moreover, also analyzes Spinoza), for the finesse with which it grasps the active abandonment of this will: "What is, however, the origin of the conversion by which a finite will, in assuming the limitations that overwhelm it, identifies itself, to the extent that this is possible, with its cause and substance? It would not be this finite will itself, except precisely insofar as we consider it to be a given part of Nature and the wise man only comes to wisdom by way of a certain eternal necessity. We are therefore necessarily necessitated to salvation and acquiescence. And again it is the secret of the strength of feeling one's effusion sustained by a source which it captured as if involuntarily, which it does not control and which it feels to be inexhaustible." Vuillemin, *Nécessité ou contingence—l'aporie de Diodore et les systèmes philosophiques* (Paris: Minuit, 1984), p. 389. To which we would add only, in order to establish a more secure link with this text, that "salvation and acquiescence" are nothing other than freedom itself.

7. Cf. Chap. 7.

8. The theme of the choice of *Dasein*'s proper possibilities, in *Being and Time*, does not refer to the classical motif of the will's choice. "To choose oneself" is not to elect one possibility among others, and it is nevertheless not a resignation to the inevitable. It is a decision to be one's own as the existent that one is, which means always, as this being whose existence *surprises* it, as existence and as its own.

9. Cf. Walter Benjamin, "Trauerspiel und Tragödie," in *Gesammelte Schriften*, vol. 2 (Frankfurt-am-Main: Suhrkamp, 1980), pp. 134, 135.

10. However, we will not pronounce these without the following warning from Adorno, from *Negative Dialectics*, E. B. Ashton, trans. (New York: Continuum, 1987), p. 369: "The deterioration of the death of metaphysics, whether into advertisements for heroic dying or to the triviality of purely restating the unmistakable fact that men must die—all this ideological mischief probably rests on the fact that human consciousness to this day is too weak to sustain the experience of death, perhaps even too weak to integrate death with the self. . . . " But we will add that "to integrate death with the self" is at least an ambiguous expression and that it is freedom itself which takes us to death and which also consequently *deprives us of every possibility of appropriating this death*, or the birth which opens onto it.

11. Cf. the entire motif of *Schicksal, schicken,* and *bestimmen,* which clearly communicates, as is well-known, with that of *Ereignis* (cf. *On Time and Being,* Joan Stambaugh, trans. [New York: Harper & Row, 1972]).

Chapter 12

1. Theodor Adorno, *Negative Dialectics,* E. B. Ashton, trans. (New York: Continuum, 1987), p. 366.

2. H. W. Petzet cites this expression in his preface to Martin Heidegger/Erhardt Kästner, *Briefwechsel* (Frankfurt-am-Main: Klostermann, 1986).

3. Cf. Philippe Lacoue-Labarthe, *La Poésie comme expérience* (Paris: Bourgois, 1986), p. 167: "This is strictly *unpardonable*"—the word relates simultaneously to Auschwitz and to Heidegger's silence. (In addition, and as a preface to later remarks, we should recall that pardon, in its Judeo-Christian tradition, needs no justification. What remains unjustifiable can, on another register, be pardoned—except when it precisely involves an attitude that leans, in one way or another, toward justifying the unjustifiable, as we might suspect the case would be at a certain level in Heidegger. Yet in the same tradition of pardon there remains an enigmatic "sin against the spirit" which cannot be pardoned. . . . (Let us add that Heidegger's silence was not absolutely total; some sentences were spoken and we will later allude to one of these on the *Unheil,* the disaster, of Nazism. But apart from this word, nothing broke Heidegger's profound silence. All the material on this point is presented and carefully analyzed by Philippe Lacoue-Labarthe in *La Fiction du politique* (Paris: Bourgois, 1988), translated as *Heidegger, Art and Politics,* Chris Turner, trans. (London: Basil Blackwell, 1990).

4. Thomas Mann, *Das Problem der Freiheit* (Stockholm, 1939).

5. As indicated earlier (Chaps. 1, 3), we are thinking of a secret complicity, in spite of fundamental differences, between the camps and everything that, by exploitation, abandonment, or torture, presents in our time what could be gathered under the names (both material and symbolic) of tenacity [*acharnement*], emaciation [*décharnement*], and the mass grave [*charnier*]. The analysis of these would have to be given elsewhere. It would be necessary to retrace what circulates between the exposing of the brutality of the primitive accumulation of capital—the exposing of the "sickness of civilization"—and the exposing of civilized and technicized barbarism.

6. One might find such a confusion of differences excessive. It is meaningful only with respect to the exhibition of a "positivity" of evil, which we will discuss. Meanwhile one should not forget, even as their necessary differences are restored, the sadistic scenes in Proust or the Bataillean project of human sacrifice: for, in spite of everything, this happened—and Bataille himself finally recognized it—outside the sacred and outside the immanent retribution of evil to which he laid claim.

7. Victor Hugo, *La Fin de Satan*.

8. Immanuel Kant, *Religion Within the Limits of Reason Alone*, pp. 32 ff. (We retain the older translation, since it seems difficult to renounce the word "wickedness" [*méchanceté*], at least for our present use, in favor of "malice" [*malignité*] even though, in its previous signification, the latter term gave its name precisely to the *Evil One* [*Malin*]; but this signification has been lost.)

9. In this sense, a simple use of the terms "good" and "evil" no doubt loses its relevance. However, the fundamental—and foundationless—discord to which they testify, without even being charged with any other determination than that of the "fury" of evil, cannot be expressed in other words. ("Fury" is not "combat," it devastates and ruins, nothing more.) And this is also why it seems to us difficult to renounce, in spite of everything, the word "freedom."

10. Doubtless, there is no longer a pure empirical figure for the "wicked being" any more than there is for the "sage" or for the "saint" (meanwhile, there are apparatuses, mechanisms, institutions, and calculations that can present wickedness as such . . .). Yet apart from the fact that we can no longer easily reason in such terms, where experience itself is transcendental, there is a total dissymmetry between the presentation of a tortured body on which maliciousness is inscribed in capital letters, and that of a body which we will not even call happy or beautiful, but which suffers from something other than wickedness. As if evil by essence imprinted its mark, and good, on the contrary, covered up its own traces. Evil must attest to its own operation, it must show its devastation. Good neither destroys nor constructs, it is not of such an order. We could therefore also conclude that good always escapes wicked destruction (as all of idealism thought, with greater or lesser difficulty): yet even this has no precise meaning. Good is not "safeguarded." Where evil occurs, there is no good on reserve. But the attestation of evil is equal to the attestation of the good that is not there, to the extent that it is not there and has no positivity.

11. Martin Heidegger, "Letter on Humanism," in *Basic Writings*, David

Farrell Krell, trans. (New York: Harper & Row, 1977), pp. 237–38 [trans. modified]. The date of this text (1946) and the use of the word "fury," in the sense whose origin we believe we can locate, lead us to believe that Heidegger at least implicitly *also* targeted Nazism here. Yet at the same time, and for fundamentally obvious motives, "fury" must also refer to an aspect of the analysis of "technology" and of *Gestell* (where the theme of fury can often be detected and sometimes explicitly read: cf., for example, "The Question Concerning Technology," in *Basic Writings*, David Farrell Krell, ed. [New York: Harper & Row, 1967]). To comprehend, not evil through technology, but the properly technological determination of technology, the one that according to Heidegger hides its essence of "disclosing" (to recall quickly one of the claims of his text), to comprehend therefore this determination by way of evil and by its fury is one of Heidegger's constant directions, even if it is rarely made explicit. The *Unheil*, the distress without safeguard, the disaster (a term employed once to designate the work of the Nazis—cf. Lacoue-Labarthe, whose entire analysis should be run through here), characterizes the world of technology. And the motif of freedom, as if in counterpoint, also runs through the entire text on technology. We simply want to point out these indications, without otherwise problematizing them.

12. G. W. F. Hegel, *The System of Ethical Life and First Philosophy of Freedom*, H. S. Harris and T. M. Knox, trans. (Albany: State University of New York Press, 1979), p. 134.

13. All figures of fury fill this abyss with the idea of a "pure race" or with every other "pure" idea, including that of freedom, even that of a violent God. We could relate them to what Lyotard calls the "absolute wrong" in *The Differend*, Georges Van Den Abbeele, trans. (Minneapolis: University of Minnesota Press, 1988). We could also relate the characterization of the evil thus attained to what Lacan designated as "the jealousy that is born in a subject in its relation to another, inasmuch as this other is thought to participate in a certain form of *jouissance*, of vital superabundance, perceived by the subject as that which he cannot apprehend by way of any affective movement, even the most elementary. Is it not truly singular, and strange, that a being should admit to envying in another, to the point of hatred, to the point of needing to destroy, what he is incapable of apprehending in any way, and by no intuitive means? The almost conceptual locating of this other may in itself suffice to produce this movement of unease. . . . " Jacques Lacan, *Le Séminaire*, Book VII, "L'Ethique de la psychanalyse" (Paris: Le Seuil, 1986), p. 278. And *existence, as such, is "superabundance."*

14. Translator's note—For the remainder of this chapter, the word

propre has been translated as "own" and "proper" interchangeably in order to register Nancy's nuancing of this term.

15. Cf. Martin Heidegger, "Letter on Humanism," in *Basic Writings*. Certainly another understanding of Heidegger's propositions on *ethos* is made possible if the *dwelling* which *ethos* must be for him is not a dwelling of the proper, and is finally not a "dwelling" at all. What we will say next about the decision will follow in this direction.

16. Martin Heidegger, *Schelling's Treatise on the Essence of Human Freedom*, Joan Stambaugh, trans. (Athens: Ohio University Press, 1985), pp. 142–43; next citation, pp. 177–78.

17. It should be noted that Hegel's analysis of good and evil in the *Phenomenology*, which dialecticizes their identity, nevertheless emphasizes in a particular tone that the simple affirmation of their identity must be juxtaposed "with an insurmountable obstinacy," namely, that of their difference.

18. Georges Bataille, "*Conférences*" in *Oeuvres Complètes*, vol. 7 (Paris: Le Seuil, 1976), p. 373.

19. Ibid., vol. 8, p. 495.

20. Cf. Chap. 3.

21. *Questions IV* (Paris: Flammarion), p. 150 [trans. of "*Die Kehre*," 1962].

22. Translator's note—*Etre-propre* translates Heidegger's "*Selbstsein*," rendered in English as "Being-its-Self" or as "Being-one's-Self" in Macquarrie and Robinson's translation of *Being and Time*.

23. "Mood—being attuned—to hear the attunement. To be able to hear: *calls* of the stillness of being." *Schelling's Treatise on the Essence of Human Freedom*, p. 189. (This call undoubtedly communicates with the one we will next discuss). [Translator's note—Nancy's discussion of tonality follows from the translation of Heidegger's *Stimmung*— "mood"—as *tonalité*.]

24. Cf. §57 and following.

25. This call and this voice have been specifically analyzed by Christopher Fynsk in *Heidegger—Thought and Historicity* (Ithaca: Cornell University Press, 1986), chap. 1. This analysis has also given rise to an essay by Mikkel Borch-Jacobsen, "*Écoute*," in *Poésie* 35, Paris, 1986. On the *call* in the constitution of *Dasein* beyond the subject, cf. Jean-Luc Marion, "L'Interloqué" in *Topoi*, in *Who Comes After the Subject?*, Eduardo Cadava, Peter Connor, Jean-Luc Nancy, eds. (New York: Routledge, 1991), pp. 236–45. And on the *call* in general in Heidegger, considered for its tele-phony and related to Heidegger's politics and his thinking on technology, see

Avital Ronell, *The Telephone Book* (Lincoln: Nebraska University Press, 1989).

26. In this way, ontological analysis yields to the "pre-ontological" comprehension of the phenomenon of *Gewissen* in ordinary experience (cf. §59). This experience is therefore only "ordinary" in that it makes the call of conscience succeed a committed act as a lived experience. *Yet it is not ordinary in that it gives primacy to bad conscience.* Moreover, the parallel analysis of an ordinary "good" conscience results entirely in the impossibility of this purported phenomenon. The good man will be the last to say "I am good" and thereby to escape from the possibility of hearing the call. Consequently, we can add to what Heidegger says, the good man is good only in receiving the "attestation of his being-wicked."

27. I owe this comment on the word to Werner Hamacher, who is preparing an important study of *Gewissen*.

28. §60, p. 345 [trans. modified]. To remain consistent with the lexicon of "factuality," we render *faktisch* as "factual" and not "factical."

29. *Questions IV* (Paris: Flammarion), p. 148 [trans. of "*Die Kehre*," 1962].

30. *Questions IV* (Paris: Flammarion), p. 284. This comes from a seminar protocol, not from one of Heidegger's texts.

Chapter 13

1. Cf. Chap. 3. Yet decision doubtless always *inscribes* itself, which means it not only says or writes something, but gives itself *as decision* (through speech or writing, or through the body, gesture, or tone). This inscription of decision is certainly not unrelated to what Jean-Claude Milner analyzes as *declaration*, which for him is precisely the material inscription of freedom (cf. *Libertés, lettres, matière*, Les conférences du Perroquet, 3, Paris, June 1985).

2. Cf. similarly Lévinas: "Violence can only aim at the face," cited by Derrida, who continues: "Further, without the thought of Being which opens the face, there would be only pure violence or pure nonviolence." Jacques Derrida, "Violence and Metaphysics" in *Writing and Difference*, Alan Bass, trans. (Chicago: University of Chicago Press, 1978), p. 147. We may add: violence also originates from a face, on which wickedness can, occasionally, be read *as the devastation of this same face.*

3. Cf. Chap. 8.

4. Blanchot: " 'Thou shalt not kill' evidently means 'do not kill him who will die anyway' and means: 'because of this, do not commit an of-

fense against dying, do not decide the undecided, do not say: "here is what is done," presumptuously claiming a right over the "not yet," do not act as if the last word has been spoken, time is finished, and the Messiah has finally arrived.'" Maurice Blanchot, *Le Pas au-delà* (Paris: Gallimard, 1973), p. 149.

5. Martin Heidegger, *Being and Time*, John Macquarrie and Edward Robinson, trans. (New York: Harper & Row, 1962), §60, p. 346. [Translator's note—Where Nancy appears explicitly to be referring to Heidegger's text, "*ouverture*" ("*Erschlossenheit*") has been translated as "disclosedness"; otherwise it has been rendered as "opening" or "openness."]

6. Cf. primarily *On Time and Being*, and *Art and Space*.

7. Yves Bonnefoy, *L'Improbable* (Paris: 1951), p. 181.

8. Gilles Deleuze and Félix Guattari, *A Thousand Plateaus*, Brian Massumi, trans. (Minneapolis: University of Minnesota Press, 1987), p. 382. This will also refer to the description of "free action" which "absolutely occupies an unpunctuated space."

9. Is it therefore inimitable? Here we will hold in reserve the mimetological question of freedom (in a general sense and with particular reference to Lacoue-Labarthe). Freedom is produced in and as the being-singular of being. The being-singular of being is for itself, in existence, neither a general essence, nor a generic substance, nor a formative force, nor an exemplary ideality. There is no reproducible contour, no model, no *schema* of practical reason in its *fact*. No non-sensible image of the sensible—but the finite transcendence of naked sensibility, existence materially deciding itself in the world. Freedom does not resemble anything and it *is* not to resemble anything. Imitation has always been considered as unfree, it has even undoubtedly furnished servility's *exemplum*, and freedom, on the contrary, would be the *exemplum* of non-imitation—the negative *exemplum* of a negation of *mimesis*. The limit of imitation, never the imitation of the limit: always *on* the limit of existence (would this be the hidden *art* of the schematism?). But this still establishes a mimetic relation, and freedom has also always been considered as exemplary: exemplary of exemplarity we could say. Exemplary of what under the name of *praxis* (excellence, virtue, revolution) can be thought of as non-*poiesis*, or as *poiesis* of the sole agent of *poiesis*. We know, moreover, that this can also be interpreted as *poetry itself.* We could investigate how freedom has been identified with poetry itself and reciprocally. Is it not at bottom for us the *exemplum*, without example, of "creation," itself exem-

plary of the unexemplifiable offering of a world and to a world? Freedom: praxical archi-mimesis and archi-poetry? If there is something of the revolutionary in art, this is because it forces one—since Plato, with and against philosophy—to think freedom. Yet perhaps it demands this more radically *of freedom.* It would be in this sense that the "archi-obligation" present in art for Lacoue-Labarthe should be understood. See Philippe Lacoue-Labarthe, *L'Imitation des modernes* (Paris: Galilée, 1986), p. 284. But if art obligates one to freedom, it is not because it gives an example of it or because there would be an "art of freedom." These determinations have all been caught up in our representation of the Greek example (in our constitution or construction of our beginnings in an exemplary origin). If there is something revolutionary, which we have kept calling "freedom," it is something that gestures toward a liberation from this very example of an art of freedom and of a freedom of art, whose chiasm signifies for us a lost Greece as well as a freedom beyond our reach. But here is a liberation for another opening, for another unexpected occurrence without example or whose only example would be surprise, the generosity of the surprise and the surprise of generosity. A surprising example. Freedom would require thinking—in a region where the demands or hopes of "art," "ethics," and "politics" would be replayed—neither an inimitable model nor a *mimesis* without model, but *the surprise of the example* as such (why does this furnish an example? Why is there an example rather than . . . ?), a surprise more originary than *mimesis* to every *poiesis,* therefore a *praxis,* we could say, but one which would not be the agent's "self-production," but rather the virtue—the force and excellence—of nothing other, but nothing less than, *existence.* An ontology of this surprising example that being gives.

Chapter 14

1. Cf. Maurice Blanchot, *The Writing of the Disaster,* Ann Smock, trans. (Lincoln: University of Nebraska Press, 1986), p. 46.

2. These fragments were added several months after this essay was drafted, and were originally given to be read for a thesis defense, and to some friends. They therefore bear traces of questions posed, of readings and of reflections made afterward. Above all, I do not want them to appear as wanting to "conclude." This classical rhetorical precaution is here more than justified. There is not "a thinking" of freedom, there are only prolegomena to a freeing of thinking.

3. Jacques Derrida, *Parages* (Paris: Galilée, 1986), p. 67. [Translator's

note—In English, there is no way to render *pas* without overlooking its multiple meanings in French, which range from its nominal designations "step, pace, footprint, trace, stride, walk, gait, dance, precedence, threshold, step of stair, passage (of arms), strait, pass, pitch, thread" to its adverbial use as a particle of negation signifying "no, not, not any."]

4. Cf. *La Jeune fille qui nous présente l'art*, forthcoming.

5. §38. I will come back to this in an essay on "opening" in the analytic of *Dasein*. Martin Heidegger, *Being and Time*, John Macquarrie and Edward Robinson, trans. (New York: Harper & Row, 1962), p. 219.

6. Translator's note—"*Technique*," in French, is open to many English translations, among which are the following: "technique," the specific style or manner in which an activity is conducted; "technics," the technological tools, methods, theories, and so forth used to carry out an action; and "technology," the terminological body relating as a whole to the technological.

7. Since these notes, Derrida has explicitly come back to the status of questioning in Heidegger: Jacques Derrida, *Of Spirit, Heidegger and the Question*, Geoffrey Bennington and Rachel Bowlby, trans. (Chicago: University of Chicago Press, 1989).

8. Blanchot, *The Writing of the Disaster*.

9. §57, Martin Heidegger, *Being and Time*, p. 323.

10. Cf. "Le Peuple juif ne rêve pas," by Philippe Lacoue-Labarthe and Jean-Luc Nancy, in *La Psychanalyse est-elle une histoire juive?* (Paris: Le Seuil, 1981); and on the Hegelian "mother," Jean-Luc Nancy, "Identité et tremblement" in *Hypnoses* (with M. Borch-Jacobsen and E. Michaud) (Paris: Galilée, 1983).

11. Maurice Blanchot, *Le Pas au-delà* (Paris: Gallimard, 1975), p. 73.

12. Robert Antelme, letter of June 21, 1945, cited in Dionys Mascolo, *Autour d'un effort de mémoire* (Paris: M. Nadeau, 1987).

13. E. M. Cioran, *Précis de décomposition* (Paris: Gallimard, 1965), p. 77.

14. Cf. Gérard Granel, "La Guerre de Sécession," *Le Débat*, no. 48, Jan.-Feb. 1988.

15. G. W. F. Hegel, *Philosophy of Right* (New York: Oxford University Press, 1967), §5, p. 22.

16. And/or the event of being. I insist here on returning to *L'Être et l'événement* by Alain Badiou (Paris: Le Seuil, 1987). Having appeared too late for me to grant it its due credit, this important book seems to me to contain, in certain respects, a thesis close to the thesis on the freedom of being.

Index of Names

In this index an "f" after a number indicates a separate reference on the next page, and an "ff" indicates separate references on the next two pages. A continuous discussion over two or more pages is indicated by a span of page numbers, e.g., "57–59." *Passim* is used for a cluster of references in close but not consecutive sequence.

Adorno, Theodor, 4, 35, 121, 184n4, 186n1, 190n11, 199n10
Arendt, Hannah, 74f, 145, 168
Aristotle, 42, 163, 193n11

Badiou, Alain, 76, 183n1, 207n16
Bataille, Georges, 12, 52, 123, 132, 134, 151, 182n11, 201n6
Baudelaire, Charles-Pierre, 123
Benjamin, Walter, 117–18, 137, 151, 165
Benveniste, Emile, 197n4
Bergson, Henri, 150, 186n1, 196–97n7
Biraud, Henri, 186–87n3
Blanchot, Maurice, 119, 148, 151, 189n3, 192n4, 204n4
Bonnefoy, Yves, 144
Borch-Jacobsen, Mikkel, 203n25

Dallmayr, Fred R., 187n3
Deleuze, Gilles, 150, 165, 190n12, 192n4

Derrida, Jacques, 7, 15, 150f, 165, 186n8, 189n3, 194n7, 197n3 (Chap. 10), 197n2 (Chap. 11), 207n7
Descartes, René, 5, 72, 87, 89f, 107

Epicurus, 191n13

Fichte, J. G., 185–86n5
Foucault, Michel, 78, 193n11
Franck, Didier, 197n8 (Chap. 9), 197n1 (Chap. 11)
Freud, Sigmund, 72, 168
Fynsk, Christopher, 203n25

Granel, Gérard, 15, 171, 188n8
Guattari, Félix, 193n4
Guilead, Reuben, 186n3

Hamacher, Werner, 204n23
Hegel, G. W. F., 1, 5, 7f, 14, 29, 33, 36, 38f, 42, 46, 49–50, 54, 76, 81ff, 88, 94, 98f, 107, 109, 118, 125,

MERIDIAN

Crossing Aesthetics

Library of Congress
Cataloging-in-Publication Data

Nancy, Jean-Luc
[Experience de la liberté. English]
The experience of freedom /
Jean-Luc Nancy ;
translated by Bridget McDonald ;
with a foreword by Peter Fenves.
p.   cm. — (Meridian)
Includes bibliographical references.
ISBN 0–8047–2175–0 (alk. paper) :
— ISBN 0–8047–2190–4 (pbk. :
alk. paper) :   1. Liberty. I. Title.
II. Series : Meridian (Stanford, Calif.)
B105.L45N3613   1993
123'.5—dc20
93–16348
CIP

♾ This book is printed on
acid-free paper. It was typeset by
Anne Cheilek in Adobe Garamond
and Lithos on a Macintosh IIci at
Stanford University Press.

Original printing 1993